DOING JUSTICE

A Trial Judge at Work

Judge Robert Satter

With an Introduction by
William Styron

American Lawyer Books/Simon and Schuster
NEW YORK · LONDON · TORONTO · SYDNEY · TOKYO · SINGAPORE

AMERICAN LAWYER BOOKS
SIMON AND SCHUSTER

Copyright © 1990 by Robert Satter

Published by American Lawyer Books/Simon & Schuster.
American Lawyer Books are published by
Am-Law Publishing Corporation.
Simon and Schuster is a division of the
Simon & Schuster Trade Division.
Rockefeller Center
1230 Avenue of the Americas
New York, New York 10020
SIMON AND SCHUSTER is a registered trademark
of Simon & Schuster Inc.
American Lawyer Books is a registered trademark
of the American Lawyer Newspaper Group, Inc.

Designed by Levavi & Levavi
Manufactured in the United States of America

1 3 5 7 9 10 8 6 4 2

Library of Congress Cataloging in Publication Data
Satter, Robert.
Doing justice: a trial judge at work/Robert Satter;
with an introduction by William Styron.
p. cm.
1. Justice, Administration of—United States.
2. Judges—United States. 3. Trials—United States. I. Title.
KF8700.S32 1990
347.73'14—dc20
[347.30714]   89-26159
CIP
ISBN 0-671-69152-X

ACKNOWLEDGMENTS

No one writes a book, however personal, without the help of others. Nancy LaRoche edited the first draft of my manuscript, adeptly using her blue pencil to collapse three sentences into one and to reduce long sentences into short ones. Linda Case also helped to cull out cant. Several lawyers read portions of the manuscript and gave good advice, among them George J. Ritter, Karl D. Fleischmann, L. Paul Sullivan, John A. Berman, and University of Connecticut law professor Hugh C. Macgill. In his typically incisive way, United States Circuit Court of Appeals judge Jon O. Newman challenged many of my assertions and thereby required me to be more accurate. Beryl Title urged me to sound less lawyerly and to put more of myself into the writing. My three daughters, Mimi Satter, Shoshana Hoose, and Jane Satter made valuable suggestions and they together with my son, Richard Satter, and his sons Bryan and Andrew Satter, were my private cheering squad. Shoshana's husband, Phillip M. Hoose, who wrote and had published two books while I tried to write this one, offered many practical hints on authoring.

I have been a member of the Writers Group for thirty-seven years. We read aloud our writing every month. The group heard every draft of every chapter. They shaped this book by their constructive criticism, given sometimes verbally and sometimes by polite silence. The members of that group are Beverly Berman, Brian Burland, Oliver Butterworth, Constance Carrier, Linda Case, Christine Lyman-Farquhar, Bill Leavy, Ellen Paullin, Penn Ritter, Scott Ritter, and Ardis Whitman Rumsey.

Steven Brill of *The American Lawyer* induced and allied with Simon and Schuster to publish this book. Alice Mayhew of Simon and Schuster proved to be the great editor she has the reputation of being. David Shipley, Alice's associate, was a delight to work with. He has a quality which is a boon to struggling authors: he returns phone calls promptly.

Kathleen Lauria typed, photostated, collated, and performed many other tasks of the superb secretary she is.

I acknowledge last my debt to the person who was always first in my life. My wife Ruth suffered through my dinnertime monologues on the cases I was trying that day and my bedtime tossings over decisions I wrestled with at night. More significantly, we shared forty-three years of a happy marriage. My deepest regret is that she could not have lived a few more months for me to place this book in her hands as an offering of my gratitude and love.

To Ruth, love of my life.

CONTENTS

Introduction   11

1. Opening Court   17

2. Here Comes the Judge   26

3. Whom to Believe?   39

4. Heart v. Mind   51

5. How I Decide a Court Case   63

6. Civil Trial by Jury   80

7. Bargaining over Pain and Disability   99

8. More on Civil Jury Trials   112

9. Does the Civil Jury System Work?   126

10. Criminal Cases   140

11. *Murder Trial* 153

12. *Dilemmas of Sentencing* 170

13. *Where Has Love Gone?* 186

14. *Prisoners of Their Future* 202

15. *The Face of Poverty* 215

16. *On Being Reversed and Sitting on the Supreme Court* 227

17. *Summing Up* 240

Index 247

INTRODUCTION

My acquaintance with Robert Satter began on an extraordinarily tense and dramatic day in June 1962, within the walls of the old Connecticut State Prison at Wethersfield. Although we had arrived separately, we were both concerned with the imminent fate of a condemned convict named Benjamin Reid. The state Board of Pardons was meeting that day; the board members had convened in order to determine whether Reid, who was black and in his early twenties and who had been convicted of murdering a black woman in Hartford five years before, was worth salvaging to the extent of having his sentence commuted to life imprisonment, or would die in the electric chair that very night. It was this quality of hovering doom that gave the session, which was held on a classically gorgeous spring day, such urgency and tension. Connecticut at that time was unusual

among the states in the way the death penalty—chiefly the
process of pardoning and commutation—was administered.
The power of commuting a sentence of death was not in the
hands of the governor but was vested in a board of five
members—a well-intentioned concept which spread the responsibility but which, from the point of view of the condemned person, had certain shortcomings. For while it was
reasonable to assume that a governor might make his comfortably remote decision well in advance of the execution
date, thus at least relieving the convict of that particular
suspense (while theoretically allowing his lawyers time for
further appeals to higher courts), the posture of the board as
a last tribunal—before which the doomed one appeared in
person, and whose decision was absolute and final—gained
an added element of dread from the fact of its being convened only a few hours before the scheduled execution. It is
unlikely that any judicial proceeding ever brought a person
so quiveringly close to the shadow line between life and
eternity.

Benjamin Reid was the quintessential American victim.
This is to say that being black, young, and destitute, he
represented the individual our society is most likely to put
to death as sacrificial atonement for its own failure to achieve
the equality proclaimed by its democratic slogans. I had once
believed in the death penalty, but had been turned around
completely, due in part to my reading Camus's remarkable
essay, "Reflections on the Guillotine," but also because my
own independent study had led me to the conviction that,
aside from the social wrong capital punishment represented,
there was nothing either morally or practically in its favor.
Besides this, there was a whole constellation of sound reasons for regarding it as a cruel perversion of justice. Using
the case of Ben Reid as an example, I wrote a long essay in
Esquire demonstrating these views, and it helped bolster interest in Reid, at the same time spurring his defense, which
had already become a rallying point for a number of people

in Connecticut, notably a group of teachers and students from Trinity College. Bob Satter, then practicing law, was also very much involved. As a result of all this activity there was considerable public interest in Ben Reid's fate when the Board of Pardons met that June day in a crowded room at the Wethersfield prison. As a spectator I was fascinated by the proceedings, which went on for an hour or so while Reid, dressed in his immaculate prison khakis, sat near the table where the board members deliberated. I recall thinking to myself that I had never been in close proximity to anyone whose life hung so precariously in the balance. Much of the testimony in Reid's behalf was fairly prosaic and predictable, and bore largely on his disadvantaged background and race (also on the fact that, if he were to be executed, he would be both the youngest in Connecticut ever tried for first-degree murder and the youngest to die); these were effective arguments but I remember feeling that no voice raised that day to plead for Reid's life was more eloquent than that of Robert Satter.

I have written elsewhere: "Satter, a prominent Hartford lawyer, had followed Reid's post-trial career with an abiding interest. It had for a long time been Satter's belief—shared by others—that of the multitude of injustices surrounding Reid's conviction one of the worst was that involving the sinister connection between Reid and the notorious mass-murderer Joseph Taborsky. It was Satter's contention that it had been the public furor and vengeful outcry attending Taborsky's trial that affected Reid's own nearby courtroom and similarly sealed Reid's fate. A mild, scholarly-looking, sandy-haired man, Satter asked the board to consider a literary allusion. 'You may recall the conclusion of *Moby Dick*,' he said, 'how, as the ship *Pequod* sinks beneath the waves, the arm of a sailor appears from the depths to hammer a pennant against the mast. Just as the nail is being driven home, a gull flies by, and its wing, interposing itself between hammer and mast, is nailed fast to the spar, so that the final glimpse of the doomed ship is this bit of fluttering life being dragged with it into the deep.' There was nothing histrionic about Satter and his manner, his words were splendidly afire. Pausing, he gestured toward Reid. 'If Benjamin Reid should die this night,' he continued, 'his life, like that of Melville's gull, would have been sacrificed just as surely as if the arm of Joseph Taborsky had reached from the grave to drag him down into oblivion.'' The silence following that speech was so complete as to be startling, and was in itself a curious lull of memorable dramatic impact. During that lull I had the feeling, for the first time, that Ben Reid's life would be saved. This was hardly a gathering where one might imagine literary allusions and references to nineteenth-century novels having much effect, but the passion in Satter's voice, and the force of his delivery, created a remarkable impression. I sensed an odd buoyancy, a mood that continued through the rest of the hearing and even through the period of waiting for the decision. The judgment, when it came, spared Reid's life and brought to most of those in the room the feeling of an ordeal's end, and immeasurable relief at death vanquished.

In the unfortunate sequel to Ben Reid's escape from the electric chair, Bob Satter's devotion to justice once more played a fascinating and, I think, instructive part. After the commutation of his sentence to life imprisonment, Reid spent eight years in prison, at which point he became eligible for parole. His time behind bars had been spent in an exemplary fashion and his parole was granted. But only a matter of days before his scheduled release, Reid, who had been on a work detail outside the walls, made his getaway into the nearby woods, spent the night eluding police dogs, and the next morning broke into a dwelling, forced a housewife into her car and later raped her. Apprehended soon after, he was brought to trial and sentenced to ten to fifteen years. Did Satter feel betrayed? He most certainly did. There was scarcely a person who had worked hard for Reid's release who did not feel utter betrayal, but unlike most of the rest of his supporters, including myself, who virtually washed their hands of Reid at this juncture, Satter summoned what has to be almost superhuman faith and compassion and, as I observed before, "went to Reid's aid . . . offering legal and moral support to a man whom most people might have written off for good." Now these many years later, having paid his debt to society, Reid is free and has become a peaceful and productive citizen—certainly living testimony to Robert Satter's invincible belief in redemption and fairness, concepts poorly apprehended in a culture that is unfairly arranged and, in matters of justice, often vindictive.

Throughout this excellent book Robert Satter demonstrates over and over again the integrity and concern for fairness that attended his arduous journey with Benjamin Reid. It should be quickly noted that *Doing Justice*, while attentive to the grave issue implicit in its title, is both instructive and entertaining; any layman whose knowledge of the workings of our judicial system is, like mine, limited to newspaper stories and an occasional television drama, will discover here a rich fund of information concerning the way courts operate and, in particular, the way in which a trial judge deals with the delicate and galling problems he is faced with day after day. The reader will gain an understanding of the Byzantine complexity of our legal system, all filtered through the perception of the man on the bench who must cope with distraught defendants, contentious lawyers, drowsy juries, dubious witnesses, and countless other courtroom vexations. Central to Judge Satter's narrative, however, is his own conscience, and it is the role played by his conscience—so crucial a factor in the destinies of those upon whom he must render judgment—that gives this book both its moral tension and its moral authority. If Satter is not a punitive man, and certainly far removed from the spirit of retribution, neither is he sentimental; and his descriptions of those troubled moments while pondering sentence and prison terms are ethical lessons in themselves. The wisdom and honesty of *Doing Justice* lie in its abiding awareness that the judge and the judged are bound inseparably by their common humanity, and it is good to hear this simple truth retold in Robert Satter's civilized voice.

William Styron

1. OPENING COURT

George Edwards stands up next to his lawyer when the sheriff shouts "All rise," and I briskly enter the courtroom. He holds his hands flat on the counsel table as he leans his long body rigidly forward. The atmosphere in court is tense, typical of a day when a sentence is to be imposed.

I settle comfortably into the high-backed chair behind the bench. The Edwards trial is vivid in my mind. He was tried before me several months ago for sexual assault first degree. The victim, Barbara Babson (name changed to disguise identity), was a woman in her late twenties and a junior executive at a Hartford insurance company. She testified that Edwards followed her into her apartment as she was entering with her arms full of groceries and raped her. Edwards denied that he used force. The jury, after deliberating only a short time, found him guilty. Now he is before me for sentencing.

Before coming on the bench, I carefully read the presentence report prepared by the probation officer. It revealed: Edwards is thirty-one years old, born of a black father and white mother. He was wounded in Vietnam and decorated for bravery under fire. At the time of the crime, he was a computer programmer at the same insurance company where Miss Babson was employed. Six months before the crime, Edwards had separated from his wife and child, and fellow employees first noticed he seemed withdrawn, depressed, and sometimes confused. His only previous criminal offense was a disorderly conduct charge that had not been prosecuted.

This morning I am surprised that Edwards appears neat and alert. He is wearing a blue suit and white shirt. At the trial he was disheveled and apathetic.

I nod to the state's attorney to begin. He asks my permission to have the victim speak first. Miss Babson expresses her fury at what Edwards has done to her. "Judge, I hope you lock him up and throw away the key," she says.

The state's attorney is equally vehement. The crime was a serious one, he says. The defendant cynically denied it and has never shown any remorse. "I urge the maximum punishment of twenty years in the state prison," the state's attorney concludes.

Edwards's lawyer starts his argument by mentioning his client's splendid Vietnam War record and his lack of any criminal record. He says that Edwards has returned to his wife and child, and they are beginning to rebuild a life together. Edwards has also begun to see a psychiatrist. The lawyer hands me a letter from the psychiatrist, whom I know to be reputable, indicating that Edwards is seriously engaged in therapy and making progress.

"If you will give George Edwards a suspended sentence, Your Honor, and place him on probation with the condition that he stay in psychiatric treatment, he won't be before this court again. George is a good risk," the lawyer pleads.

The maximum sentence for sexual assault first degree is twenty years. There is no minimum. My alternatives are to impose a prison term of any number of years up to twenty or to suspend any time in prison and put Edwards on probation with conditions. What should my sentence be?

.   .   .

I am sitting on the bench in the family part of the superior court in Hartford. The third-floor courtroom is small, too small for the crowd of litigants and attorneys pressing to have their cases heard. I feel hemmed in and keep wanting to push my chair backward. Today is motion day, and I am hearing a motion for change of custody.

Susan Fletcher is on the stand, an attractive, brown-haired woman in her mid-twenties. She testifies in a pleasant but precise manner, completing each sentence before starting the next. Yet as I listen, it occurs to me that what she is saying is like the story line of a soap opera.

When she was in college, Susan became pregnant by Tim, her co-worker at a summer restaurant job. Her mother refused to have her remain at home, so Susan went to live with Tim's family. After the child, Richard, was born, the couple moved into their own apartment. Susan and Tim did not get along, but they nevertheless got married. The fights continued. Susan went back to her mother, who allowed her home only on the condition that she leave Tim and abandon her son. At the divorce Susan let custody of the boy be awarded to Tim. For a whole year afterward she did not see the child, but then she began visiting him once a week.

Over the next four years, Susan became pregnant again, had an abortion, and then married the father of the aborted child. She and her new husband moved to a semirural town where he has a flourishing business. With Tim's concurrence, she started having Richard stay over twice a week and every other weekend.

Susan says her life is now in order; she has a loving husband, a comfortable home, and wants to reclaim her boy. "When Richard visits us, he has his own room. My husband and I read to him every night. We are also teaching him to read. The school in our town is excellent, and he will enjoy going to it with his friends in the neighborhood."

Tim is a stolid, almost grim sort of man. He describes how over the last five years he raised Richard with the help of members of his extended family. He holds a modest job as the manager of a fast-food restaurant, and lives in a small Hartford apartment with his wife and a newly born baby. Recently he enrolled Richard in a Catholic elementary school.

Tim is defensive about Susan's superior education and position. He testifies: "I may not be able to provide Richard with all the things Susan can. But I and my family have cared for the boy from birth. He is happy with us and loves the new baby. He'll start in our parish school next month. I don't want to lose him now when he is just turning five."

The legal standard I am to apply is "the best interest of the child." The family relations officer's report reveals that both Susan and Tim are capable of raising Richard in a loving way. The real issue is who should be the live-in parent, from whose home the boy will go to school, and who should be the visiting parent. What should my decision be?

· · ·

The trial of the medical malpractice suit of Brian Morgan against the St. Francis Hospital and Dr. Alvaro Oviedo lasted ten weeks. It ended with a jury verdict for the hospital and the doctor. When Brian's attorney moved to set aside the verdict and for a new trial, I thought it was a routine motion I could readily deny. But Brian's attorney raised an issue that surprised me and gave me pause. He claimed that two members of the jury were employees of Aetna Surety and Casualty Company, which insured both of the defendants. He had objected to these jurors when the jury had been picked, but another judge, who had supervised the jury selection, had overruled his objection. This was the first I learned of that ruling. Now, after the trial, Brian's lawyer asserted in his motion that the presence of those persons on the jury was unfair, and required that the verdict be overturned and his client be given another trial before an impartial jury. After reading the briefs of both sides, I set the motion down for argument.

Brian's lawyer starts by citing the common law rule that bars anyone from being a juror in a case in which his employer is a party. "In fact," he says, "a leading Connecticut case holds that such an employment relationship automatically disqualifies the juror without any necessity to show actual bias, and if he is allowed to sit, the verdict must be thrown out."

"What do you say to that?" I ask the hospital lawyer.

"The case referred to by the plaintiff's counsel is distinguishable from this one, Your Honor. It speaks of a juror as an employee of a party. The jurors here were not employees of the hospital or the doctor."

"How can that make a difference," counters Brian's attorney. "Aetna has even more interest in the outcome of the case than the defendants because it, not the hospital or doctor, must pay the dollar amount of any verdict."

"But," I ask, "isn't there a fundamental distinction between a juror being an employee of a party and being an employee of an insurance company insuring a party? The employee of a party knows his boss is in the case. The employee of an insurance company doesn't know his company insures one of the parties. Thus, the insurance company employee is not influenced by his employment relationship."

"That may be so, Judge," Brian's lawyer says, "but in my brief I cite four or five cases from other states that specifically hold that employees of insurance companies that insure one of the parties should not sit as jurors."

"What's your response?" I ask the doctor's lawyer.

"Well, Your Honor, whatever the rule in other states, in Connecticut, and especially in Hartford, where so many people work for insurance companies, jurors have never been disqualified for that reason. Moreover, insurance was never once mentioned during the trial, so as you said, the two Aetna employees never knew their company was involved."

"Let me shift gears," I say, "and ask you defendant lawyers this. If I held three shares of Aetna stock, under the Code of Judicial Conduct I could not have been the judge in the case. The reason is not that those three shares would influence my rulings, but that there would be an appearance of partiality. Why shouldn't that principle apply as well to jurors? Certainly from the point of view of the plaintiff who lost the case, having two Aetna people out of the six jurors doesn't seem fair."

The lawyer for the hospital pauses to reflect and then answers, "Jurors are from the community and are not required to be as isolated as judges. But most important, there has been no showing of favoritism by those jurors. The plaintiff got a fair trial, and in the end, that's the bottom line."

The argument has aired the issues but not resolved them for me. I realize I will have to study the cases cited in the briefs and research the law myself. Clearly, the parties feel a great deal is at stake. Brian rejected a $200,000 offer of settlement during the trial and desperately wants another chance to prove his case. Aetna provided the lawyers for the hospital and doctor, by my guess expended well over $100,000 in their defense, and is determined to retain the verdict. However I decide the motion, there is certain to be an appeal. So I'd better be right.

•   •   •

These are examples of dilemmas I face as a judge of the Connecticut Superior Court. The Connecticut court system is unique in the country, in that the superior court is a statewide, one-tier, trial court of general and unlimited jurisdiction. This contrasts with the court system of other states in which trial jurisdiction is segmented among several different tribunals, such as traffic courts, felony courts, family courts, and so on. A Connecticut Superior Court judge hears all kinds of cases.

These cases fall into these natural categories: *civil court cases*—mainly disputes between private parties over commercial transactions or over rulings of administrative agencies, decided by a judge; *civil jury cases*—mainly personal injury claims, decided by a jury; *criminal cases*—cases in which the state accuses a person of a misdemeanor or felony and endeavors to prove it, decided usually by a jury; *family matters*—disputes over divorce, alimony, child support, visitation, and custody, decided by a judge; *juvenile matters*—cases involving children under sixteen who are accused of crimes or who are neglected or abused by their parents, decided by a judge; and *housing matters*—landlord-tenant disputes and claims of housing code violations, decided by a judge.

Some of the dilemmas these cases create arise in the course of the trial: Should I intervene when an incompetent lawyer is mangling his client's case? How can I make my instructions on complicated legal principles understandable to members of the jury? Above all, how can I create an atmosphere in the courtroom that justice is being sought?

Some of the dilemmas these cases present are questions of substantive law: Should the step-grandchildren of a decedent get his estate when all the beneficiaries named in the will died before the decedent and he left no other heirs? Should a "rainy day" fund be created to protect the customers of an electric light company from future rate increases when the company's current earnings exceed a fair rate of return?

But the most challenging decisions I must make are those that have a direct human impact, such as what sentence to impose, to whom to award custody of children, and most difficult of all, whether or not to declare that a woman who has neglected or abused her children shall no longer be their mother. Those are the dilemmas that disturb my sleep and in the dead of night have me asking: Who am I to judge? Where do I get the wisdom? What right do I have to play God with other people's lives?

This book is about decision making. "What should my decision be?" is a frequent refrain. It is meant not only to reveal my own internal struggle, but to act as a challenge to the reader as well.

"How do I decide?" is an even more fundamental question. What factors play a part in decision making? How are conflicting factors balanced against each other? What finally clicks to resolve doubts and create confidence that a right decision has been made?

In the usual run of cases, issues of law are determined by clearly worded statutes and authoritative precedents. But occasionally the applicable statute is ambiguous, or precedents conflict, or there is no statute and no precedent. Then the judge's scholarship, his judgment, and ultimately his values come into play.

The resolution of human dilemmas, I find, rests on clear reasoning, as far as it will take me, but, in the final analysis, on heeding the stirrings of my heart, trusting the feelings in my gut, making a courageous leap of faith. Moreover, because the law is so general—"the best interest of the child" —and the discretion of the judge is so broad in such cases, appeals courts rarely disturb these decisions.

Thus, a theme of this book is that the judge is often a part of his judgment. Who he* is makes a difference in his decisions and also in the atmosphere he creates in the court-

* The use of the male pronoun is for editorial convenience only. In Connecticut, the chief justice of the state supreme court, the chief judges of the state appellate court and of the federal district court are all women.

room. His body language and tone of voice, his reactions to witnesses, his manner of ruling on objections, his treatment of lawyers all affect a perception of the fairness of the trial.

Because a judge's personality and values are significant, I must reveal a little about myself: experiences that shaped me, the kind of law I practiced, twists of fate that resulted in my becoming a judge. These will give clues to why I decide the way I do and provide a benchmark for the reader to evaluate my decisions.

Another theme is telling what it is like to be a judge. One day I was a lawyer. The next day I was a judge. Did I suddenly metamorphose into an impassive and objective figure on the bench, repressing old passions and convictions? What are my feelings when I exercise the awesome power of sending a person to prison? What goes on within me when I must decide a case in which law and fairness conflict?

This book, then, is a view outward from the bench and inward into the heart of a judge. It depicts the dramas in the courtroom, the struggles to resolve judicial dilemmas, and the feelings that churn beneath the black robe.

Let me begin.

2. HERE COMES THE JUDGE

When I was appointed to the bench, new judges were given no indoctrination or training. I did receive two valuable bits of advice from a wise veteran. "Bob," he said, "never put your judicial robe on over your suit coat, and always go to the bathroom before going on the bench." Feeling I needed more lofty counsel, I went to the chief judge on my own initiative. His only words were, "There are many styles of judging. You will have to develop your own Satter style." The next day I was on the bench.

My first assignment was to the criminal court on Morgan Street in Hartford. It was a grimy building at the junction of two interstate highways. Peeling paint dropped from courtroom walls, the air-conditioning rarely worked, and through the open windows came the constant roar of speeding traffic. At Morgan Street everything smelled of crime, poverty, and defeat.

In the early years of my practice I had represented clients there, mostly when they were charged with petty offenses and traffic violations. Later on I usually sent an associate. Whenever I went myself, I always wanted to get out as quickly as possible.

Now a judge, I entered the Morgan Street courthouse that first morning as into a hallowed Hall of Justice. In the small chambers assigned to me, I put on my black robe. Gazing in a mirror, I liked the way the robe looked. I reflected briefly on the twists of fate that had brought me to this moment. I had no illusion that I had been appointed on the basis of my legal ability alone. I knew that luck and political connections had played a far more significant part.

I entered the courtroom, excited but not a bit nervous. A sheriff shouted, "All rise. The Hartford Court of Common Pleas is in session. Judge Robert Satter presiding. Be seated." Lowering myself into the armchair behind the bench, I was surprised at how high I was above the room. My robe felt comfortable, even though the air-conditioning, as usual, was not working that hot July morning. I had an instant consciousness of power as I looked out over the large green room and sensed everyone was waiting for me to indicate that the proceedings could start.

This was arraignment day. The courtroom was filled with a motley collection of Hartford's underclass who had been arrested over the weekend for a variety of minor crimes and were being presented for the first time.

I nodded to the prosecutor to begin the first case. The clerk shot up from his desk below the bench and whispered to me that I must first advise those accused of crimes of their constitutional rights. I strained to remember what they were: the right to remain silent, to have a lawyer appointed if they couldn't afford one, to have reasonable bail set. Later I realized I had left about half out.

The first defendant called was a teenager accused of stealing a car. His lawyer asked for an adjournment. I granted it. There then paraded in front of me accused shoplifters, petty thieves, prostitutes—the shifty, poor, and unlucky of the city. I granted continuances, set bail, appointed public defenders, heard pleas, set a trial date for those who pleaded not guilty, and imposed on those who pleaded guilty the sentence agreed upon by the prosecutor and defense counsel. I was having a great time. Before I knew it the court day was over.

I had been so engrossed in my new role that not until I was driving home did the thought strike me that most of the defendants in that courtroom had been black or Puerto Rican. The next day, to check that impression, I recorded on a pad on the bench the color of those who appeared before me: 78 percent were members of those two minorities. Was it because they were the ones who committed the crimes or the ones whom the police more readily arrested? Or, more likely, was I seeing the grim connection between city poverty and street crimes?

Before I could pursue the implications of those questions, I was assigned for a week to the court in rural Winsted. Then I began three-month stints in small towns and big cities throughout the state. I heard a variety of criminal and civil cases. The novelty of people standing when I entered the courtroom and calling me "Your Honor" wore off. Gradually reality of the judicial life set in. I came to realize the vast difference between being a lawyer and being a judge.

.   .   .

As a boy growing up, I never dreamed of becoming a judge. Does anyone? Judgeships are not the stuff boyhood dreams are made of.

In fact, becoming a lawyer never even crossed my mind until one day, late in my senior year at Rutgers, I chanced to meet the dean of men walking on campus. Out of the blue, he said, "Bob, the New Jersey Columbia Law School Alumni Association wants me to suggest a Rutgers student for a scholarship to Columbia Law School. I'd be glad to recommend you, if you are interested."

I had been thinking of pursuing a graduate degree in economics but decided on the spot to accept the dean's offer. It was the spring of 1941; I had just registered for the draft and figured it really did not matter what I did for the next several months until I was called up.

On my first day at Columbia, I sat in the library, aimlessly leafing through the stern volumes and asking myself, "What am I doing here?" In class, I quickly recognized that what mattered was understanding what a case meant, not remembering what the opinion said: analysis, not regurgitation. But I resisted the hairsplitting, resented professors attempting to sharpen my mind by narrowing it. That whole first year I never got the hang of legal reasoning.

A month after the spring semester ended, I was in the navy. I spent the next three and a half years as an antiaircraft gunnery officer on a cruiser and battleship in the Pacific. At sea I read *The Common Law* by Oliver Wendell Holmes, *The Nature of the Judicial Process* by Benjamin N. Cardozo, and the biographies of several Supreme Court justices. These broadened my perspective of the law. When I returned to Columbia, I had a strong desire to be a lawyer and studied seriously.

My first job was with a firm located on the fortieth floor of a skyscraper in the Wall Street district. I arrived eager to begin my new career. A partner gave me my first assignment: write to an airline company about the lost luggage of a client's wife. I sat behind my shiny desk, gazed out the window at the magnificent view of the New York harbor, and casually rang for the stenographer. A pleasant middle-aged woman entered.

"Take a letter," I said somewhat imperiously. I had seen people dictate. It seemed easy enough. The secretary sat in front of my desk, steno pad open, pen poised. I started:

"Your company has negligently . . . No, that's not right.

"Please be advised that . . . No, cross that out.

"I write on behalf of my client . . . No, let me start again."

After a few more of my attempts, the secretary closed her

pad and said gently, "Don't you think you should handwrite your letter first?"

An early task was to draft a legal memorandum for the firm's trusts and estates partner in a case involving the rule against perpetuities. That rule is a perplexing common law principle that restricts the time into the future a testator can tie up his property in trust. A visiting professor teaching future interests at Columbia the year I took the course spent the whole semester ridiculing the rule, without ever enlightening us on how to apply it. I struggled over that memo for days and nights. Finally I brought it to the partner. As he read it, a more and more puzzled expression came over his face. When he finished he held the memo with his thumb and index finger over a wastepaper basket. He opened his fingers, and my first attempt at legal research floated to the bottom.

Despite that ignominious beginning, I plunged into the New York practice, acquiring legal skills as I drafted partnership agreements, incorporated businesses, tried cases, argued appeals. But over the years, as my competence grew, I found myself questioning the purpose of it all. Our firm mainly represented corporations and wealthy people. My efforts seemed only to make the rich richer. And the city itself—the towering city of steel and brick—accentuated my sense of insignificance. I felt I could never scale its peaks, have my name carved in its stone.

At that propitious moment in my thinking, a college friend asked me to form a law partnership with him in Hartford. I jumped at the chance. Hartford, as it quickly became apparent, was a wonderful place to practice. Lawyers were friendly; the city was small enough for me to make a reputation, have an impact.

Our firm grew in the typical way general practices do: one client recommending a new one, one case leading to another, all without pattern or order. Because early on I helped organize a Hartford chapter of the American Civil Liberties

Union and was its first president, I attracted civil rights cases.

One such case I was always proud of involved a Hartford Theological Seminary student from Norway, named Eric Leidenfrost. He was a conscientious objector who had applied to become a United States citizen. The law then required that conscientious objectors seeking citizenship, who would not swear to serve in the military service, had to take an oath that they would do "work of national importance." The United States Immigration Department at that time had a practice of asking c.o.'s whether they would work in a munitions factory and denying their applications when they said they would not. This happened to Leidenfrost. The department justified its practice on the ground that the law allowed no exception to the obligation to do work of national importance. A federal district court in northern California had upheld the department's interpretation of the law, and all over the country c.o.'s were being refused citizenship on that basis.

I appealed the denial of Leidenfrost's application to the Connecticut United States District Court. A renowned Quaker and recognized expert on conscientious objection, whom I put on the stand, testified that no c.o. would agree to work in a munitions factory, and this was known to Congress at the time it enacted the law allowing c.o.'s to become citizens. I argued to the court that to deny citizenship on the ground of refusal to do such work made a mockery of the law and was contrary to congressional intent.

The wonderful judge agreed. In an oral opinion from the bench, he rejected the reasoning of the California court and reversed the department's denial of Leidenfrost's application. Then he dramatically swore in Leidenfrost as a citizen. That decision was followed by other district courts throughout the country. The department was forced to change its nasty policy.

As busy as our practice became, particularly as we started

to represent labor unions, I always found time to involve myself in the community. I was on the boards of several social service organizations, president of the Greater Hartford Community Council, and a founder of Hartford's anti-poverty agency, the Community Renewal Team. Such activities led me inevitably into politics.

My political career, such as it was, included two successive events that qualify for *Ripley's Believe It or Not*. In 1962 I won a primary election for nomination as representative to the Connecticut state legislature by one vote. Six weeks later I won the general election over a Republican opponent, again, by one vote, 4,164, to 4,163. That earned me the nickname "Landslide Satter" and made me a legend in Connecticut politics. All told, I served three terms in the state house of representatives.

I loved the legislature—jousting in floor debates, grappling with important state issues, feeling I was engaged in "enterprises of great pitch and moment." And I championed my own pet causes. One was the abolition of capital punishment. My bills on that issue never succeeded (although once the vote in the house was close), but I did make one contribution to the trial of capital cases.

It always seemed unfair to me that an accused, charged with a crime for which he faced the death penalty, ran the risk of implying he was guilty of the crime itself if, during the trial, he put on exculpating evidence to avoid execution. A better procedure, I thought, would be first to have a trial on the issue of the accused's guilt or innocence; then, if the jury rendered a guilty verdict, continue the trial before the same jury to allow the accused to show mitigating circumstances why the death penalty should not be imposed.

In the 1965 session I sponsored a bill incorporating this idea of a split trial and verdict in capital cases, shepherded it through the legislature's judiciary committee, and got it passed by both houses. The effect has been virtually to preclude capital punishment in Connecticut because juries, having found an accused guilty, are reluctant to take responsibility for voting for his death.

In those days strong political parties ran the legislature, and strong leaders ran the political parties. State Chairman John M. Bailey ruled the Democratic party by his political acumen, by the force of his personality, and, as a result of his arrangement with Democratic governors, by his control of patronage. In particular, Bailey effectively selected all state judges. He rewarded with judicial appointments those politicians, or friends of politicians, who voted at state nominating conventions for the candidates Bailey favored. He similarly rewarded those who served the Democratic party.

After my last term in the state house of representatives, Bailey picked me to be general counsel to the Democratic party legislators. The two previous party counsels had been appointed judges. He led me to believe that I would be selected also.

By then I passionately yearned for the position. I loved practicing law. I cared about my clients. I especially enjoyed representing my union clients. But after more than twenty years at the bar, I felt I was repeating myself. The pace and pressure of the practice, particularly the tyranny of the telephone, were wearing me down.

Then there was Mrs. Gold. Every lawyer in general practice, after only a few years, acquires the equivalent of a Mrs. Gold. She is the client whose case the lawyer thought he had completed but who continues to call about the troubles of her life. I had obtained a divorce for my Mrs. Gold on the precise terms she wanted. The day after the entry of the decree she was on the phone demanding changes. I made motions for modification, and some even succeeded. But nothing I did satisfied her, for her problems were more fundamental than I could solve as a lawyer. But that did not deter her calling me regularly, launching into unstoppable monologues, invariably when I was most busy. Harassment by Mrs. Gold and clients like her made the bench seem an attractive refuge.

Finally, having made innumerable futile attempts to persuade "dumbjudges," I wanted to decide cases my way, to leave my imprint on the law.

The legislative counsel job to which Bailey appointed me put me in the center of the political swirl at the capital. I had the responsibility of shaping the major Democratic administration bills of each session. This meant not only drafting the bills, but, when opposition arose among Democratic legislators, negotiating compromises and revising the language to garner the votes for passage. When Bailey did not make me a judge after my productive service during the 1967 session, I was disappointed. When he did not do so after the 1969 session, I was devastated. He seemed to be keeping the prospect of a judgeship before me like the mechanical rabbit at the dog track.

Bailey had no power of patronage from 1970 to 1974, when Republican Governor Thomas Meskill was in office. During those years I represented the Democratic party in a suit brought in the federal district court challenging a Republican plan to redistrict the Connecticut legislature. The case involved the constitutional doctrine of one man, one vote. It went all the way to the United States Supreme Court. Arguing in that historic courtroom, fielding the questions of those august justices, was the high point of my legal career.

Bailey was dying of cancer in Hartford Hospital when Democratic Governor Ella Grasso was inaugurated in January 1975. Just a few days before his death, he kept his implied promise to me by penciling my name on a list of recommended judicial candidates. Ella nominated me in the spring, and, after being approved by the legislature, I was sworn in on July 1, 1975, as a judge of the court of common pleas.

·   ·   ·

Some aspects of the transition from lawyer to judge I anticipated, such as the shift from advocacy to neutrality, from causing the storm in the courtroom to being the calm at the center of the storm. A real surprise was instantaneously becoming a member of the state bureaucracy. As a lawyer and senior partner in my firm, my time had been my own. On the spur of the moment I could be off to a ball game at Fenway Park or to the tennis matches at Forest Hills. As a judge I had fixed hours and a fixed schedule. I had to be at a specific place every day, all day, and to request days off and vacations months in advance.

But the biggest jolt was discovering the loneliness of being a judge. Everything about the job conspired to isolate me—physically, socially, emotionally. Sometimes I felt like a quarantined child looking wistfully out the window at playing friends.

The judicial status that had seemed attractive when I was an attorney proved to be imprisoning. People kept their distance. Court clerks were deferential, jurors and litigants remote. Lawyers, with whom I dealt in chambers in an effort to settle cases or discuss aspects of the trial, were constrained. I was the one who held them captive after the business at hand was completed, regaling them with stories of my past triumphs, while they, I sensed, fretted to get free.

Connecticut's practice of rotating judges geographically added to the sense of isolation. Every three months I was assigned to a different court location. Over several years I sat in almost every courthouse in the state. As one of my colleagues put it, "Have gavel, will travel."

Frequently I went to lunch alone. In the small towns where I was the only judge, eating with the prosecutor or other lawyers gave an appearance of partiality.

Each morning when I arrived at the courthouse, I went straight to my chambers and then spent the day on the bench. During recesses, lawyers lined up outside my chambers door for me to sign ex parte orders. There was no time for coffee breaks or chats with colleagues. At the end of the day I reviewed my trial notes and signed the arrest warrants placed on my desk. By then the courthouse was deserted. I left with laden briefcase. There was nobody to say good night to.

In the evening I retired to my study to look up a puzzling point of law that had come up at the trial, prepare a jury charge for the next day, or, if I had the energy, attack my backlog of undecided cases. I wrestled with my dilemmas alone, reflecting in solitude and reaching solitary decisions.

The political activities I had engaged in before becoming a judge I expected to give up. I also had to resign my membership on community and social service organization boards because most of their meetings were held at times that conflicted with my rigid court schedule. Divorcing myself from such activities cut me off from the vibrancy of society.

Such professional solitude made me treasure home and personal life even more. My wife, Ruth, was the one who listened as I related the amusing incidents and unexpected twists of a trial, who provided support as I agonized over the dilemmas of decision making. Being with friends on weekends also fortified me to face the monastic week ahead.

In the early years there was another unexpected irritant. Governor Grasso had initiated the policy of appointing new judges only to the court of common pleas. It was a court of limited criminal and civil jurisdiction, empowered to hear only misdemeanor crimes, civil cases in which the amount claimed did not exceed $15,000, and appeals of the decisions of administrative agencies. It was distinctly inferior to the superior court, which had unlimited civil and criminal jurisdiction. I found myself chafing under my court's lesser responsibility and status.

I also resented the snobbery of superior court judges. Many of them pointedly avoided going to lunch with court of common pleas judges who sat in the same courthouse. What was infuriating was that they had been appointed on the same political basis as we, and they were not a jot more competent.

In 1978, however, the court of common pleas was merged into the superior court to form a one-tier, statewide trial court. This eliminated the caste system among judges and improved morale immensely.

Imperceptibly, over time, I became more accepting of my lot. Nostalgia for my life as a lawyer waned when attorneys kept telling me how the practice was changing: clients showed little loyalty and, when their cases went poorly, threatened malpractice suits. And with law schools pouring out graduates, the profession was becoming overcrowded. Again and again I heard, "It's a jungle out there."

I hunkered down with my fellow judges, realizing that, after all, we had only each other. I lunched with them more often. They were not as lively as legislators, but I began to see them as comrades, sharing with me the same burdens and challenges. I especially appreciated the concern they had for each other and their spirit of cooperation. When puzzled over a point of law, I could drop into another judge's chambers and get helpful pointers.

Although the judicial abilities of my colleagues varied, each in his own way made a contribution to the multiple functions of judging. Some were good at writing learned opinions, some at sentencing criminals, some at handling family and juvenile matters, and some at trying simple traffic violations with dignity. I recognized that I lacked many of those skills.

And my colleagues were honest. Over Connecticut's three-hundred-fifty-year history, not even a hint of corruption has tarnished a single superior court judge. That cannot be said of judges of the neighboring states of New York, Massachusetts, and Rhode Island. I was proud to be part of that tradition of integrity.

I overcame the sense of loneliness I felt so deeply in the beginning. In my second year on the bench I organized a

colloquium of judges to explore fundamental issues of jurisprudence. If legal philosophy is the theory of how law
works, who better than judges to test those theories against
reality? About fifteen of us began meeting regularly six times
a year over dinner to engage in spirited discussions of serious topics.

I started teaching a course on legislative process at the
University of Connecticut School of Law. I loved the contact
with young, eager students and felt that by training them I
was helping to shape the future of the profession.

The practice of geographical rotation was curtailed. Judges
were kept closer to their homes. I was assigned to the Hartford courthouse, where I have stayed for years. That judicial
district gets the most challenging cases in the state, and I
have been given more than my share.

I found I no longer missed the fray. The contemplative life
of a judge had its advantages. I enjoyed wrestling with difficult legal issues, probing for the resolution of human problems, having my opinions published in the case reports and
thus stitched into the fabric of the law.

I had given up the practice because I wanted more meaning in my life. Now the most meaningful thing I could do
was to strive for justice.

3. WHOM TO BELIEVE?

The phone rings in my chambers a few minutes after ten. The calendar judge for the civil part of Hartford Superior Court is on the line.

"Bob, I'm sending you a court case to try. *Romano* v. *Costello*. Your clerk is bringing you the file. The lawyers say it's a short trial."

A court case means I will hear it without a jury and I alone will determine the facts, resolve the issues of law, and render a final judgment. Determining the facts is often the most difficult.

The facts of a case are the conclusions drawn from the evidence. The evidence is mainly in the form of testimony, so finding the facts requires assessing not only what witnesses say on the stand, but which are telling the truth. Since people on each side of a case often give contradictory versions of the same event, the subtext of a trial is credibility —which witnesses, and to what extent, are to be believed. I suspect it will be so in the trial being sent to me.

Certain kinds of cases are required to be tried by a judge alone. Among them are so-called equity actions, in which one party seeks an injunction to forbid the other party from doing an illegal or harmful act or seeks to compel the other party to specifically perform a contract. Others are appeals from decisions of administrative agencies. Actually, any case can be tried to the court without a jury if the parties so desire and they often do when they want a quicker hearing, or when the issues are complicated and they do not trust a jury to decide them. Businessmen in particular prefer to have their commercial and corporate controversies resolved by judges.

The lawyers appear at my chambers. I know them both as hardworking practitioners. We chat informally for a few moments, I calling them by their first names. I glance at the complaint in the file. It alleges that the plaintiff has loaned the defendant $10,000; the defendant has failed to pay on time; the plaintiff demands damages equal to the amount of the loan plus interest and costs.

"Do you have a defense?" I ask the defendant's lawyer.

"You bet, Your Honor. My client claims—"

"Wait a minute," the plaintiff's lawyer interrupts, bristling, "we can't discuss the case before the judge who's going to hear it."

"Take it easy, fellows. I just want to know what the issue is. Any chance of settling the case? If so, I will send you to another judge who can help you reach an agreement."

The trying judge in a court case cannot get involved in settlement negotiations with the attorneys. He may learn facts not admissible into evidence or learn the parties' compromise positions, which may improperly influence his ultimate decision.

Both lawyers shake their heads. The plaintiff's attorney

says, "We've tried to settle, Judge, but there's no chance. The case has to be tried."

"Okay, let's try it," I say.

The next moment I am on the bench. The courtroom is small and spare, as unpretentious as the waiting room of a rural railroad station. None of the splendor of a jury court-room. Aside from the court clerk and reporter, the only others present are the two lawyers and their clients. I have just finished bantering with the lawyers and am now conducting the trial with strict formality. I am amazed at how quickly all of us assume our roles.

Since this is a court case, lawyers will forgo the hammy vaudeville gestures they pull before jurors: the dramatic thrusting of a document at the witness as if piercing his heart; the rolling of the eyes upward and the incredulous shaking of the head at the witness's last answer. They will also eschew hackneyed tactics, such as asking witnesses called by the other attorney whether they talked to the attorney before testifying. They know judges understand that lawyers must speak to witnesses in order to prepare them for trial. If the attorneys do engage in such playacting, I will say, "Counsel, please don't waste my time with this nonsense. Let's get on with the case."

I also try court cases differently from jury cases. For example, although the rules of evidence are supposed to be applied alike in both, I, and most judges, apply them with less rigor in court cases. The analogy can be made between the difference in adult conversation when children are in the room and when they are out of earshot. In court cases, where there is no jury, I tend to be more liberal in letting in evidence that the rules might exclude as unreliable, because, as an experienced trier, I feel capable of disregarding such evidence.

The plaintiff's attorney motions to his client to take the stand. The clerk asks the short, gray-haired man to raise his right hand and intones, "You solemnly swear that the evidence you shall give, concerning the case now in question, shall be the truth, the whole truth, and nothing but the truth, so help you God?"

"I do."

"Give your name and address."

"Frank Romano, Thirty-nine Preston Street, Hartford."

The witness takes his seat in the chair on the raised stand next to the bench. He sits stiffly, ceaselessly kneading his thick hands in his lap. Under questioning by his attorney, he testifies that his niece's husband wanted to start a sidewalk construction business. "That's Joe," he says, pointing to the defendant. "He asked me to loan him ten thousand dollars, and promised to pay me back in two years. I was glad to help him get going in a new business."

The $10,000 check to the order of Joseph Costello is introduced into evidence; it has been duly endorsed and cashed. Mr. Romano's lawyer asks:

"Was your agreement with Mr. Costello in writing?"

"No. I trusted him. He was my *paisan*."

Mr. Romano concludes by saying that after three years he demanded payment, and when it was not forthcoming, he started this suit.

I have been listening and observing the witness. I notice that he holds his head slantwise and seems to speak into space rather than directly to his lawyer.

The defendant's attorney begins his cross-examination of Romano by eliciting from him that he has no children and Joe's wife, Felicia, is his favorite niece. Then the lawyer asks, "Didn't you really give the money to Mr. Costello so he could provide a better living for Felicia?"

"Yes, I wanted to help Felicia. But the money was a loan to Joe."

"Yet you waited three years to ask for the money back when you said the loan was for two years, isn't that so?"

"I wanted to see if Joe would pay me back on his own."

"Isn't it a fact that you didn't demand payment until after Joe left Felicia and started the divorce?"

"That had nothing to do with it," Mr. Romano retorts angrily. "It was a loan, and I wanted my money back."

After both counsel finish with the witness, I have a question to ask him. Although in a jury case I intervene as little as possible in order to permit the attorneys to convince the jury in their own way, in court cases they have to convince me, and the decision is my responsibility. I am more interested in finding out all the information that will help me decide than I am in protecting the trial strategy of the lawyers. So I ask from the bench, "Tell me, Mr. Romano, if there had not been a divorce between Joe and Felicia, would you still be asking for the money?"

"Well, Judge . . . I don' . . . I love Felicia. . . ." Mr. Romano looks at his attorney. "But it was a loan, Judge," he says in a rising voice. "Joe promised to pay me back, and he didn't."

Mr. Costello is called by his attorney to the stand. He is a muscular man of about thirty, with wavy black hair and blue eyes. The clerk recites: "You solemnly swear that the evidence you shall give, concerning the case now in question, shall be the truth, the whole truth, and nothing but the truth, so help you God?"

"I do."

He is at ease on the witness chair, but I notice he speaks slightly out of the side of his mouth. After some preliminary questions, his lawyer asks, "What was the arrangement concerning the ten thousand dollars with your uncle-in-law?"

"He knew I was going into the construction business and offered to help me. I said I didn't know if I could pay him back. He said, 'Don't worry about it, Joe. This is a gift. Felicia is my favorite niece. I'm glad to help her in this way.' I thanked him. A few days later he gave me the check."

"What happened next?" asks his lawyer.

"Three years later Felicia and I got divorced. Then for the first time he started pestering me for the money. I woulda paid him just to get him off my back. But the business is barely breaking even, and I just don't have the dough."

Cross-examination does not shake the essentials of his story. That is the case. Simple set of facts. The only thing difficult is the decision.

Was the money given as a loan or a gift? Whom am I to believe, the uncle or the nephew? On what basis can I decide who was telling the truth?

In olden days the sworn oath of a witness as a God-fearing man was thought to assure his telling the truth. Now God is not so feared. We rely on the tendency of people generally to be truthful, on the professional ethics of lawyers not to suborn perjury, and on the weapon of cross-examination. In practice, all are slender reeds.

Professor John Henry Wigmore, leading authority on evidence, warns of the latent errors in oral testimony of "Perception, Recollection or Narration." Witnesses may testify erroneously because they perceive an event incompletely, recall it imperfectly, or tell it inaccurately. Clues to such errors can sometimes be revealed by artful cross-examination. However, the best of cross-examination can rarely crack deliberate perjury or its next of kin, the conscious shading of the truth by a witness out of his own self-interest. Here the uncle and the nephew have equal self-interest to remember the facts in the way that favored each of them.

Can I decide credibility on my observations of the demeanor of the uncle and nephew on the stand: the uncle's tenseness, his way of never looking at his lawyer; the nephew's ease, his manner of speaking out of the side of his mouth? Can I, in Shakespeare's felicitous words, "find the mind's construction in the face"? Are external signs— squints of the eye, twitches in the cheek, nervous gestures of the hands—reliable clues of the speaker's truth or falsity?

I know so little about the uncle and nephew. The uncle has been on the stand about thirty minutes, the nephew twenty. A friend who served on a jury once complained about his lack of information about the background of the witnesses.

"What did you want to know?" I asked.

"For one thing, what people who know the witness think of him. People like his neighbors, his pastor, his banker. For another, what kind of person the witness is. Things like does he pay his debts, give to charities, drink to excess."

"But," I protested, "that would open up so many areas that the trial would never end."

Yet my friend was right in his essential point. Witnesses on the stand appear two-dimensional. Rarely is the third dimension of their character revealed.

Forced to decide in the uncle-nephew case, I choose to believe the nephew. It rings truer to me that the divorce, and not the original understanding about the money, is the real reason the uncle wants to be repaid. I do so despite the uncle's heated denial. But my decision in favor of the nephew has no solid, objective basis; it is founded not on analysis, but on a hunch.

Direct conflict of testimony is not confined to simple cases in which the only witnesses are the plaintiff and the defendant. Such conflict is endemic in court proceedings. I have conducted trials involving a maze of complex legal issues and lasting months, in which the outcome hung on the credibility to be accorded opposing witnesses on a key point. In a hotly contested fraud action, the decision rested on whether to believe the plaintiff's witnesses that certain disclosures were made at a certain meeting between the parties held at a certain time and place or to believe the defendant's witnesses that no disclosures were ever made and no such meeting was ever held.

In most court cases only money is involved. But in the Rosado extradition proceeding the issue is whether a man should be required to stand trial for murder in a distant place, and the credibility question presented is not which group of witnesses to believe, but whether to believe any of the witnesses.

In this case the governor of Puerto Rico requested that the

governor of Connecticut return Luis M. Rosado Cintron to
Puerto Rico because he is charged with first-degree murder,
"was present in the Island at the time of the commission of
the crime, and is now a fugitive from the Justice of the Commonwealth." The extradition papers contain the sworn
statement of a witness who affirms he saw Rosado shoot and
kill one Edwin Zambrana Torres on April 25, 1987, at 8:20
P.M. at a Gulf station in Santa Isabel. The witness identified
Rosado as the person shown in the attached photograph.

After being arrested in Hartford on the warrant issued by
the Connecticut governor, Rosado refused to waive extradition and filed a habeas corpus application to test the legality
of the proceedings. Under our law there is a strong presumption in favor of granting extradition and returning the
accused to the state requesting him. The accused cannot resist on the ground that he did not commit the crime. But he
can claim that he is not a fugitive because he was not in the
requesting state at the time of the alleged crime. That is
Rosado's defense in this case: that on April 25, 1987, he was
in Hartford.

Rosado appears in court accompanied by two burly policemen in plain clothes who keep their eyes on him from the
first spectator row. He is a thin, light-skinned man of about
forty who clearly matches the photograph in the extradition
papers.

His attorney calls the first witness. After being sworn in,
the pretty adolescent identifies herself as Maly Rosado, the
petitioner's daughter. She testifies in a self-assured voice
that her family came to Hartford in 1986 to live with the
family of Maria Martinez. They were all living there on April
25, 1987.

"That day," she said, "was Maria's son Alexander's birthday. While he was playing football, we planned a surprise
party for him. In the late afternoon my father and I went to
a bakery to buy a birthday cake. The party was from six until
eight-thirty that night, and my father was there all the time."

Alexander next takes the stand. He is a well-built boy who speaks with a slight Spanish accent. "April 25, 1987, was my fifteenth birthday. It was a Saturday and I played football. After the game, when I came home about three-thirty in the afternoon, I found a party had been planned for me. Mr. Rosado and his daughter went out to get the cake. The party was from six until eight-thirty that night, and Mr. Rosado was there all the time."

Maria Martinez, a short, stout woman, testifies that the Rosados came to live with her in September 1986 and remained until August 1987. During that time Rosado never left for any long period of time. She produces a birth certificate that showed Alexander was born on April 25, 1972.

"On that day in 1987," she says, "Mr. Rosado asked me if I was going to bake a cake for Alexander's party. I said I had no money, so Mr. Rosado bought a cake. The party was from six until eight-thirty that night, and Mr. Rosado was there all the time."

Mr. Rosado testifies that on April 25, 1987, he was at Maria's house all day and night and he was not in Puerto Rico. He says he is a carpenter and member of a local construction union. In April 1987 he was working on the construction of an apartment house in Hartford, but on April 18 the masons went on strike. The next week he worked two days for a company doing scaffolding and one day at the new legislative building doing general cleaning.

The state's attorney cross-examines Rosado and his witnesses but puts on no witnesses of his own. At the end of the evidence I say that I am puzzled by the testimony of Mr. Rosado's daughter and Alexander that Alexander was playing football in late April since that is a fall sport. "Couldn't you have a coach or teammate clear up that question in my mind?" I ask Rosado's lawyer. "Also, it seems to me Mr. Rosado could present some evidence—wage receipts or the testimony of an employer or union hiring hall official—that he was working some days the week of which April twenty-

fifth was a Saturday and the following week. Finally, since
the state claims Mr. Rosado was in Puerto Rico on April 25,
it might be able to obtain evidence from an airline that he
took a plane there before that date. There aren't that many
airlines traveling from Hartford to the Island. I'll adjourn the
case until next Tuesday for the attorneys to present this ad-
ditional evidence."

At the adjourned day, Rosado's lawyer says that Alexander's coach kept no records so he cannot testify to football
practice or a game on April 25. He adds that the construction
job Rosado worked was on strike from April 11 to May 8,
1987, and he did not work in that period. The state's attorney
says the airline companies do not keep passenger lists after
flights are completed.

So I am left with the testimony of the witnesses. There is
no conflict among them, but still I am not obligated to believe them.

The public policy is so strong in favor of extradition that
the accused must prove his defense that he is not a fugitive
from justice by the highest standard of proof in the law:
proof beyond a reasonable doubt. That high standard impli-
cates the issue of credibility. If I am in doubt about the credibility of Rosado's witnesses, I can decide that he has failed
to meet his burden of proof. If I believe his witnesses, I can
decide he has met his burden and deny extradition.

The state's attorney argues that mere oral testimony is
insufficient to establish proof beyond a reasonable doubt. I
retort, "The state relies upon the testimony of witnesses to
prove the commission of a crime all the time. If that testimony can support a finding of guilty in a criminal case, it
can support a finding that Rosado was not a fugitive in an
extradition proceeding."

But the question remains: Shall I believe the witnesses?
Two exactly opposite but equally valid inferences can be
drawn from each aspect of their testimony. On the one
hand, all the witnesses are either Rosado's relatives or his
close family friends. On the other hand, that alone is not a

basis for discrediting them, for often an accused can only rely on the testimony of family and friends to prove he was not at the scene of a crime. Whether or not Alexander was playing football on the Saturday in April is not material in and of itself, except that inferences about credibility can be drawn from the accuracy of irrelevant evidence. But too much should not be made of that testimony because the witnesses could have meant soccer, which is played in the spring. The testimony about Maly and Mr. Rosado getting the birthday cake and about the party rings true. But when all the witnesses spoke of the duration of the party and Mr. Rosado being there, I heard them use exactly the same words, indicating they might have been coached. Mr. Rosado first testified that he worked a few days during the week of which April 25 was a Saturday and then produced no evidence. But I wonder how I can prove what I was doing on any given day a year ago.

I think long and hard about the case. I go back and forth: one day deciding for Rosado and the next against him. I am aware that if I send him to Puerto Rico, the commonwealth will still have to prove him guilty. But requiring him to defend himself on a murder charge if he was not there when the crime was committed is imposing a serious hardship. The more I reflect, the more I realize that the answer lies not in analysis but in intuition. Facts determine the outcome of most cases, and the credibility accorded the witnesses determines what the facts are. But what determines credibility?

Despite the vast number of cases judges hear, they have no special ability to discern testimonial truth. Intuiting the reliability of what people say is an innate rather than acquired skill. Judges, like everyone else, tend overly to believe the members of their own social class. Six jurors of various backgrounds, applying their combined common sense, are better at assessing witnesses than a single, lonely judge. Painfully aware of that, I wish that a jury was deciding this case.

In the end I conclude that I do not believe the witnesses

when they place Rosado in Hartford on April 25, 1987. So I
deny the application for a writ of habeas corpus and order
Rosado extradited to Puerto Rico to stand trial for first
degree murder.

But if I am honest with myself in the Rosado case and in
all cases in which a determination of credibility must be
made, I have no stronger basis for my decision than a guess.
And, it is important to note, if I am wrong in that guess,
I am dead wrong in my final judgment of the case. Nor do
the losers have recourse on appeal. An appellate court always defers to the trial judge who sees and hears the witnesses, and it never reverses on the basis of his assessment
of credibility.

Thus, when deciding a court case, I live with the possibility—probability—of making a total, irredeemable, and
costly mistake. Even worse, of causing a serious, grievous
injustice. That is scary.

4. HEART V. MIND

After I decide, on any basis I can, what witnesses to believe, and so determine the facts of a court case, I must deal with the legal issues presented. The applicable law that my research discovers almost always makes sense and directs a decision in my case with which I am comfortable.

Occasionally, however, cases come before me in which my sympathies impel me toward one result and the law seems to compel a different result—cases, in short, that generate a war between my heart and mind. Resolving them satisfactorily is an especial challenge. The true art of judging, I believe, is a judge using his mind to find *valid* ways to implement the stirrings of his heart.

An example of a case that engendered a conflict between my heart and mind was the Charles Bush estate matter. I had to decide who should get the assets of a deceased nonagenarian who had outlived the beneficiaries named in his will.

In 1910 Charles Bush married Mary Somers. Raymond, her five-year-old son by a previous marriage, came to live with the couple but was never adopted by Charles. In 1933 Raymond Somers married Helen; they had two children, Jack and June.

In 1965, at the age of seventy-six and in poor health, Charles made out his will. He gave his entire estate to his wife, Mary. If she predeceased him, everything was to go to her son, Raymond. If both Mary and Raymond died before Charles, everything was to go to Raymond's wife, Helen. The will did not provide for the contingency of their all dying before Charles. But they did.

In the late 1960s Mary died. Charles continued to live through the 1970s and into the 1980s. In 1983, within a span of seven weeks, Raymond's wife, Helen, and then Raymond himself died, and finally, two weeks later, Charles died at the age of ninety-four.

Raymond's son, Jack Somers, filed Charles's will in the East Hartford Probate Court. He had himself appointed administrator and claimed that he and his sister, June, were entitled to Charles's estate, then worth $80,000. The probate court appointed an attorney to search for any other members of Charles's family. None were found. The court determined that Jack and June, being Charles's stepgrandchildren, were not his legal heirs. Since there were no other heirs, the court ruled that Charles's estate escheated—that is, it was deemed abandoned and must be paid over to the state of Connecticut.

Jack appealed the probate judge's decision to the superior court. Because Connecticut probate courts are not courts of record, their cases are tried by the superior court de novo— that is, as if for the first time and without any weight being given to the probate court decision.

At the trial before me, Jack's lawyer seeks to introduce

evidence about the relationships between Charles and Raymond and between Charles and Jack and June. The assistant attorney general representing the state, now a party in the suit because of the probate court ruling, argues that such evidence is irrelevant in a will construction case. If this were a jury trial, I would have to decide the evidentiary question right then. But since it is a court case, I tell the attorneys I will allow in the evidence, subject to my later deciding its relevance and probative value.

Jack testifies that Charles raised Raymond as his son. After Raymond married Helen and they had their children, the Bush and Somers families lived on the same street in East Hartford. They went on picnics and outings and had many happy times together. Charles treated Jack and June as his grandchildren. After Charles's wife died, Charles became even closer to Raymond's family.

As the evidence unfolds, so does my feeling that Charles's estate should surely go to Jack and June rather than to the state.

Since the facts in the case are not in dispute, I do not have to wrestle with credibility of witnesses or to unravel tangled strands of evidence. The only question is the law.

The legal issues that arise in court trials differ from those in jury trials, and the judge's role in dealing with them also differs. In jury cases the relevant law is usually confined to the few repetitive areas of negligence, malpractice, and product liability. It is a broad highway with clear markers. The judge's function is to express the law clearly to the jury and let the jury decide the case. In court cases, on the other hand, the applicable law spans the legal encyclopedias from abatement to zoning. It is often a rural trail in the hinterlands. The judge's task is to master unfamiliar legal realms and to decide the case himself.

Law generally falls into three broad categories: common law, which rests on the precedent of previously decided cases but can also be molded by judges on the basis of experience and common sense; statutes enacted by Congress and the state legislature; and constitutions of the nation and the state.

The Bush estate case involves the first two categories. There is a common law question—how to construe Charles's will. And there is a statutory question—how to interpret the state statute governing the situation when beneficiaries named in a will die before the testator.

When the trial concludes, I ask the lawyers to file briefs. I know they will be helpful in identifying relevant cases and marshaling arguments on each side of the issues. Serious lawyers put substantial scholarship into their briefs, and I consider them seriously. But lawyers are advocates. Their partisanship narrows their focus; they cite and interpret only authorities that advance their clients' positions. My job is to decide not on the basis of the better brief, but on the basis of the law itself. Yet whenever I am inclined to rest a decision on a point not raised by counsel, I remind myself that the lawyers have worked on the case longer than I and probably know it better than I do, so I proceed cautiously.

As it turns out, the lawyers in the Bush estate case file superb briefs. Jack's lawyer claims that the basic common law rule for construing a will is to effectuate the testator's intent. By giving everything to Raymond and then to Helen, Charles indicated a testamentary scheme from which it can be inferred that if these beneficiaries died before him, his estate should go to their descendants. The state, on the other hand, asserts that the words of the will are the sole evidence of Charles's intent. No words in the will make any bequests to Jack and June.

Jack's attorney also seeks to invoke what is called the anti-lapse statute. The law generally is that a bequest to a person who dies before the testator lapses if the will does not provide for any other disposition, and the estate is distributed as if the bequest had not been made. The Connecticut anti-lapse statute is designed to prevent that from occurring in certain situations. It provides that when a bequest in a will is made to the testator's "child, grandchild, brother, or sister," and any of them dies before the testator, with no provision in the will for such contingency, then the bequest to any of them shall go to that person's children. But the Connecticut statute does not save a bequest to a person other than the testator's child, grandchild, or sibling; if such other legatee dies before the testator, the bequest to him lapses.

Jack's lawyer asserts in his brief that the word *child* in the statute should also mean stepchild; or at least it should mean it in this case when the evidence indicates that Charles raised Raymond as his son. The state asserts that the word *child* in the statute means only a natural child and thus the statute does not operate to save Raymond's bequest for Jack and June.

After reading the briefs, I call both lawyers into court to argue their positions. Oral argument almost always illuminates the turgid prose of briefs. But I do not let the lawyers argue by making speeches. Rather, I engage them in a Socratic dialogue, requiring each, under my questioning, to overcome the weakest points of his side of the case and to respond to the strongest points of the other side.

"Why should I consider any evidence about how Charles intended his estate to be distributed, other than the words he himself used in his will?" I ask Jack's lawyer.

"Courts always consider evidence of the circumstances surrounding the formation of a contract in order to effectuate the true agreement of the parties," she says. "We also accept evidence as to intent in connection with inter vivos trusts and insurance policies even after the maker of those instruments has died. Why not in will construction cases?"

"Do you agree?" I ask the assistant attorney general.

"No, sir, I don't. The law is clear. A court can determine the testator's intent only from the words of the will. Otherwise the floodgates would be open for every disappointed relative or friend to produce evidence that the testator intended to make a gift to him."

Jack's lawyer responds quickly. "The floodgates argument

amounts to saying, 'If we do justice in this case, we will have to do it in other cases.' What's wrong with doing justice in this *and* in other cases?"

I take another tack. "Why should I infer Charles intended to give his estate to Jack and June?" I ask Jack's lawyer. "If he had such a fine relationship with them at the very time he wrote his will, why didn't he make bequests to them then, when he could easily have done so?"

"Well, Judge, Charles was not only seventy-six when he wrote his will, but also in poor health. He never dreamed both Raymond and Helen would die before him. And he never had a chance to change his will because Raymond died just two weeks before he did."

"How do you answer that?" I ask the state's lawyer.

"Very easily. The court can't consider all the reasons Charles didn't make bequests to any particular logical legatee. Besides, the court is simply not in the business of rewriting wills."

Again I change the course of questioning. "Why," I ask the state's lawyer, "can't Raymond be considered Charles's child so that, under the anti-lapse statute, the gift to Raymond goes to his children?"

"A number of states have the same statute," he replies. "In every case in which children of a stepchild of the testator tried to claim a bequest under that statute, the courts have turned them down."

"Is that true?" I ask Jack's lawyer.

"Other state courts have decided that way," she acknowledges. "But those decisions are not binding on you. No Connecticut court has ruled on the question, so you can interpret our statute as you see fit. Moreover, there is a special reason in this case why you should not follow those rulings. In all those other cases, the fight over shares of the estate was between children of a stepchild and other heirs of the testator. If the court decided for the stepgrandchildren, it would be at the expense of those other heirs. Here, if Charles's money doesn't go to Jack and June Somers, it goes to the state of Connecticut. Clearly Jack and June's claim is superior to that of the state."

"How about that?" I query the state's lawyer. "Do any of those cases which you rely on reject the claims of stepgrandchildren in favor of escheat to the state?"

"I don't think so, Judge. But the ruling that a stepchild is not a child within the meaning of the statute should apply regardless of whom the estate is going to."

The argument has proven immensely helpful. I have raised the questions that puzzle me and given counsel the opportunity to answer them. All of us are stimulated by grappling with the knotty intellectual and human issues of the case.

Now it is my turn to research the law. Superior court judges in Connecticut do not have their own law clerks to help with such tasks, as do judges in the federal courts and courts of other states. We do have access to a pool of recent law school graduates hired by the judicial department, but these clerks are of varying competence, and I never work with any one of them long enough to develop confidence in them. I do have a secret "law clerk," my former partner and now a judge on the United States Court of Appeals, Jon Newman. I call him occasionally when I have a particularly difficult legal problem, and he is always helpful. In this case, however, I am actually pleased to plunge into the books because I know that I can get the nuances of the law best by reading the authorities myself. Those subtleties often cannot be conveyed by the research of others.

My investigation reveals that the testator's intent of how he wants his estate distributed can be inferred only from the words of the will. Connecticut law excludes all other evidence. How strictly the rule is applied is indicated by a case in which a testator directed his lawyer to rewrite his will to eliminate from his previous will one set of charities and give his residuary estate to a new set of charities. The lawyer

mistakenly drafted the new will to include both sets of charities, and the testator, without noticing the error, executed
it. The Connecticut Supreme Court held that the will had to
be carried out as written; no evidence of the mistake could
even be considered. However, it is a three-to-two decision;
the dissent indicated that extraneous evidence should be
taken into account to show the true facts about the making
of the new will.

My research also reveals that the courts of at least ten
other states have denied claims of stepgrandchildren seeking
a share of an estate under an anti-lapse statute. The rationale
of all those decisions is that by the statute specifying that
only bequests to particular relatives of the testator—his children, grandchildren, or siblings—are to be saved, the legislature intended the testator's property to devolve only along
his bloodline.

I puzzle and puzzle over the case. Can I get any mileage
out of the dissent in the supreme court case indicating that
under some circumstances extraneous evidence outside of
the will can be considered? But a dissenting opinion does
not express the law. It can sometimes be relied upon if it was
written a number of years earlier and the supreme court has
indicated in later opinions an inclination to adopt the dissent's reasoning. But the dissent I seek to rely on has been
written only a few years ago, and there is no basis for thinking it might become the majority opinion of the court.

Moreover, even if I can consider the close relationship
between Charles and Jack and June, an inference that Jack
and June are the likely beneficiaries of Charles's estate when
their parents died before Charles is no stronger than an inference that they are not his intended beneficiaries when his
will does not provide for them. Although Charles may have
expected Raymond and Helen to survive him, and although
he did not have much time to make a new will when they
predeceased him, still a court cannot guess how such a will
would have been written.

The nub of the matter is that Charles's will was poorly

drafted. It does not cover a foreseeable contingency that has indeed occurred: all the named beneficiaries dying before Charles. But the fact that Charles's lawyer has bungled does not entitle me to rewrite the will to correct his mistake.

Can I interpret the anti-lapse statute in a way that will justify getting the money to Jack and June? Now I am shifting the focus from Charles's intent, as inadequately expressed in his will, to the legislature's intent, as expressed in the statute. Specifically, when the statute provides that a bequest to the testator's "child," who dies before the testator, shall go to the child's descendants, does the legislature mean that a bequest to the testator's stepchild, who dies before the testator, shall go to the stepgrandchildren?

In some instances the law treats a step relationship as it does a blood relationship. In divorce law, for example, when a stepparent assumes the role of emotional parent, that person may be awarded custody of the child. Similarly, in tort law a stepparent who stands in loco parentis may be held liable to third parties injured by deliberate acts of the child. With divorces so common and the children of one spouse so frequently going to live with the new spouse, the tendency is to assimilate the legal status of the stepchild with that of the natural child.

However, that liberalizing trend has not extended to the law of wills and estates, mainly because the underlying premise of that law is that property should pass along bloodlines. Another reason is that a testator can clearly state in his will that gifts to children shall include gifts to stepchildren or their descendants. If he does not do so, the law will not assume that is his intent. To construe "child" in the anti-lapse statute as including stepchild might be establishing a dangerous precedent. My zealous desire to do justice for Jack and June could create a general rule that might do injustice in many other situations where the testator, by not mentioning stepchildren, intended that they not become beneficiaries of his estate.

The courts of other states have consistently denied stepgrandchildren, whose parents died before the testator, any rights under the anti-lapse statute. There is not a single case holding the other way. These decisions are not binding on me, as are the decisions of Connecticut's appellate and supreme courts. But wisdom does not stop at state borders. Although there are exceptions, the reasoning and holdings of the courts of one state are generally followed by courts of other states. Furthermore, even if I differ with those decisions, the higher courts of Connecticut are likely to find them persuasive and so reverse me.

The thought I originally had that this case is unique because the money goes to the state proves to be false. My research unearths cases in Ohio and in Washington (not found by the lawyers) in which the courts allowed the estate to escheat rather than award it to the stepgrandchildren under the anti-lapse statute. The legislatures in both states subsequently amended their statutes to provide that if the testator dies without any living heirs, instead of escheating, his estate goes to his stepchildren or their descendants. Amending the anti-lapse statute appeared to be a better way to develop the law than my interpreting the word *child* to include stepchild.

The case becomes an obsession. I awaken in the middle of the night thinking about it. At meals with my wife I either talk nonstop or fall into long periods of thought. "You'll find a way," Ruth says encouragingly. But the law is a steel barrier I cannot figure how to go over, under, or around.

After resisting the thought of that $80,000 sinking into the bottomless pit of the state's general fund, and after straining to fulfill my heart's desire, I have to concede to myself that there is no valid way to rule that Charles's money shall go to Jack and June.

I put off writing the painful opinion, as one usually does with things one does not like doing. When I finally get down to it, I suddenly think of a way out of the dilemma: settle the matter. I remember that I have never explored that possibility with the lawyers. Even now, because it is a court case, I cannot participate in negotiations, but I can initiate them. I call Jack's lawyer and ask if she has tried to settle with the state.

"Goodness, yes," she replies. "We have tried all along. But the assistant attorney general won't consider it."

I sensed that righteousness in the state's lawyer from the argument. But Attorney General Joseph Lieberman, whom I know from my legislative days, when he had been Senate majority leader and I general counsel to the Democrats, is a generous and compassionate man. He may be inclined to compromise a case of this nature.

"I have in mind speaking to Joe Lieberman," I say. "If I can get him to call you, will you discuss settlement with him?"

"Of course, Your Honor."

After asking the assistant attorney general to show the case file to his chief, I wait a few days and finally get the attorney general on the phone.

"Joe, in the Bush estate case, it just doesn't seem fair for the state to take that whole eighty thousand dollars. Would you be willing to work out some sharing arrangement with the attorney for the grandchildren?"

"But Bob," he says, "if our office settles, we'll have to give in to every stepchild in the state whenever a lapsed legacy occurs."

"There hasn't been a single case in Connecticut with these facts," I reply. "You won't be setting a precedent. You'll be doing the right thing."

Several weeks later Joe calls back to say that he has had more of a battle with the attorneys on his staff than with the plaintiff's lawyer. But he has prevailed, and the case has been settled by splitting the $80,000, half to the state and half to the children.

"Joe," I say, "what you have done may not make the state richer, but it sure makes it better."

I am delighted. When the law proved intractable, I called upon the parties' own sense of fairness to bring about the desired result.

I do one thing more: ever the ex-legislator, I write up a summary of the case and send it, along with copies of the Ohio and Washington statutes, to the chairman of the legislature's judiciary committee, suggesting a legislative solution to a problem I could not solve judicially. In the 1987 session the legislature adopts my suggestion. It amends the anti-lapse statute to add a stepchild as one whose bequest will not lapse if he predeceases the testator, and it enacts a new statute providing that if a testator has no heirs, his estate goes to his stepchildren or their descendants before escheating to the state.

So the problem of future Jacks and Junes is solved. But for me the challenge to find valid ways to implement the stirrings of my heart goes on. Meeting that challenge is the most satisfying and worthwhile function I perform on the bench.

5. HOW I DECIDE A COURT CASE

Hard cases like the Bush estate case raise a fundamental question of judicial decision making. That question, when asked by litigants, is: Do all judges decide the same way? If they do, it does not matter before whom their cases come. That question, when asked by a judge, is: Can he decide differently because he is different from all other judges?

When I first came on the bench, I felt that my social concerns and perceptions of justice, derived from fighting civil liberties battles, leading community and antipoverty organizations, representing labor unions, and participating in politics were as much a part of me as the color of my eyes. I asked myself: Did I as a judge have to repress those values and allow them no influence over my act of deciding?

The question is not a new one. Jurisprudence has long

divided into two schools over the role of a judge's values in decision making. The legal positivists assert that law is an all-embracing body of principles; the judge's duty is to discover the correct rule within that body of principles and to apply it inexorably. They consider the judge's values inconsequential. The legal realists, on the other hand, assert that a judge exercises unbridled discretion in making decisions; he works backward from conclusion to principles and uses principles only to rationalize his conclusions. They consider the judge's values all-important.

Experience has taught me that in some kinds of cases the positivists are right; in others the realists are right; and in still others it very much depends upon the judge.

In those cases in which the applicable law is certain, the positivists are right, and my values have no influence on my decision. When a clearly worded statute or my analysis of authoritative precedents points toward only one result, I decide that way. It is my duty to do so, not only as a trial judge who will otherwise be reversed by an appeals court, but also as a principled judge whose individual notions of fairness must give way to the law. The Bush estate case illustrates this. I struggled to reach what I felt to be a just result but, in the end, was about to bow to the dominating force of the law when I found another way to resolve the dilemma.

Another example of my applying the law in disregard of my own predilection was my ruling in an appeal from a decision of the state agency regulating public utilities. That agency, finding that an electric company was making profits in excess of those deemed reasonable when its rates to consumers were approved the previous year, ordered that the excess profits be placed in a reserve fund to be used as an offset to the company's next request for a rate increase. At the trial, consumer groups argued that since the company was earning more than a fair return on its investment, a ratepayers' fund should be created to reduce future rates. The argument had an appealing ring of fairness. Why should the utility company reap bloated profits at the expense of the ratepayers?

My research into the law of public utilities, however, revealed that once rates are set by a regulatory agency, the revenues realized belong to the company. The principle is two-edged. A utility both bears past losses incurred below a reasonable return and retains past profits realized above a reasonable return. Neither may be taken into account in fixing rates to be charged in the future.

One lone decision, by the Rhode Island Supreme Court, holds that the rule should apply only to protect ratepayers against utility losses, but not to allow a utility to retain excess profits. Although there is a Robin Hood attractiveness to that one-sided policy, I saw no legal merit to it.

So I rescinded the order creating the ratepayers' fund. Finding the law to be clear, I applied it rigorously.

In *Morgan* v. *Saint Francis Hospital, et al.* the law was not that clear, but my guess of how a higher appeals court was likely to rule dictated my decision.

Brian Morgan brought a medical malpractice suit against a hospital and doctor. During the picking of the jury, Brian's lawyer used up all his peremptory challenges (the right to excuse a prospective juror for any reason whatsoever). Then in succession two people who worked for Aetna Surety & Casualty Company presented themselves for selection. Brian's lawyer challenged them for cause, claiming they should not be allowed to sit as a matter of law because Aetna insured both defendants.

In Connecticut the lawyers pick the jury by themselves with only a clerk present. If a challenge for cause is raised, counsel go before any judge who happens to be available for a ruling. A judge denied Brian's lawyer's challenges.

The case came before me to be tried. Throughout the trial no mention was made of insurance in general or of Aetna in particular. The trial lasted ten weeks. An Aetna claims representative was in the courtroom during much of that time. The jury returned a verdict for the hospital and doctor.

Brian's lawyer moved to set aside the verdict against his client and for a new trial on the ground that legal error was committed in permitting the two Aetna employees to be members of the jury. Brian had turned down a $200,000 settlement offer and desperately wanted another trial. Aetna, which had hired the lawyers for the hospital and doctor and paid out, by my estimate, over $100,000 to defend the case, was determined to retain the verdict. I sensed that however I decided, an appeal was inevitable.

In Connecticut there are two kinds of challenges for cause: a so-called "challenge to the favor," which is granted on a showing of actual bias by the prospective juror, and a so-called "principal challenge," which is granted on a showing of such a close relationship of the prospective juror to the parties or the suit that bias is conclusively presumed. An example of a close relationship is the venireman being an employee of the defendant. The law deems that an employee would be under such pressure sitting on a case in which his employer was a party that he could not be impartial and therefore requires, on the basis of the relationship alone, that he be excused.

Brian's lawyer argued that he was entitled to a principal challenge as to the Aetna veniremen. His point was that if an employee of a party must be disqualified from serving as a juror, then there is even more reason for disqualifying an employee of the company insuring the defendant, because the insurance company is obligated to pay the judgment and has a greater interest than the defendant in the outcome of the case.

That argument, I felt, had a surface attraction that did not bear up under analysis. In Connecticut, at least, there is a critical distinction between a juror who is the employee of a party and one who is the employee of the company insuring the defendant. The employee of a party knows his boss is in the case and consequently is subject to all the pressures of the relationship. In Connecticut, however, the existence of insurance is zealously kept out of the case, so an employee of an insurance company does not know his employer is involved and is not susceptible to those biases.

In his brief, Brian's lawyer cited cases from at least four states that an employee, officer, or stockholder of an insurance company indemnifying one of the parties is disqualified from sitting as a juror. In reading those cases, I noted that in each of those states the practice was for counsel to question prospective jurors about their connection with the company covering the defendant. The jurors were, thus, alerted to the insurance company involved. Under those circumstances, it was as appropriate to disqualify employees of the insurance company as employees of a party. In the *Morgan* case, Brian's lawyer was not allowed to make that inquiry of the Aetna people, so those cases of the other states were distinguishable.

Despite this ratiocination, I was sympathetic to Brian's outraged cry of foul when two of the six jurors deciding his case were employees of the company that had the biggest stake in its resolution. The appearance of impropriety alone seemed to me to jeopardize confidence in the system.

I was disturbed by the possibility that Aetna veniremen could have inferred their company was the insurer from their recognizing as a fellow employee the Aetna claims representative who attended much of the trial, or from their awareness that Aetna is the largest medical malpractice carrier in Connecticut. But this was speculation on my part because Brian's lawyer had produced no evidence on these points in his motion to set aside the verdict.

I was also disturbed that Aetna knew from its attorneys that the two members of the jury were its employees. Wasn't there a risk that Aetna could find ways to communicate to the jurors that it was the carrier? Large corporations have not proven themselves to be paragons of virtue these days.

The better practice might well be to exclude automatically from the jury employees of involved insurance companies so as to avoid that possibility of overreaching. The virtue of an absolute rule is that it simplifies the jury selection process at the beginning of the trial and reduces attacks on verdicts after they are rendered.

My research, however, revealed that the Connecticut Supreme Court is opposed to expanding the list of relationships that automatically disqualify prospective jurors. It has said in several cases, "This court does not choose to create a set of unreasonably constricting presumptions that jurors be excused for cause due to occupational or other special relationships which might bear directly or indirectly on the circumstances of a given case, where, as here, there is no showing of actual bias or prejudice."

Forced to recognize that an appeals court would not approve my enlarging the scope of principal challenges, I suppressed my misgivings and denied Brian's motion to set aside the verdict.

But in a class of cases called equity cases in which the law permits me to apply equitable principles to achieve essential fairness, the legal realists are right and my own sense of justice can dominate. *Green* v. *DeWeese* is such a case. A court order is being sought to compel the defendants to live up to their contract to sell their house to the plaintiffs.

One of the plaintiffs, Constance Green, is the first witness. Black and beautiful, she makes a striking appearance on the stand. She testifies that she and her husband have been looking for a larger house in a nicer neighborhood in their town for more than two years. When they were shown the house owned by the defendants, they felt it met all their needs.

"It is in Bloomfield," she explains, "where we have to live because I am vice president of the town board of education. It has the right number of bedrooms for our growing daughters, and its three-acre lot on a cul-de-sac gives us the privacy we want."

That afternoon she and her husband signed an offer to buy at $100 more than the asking price and gave the agent a $1,000 deposit. A few days later, when their offer was accepted, they paid the balance of the deposit of $18,000 to the agent and applied for a mortgage.

"What happened next?" asks Green's lawyer.

"Well, several days passed and then I got a call from Mr. DeWeese at my law office. He said he had made a mistake about the real estate contract. He and his girlfriend had reconciled and they wanted to stay in the house. He apologized and offered to pay for any expenses we had incurred."

"What did you say?"

"I told him we loved the house and would not cancel the contract."

"What then occurred?"

"When we finally realized Mr. DeWeese did not intend to sell to us, we went to you to start this action to compel the defendants to comply with the contract."

"Are you ready, willing, and able to buy the house in accordance with the terms of the agreement?"

"We certainly are ready and willing. It is a dream house for us, one we never expected to find or to afford. We are also able. We are assured our bank mortgage will be approved, and we have enough money to pay the balance of the purchase price."

Some exhibits are introduced—deposit checks and mortgage application—and the plaintiffs rest.

The defendant, Charles DeWeese, takes the stand. He is clean-cut, neatly dressed, looking very much the engineer he reveals he is. He tells how he and his friend, Marjorie Alexander, purchased the house together and have lived there with his high-school–aged son for five years. They have remodeled some of the rooms and redecorated the whole house to their liking. After a sudden, serious quarrel, Charles and Marjorie discussed putting the house on the market.

"I didn't want to do it because I felt we could overcome

our differences," says Charles, "but Marjorie insisted. We went to a real estate agent who told us a price he thought the house could bring. I demanded the house be listed for five thousand dollars more. I wanted to discourage offers so I would have more time to convince Marjorie to stay with me."

"What happened next?" asks DeWeese's lawyer.

"I was shocked when the evening of the day we put the house on the market, the agent brought us a signed offer from the Greens for a higher price than we had asked for. Marjorie and I discussed accepting the offer well into the night. I was sure we could live happily together. Marjorie wanted to sell. I pleaded that we let more time pass and not rush into things. She refused. I was terribly upset. Finally, I gave in and we signed the contract."

"Then what happened?"

"Marjorie went off on a business trip for a few days. When she came back, everything had changed. She said she realized she had loved me all along. We agreed to get married and to hold on to the house. I called Mrs. Green the next morning, told her a terrible mistake had been made, and offered to pay any of her expenses. I also instructed the agent to return the deposit to the Greens."

Marjorie Alexander, an attractive woman with an open face and a sincere manner, confirms Charles's testimony and adds that their wedding date is set for a day three months away.

All the evidence in, the Greens' lawyer makes closing argument. "Mr. DeWeese may have been unhappy about signing the real estate agreement, but both defendants knew what they were signing, and it is a valid contract. Clearly the defendants have breached it. My clients do not want money damages; they want what the law entitles them to: an order of this court directing that the defendants convey the property to them at the price set forth in the contract."

Defendants' lawyer responds, "A claim for specific performance of a contract is an action in equity, one which calls upon the court to treat the parties fairly. The remedy is not granted as a matter of right but is within the discretion of the court. The court can refuse to order that a real estate contract be enforced if the sale will cause unreasonable or disproportionate hardship on the seller. That is certainly the case here. During the time my clients had a temporary falling-out, they improvidently signed the agreement to sell their house. A few days later they patched up their quarrel and now plan to get married. It would be a terrible injustice to require them to move from the house that has been their home and where they hope to live happily ever afterward."

"How about my clients?" replies plaintiffs' lawyer. "They didn't know of the defendants' problems. They have bought a house that is perfect in their eyes and fulfills their highest hopes. They should not be deprived of the benefits of an agreement which they entered into in good faith and the terms of which they are ready to fulfill."

I feel the deepest sympathy for both couples. As I worry over my decision, I am reminded of the observation of Justice Bernard Botein, formerly of the Appellate Division of the New York Supreme Court, that a trial judge cannot decide his cases the way he solves a crossword puzzle. "He may not enter his findings of facts across, and his conclusions of law down, and call the result a decision. Too often they may be blended only by a knowing heart and disciplined mind— often accompanied by much anguish of spirit."

In a case like this the discretion vested in a judge is so broad, he can decide either way without fear of reversal by an appeals court. How he does decide very much depends on the kind of person he is and his prior life experiences. A rigid, law-and-order type of personality is likely to conclude that the contract was freely and knowingly entered into and the defendants' distress, which they brought upon themselves, does not excuse enforcing the contract. A flexible and forgiving type of personality is likely to conclude that the defendants made an understandable mistake and should not suffer its full consequences by losing their home.

What tips the scale for me is an experience I had as a lawyer representing a black person purchasing a house in that very town of Bloomfield. My client was so fearful he would not get the property, he had a white person negotiate the price with the owner; the house being vacant, he visited it only late at night when he could not be seen by the neighbors; he arranged a loan beforehand and did not even appear at the closing. The happiest moment of his life, he told me, was when I handed him the deed to the house.

In the case before me I discern no discrimination in Charles and Marjorie withholding the property from the Greens. But that experience taught me that if the Greens are denied this house, whatever other beautiful house they try to buy in another lovely suburban neighborhood, they are likely to encounter invisible, but real, barriers. The hardship they may suffer is greater than the inconvenience imposed on Charles and Marjorie by being forced to move. So I balance the equities in favor of the Greens and order specific performance of the contract.

My ruling is affirmed when appealed to the appellate court. The Greens move into their dream house; Charles and Marjorie marry, I learn from their lawyer, and continue their life together in another town. The affirmance validates that in equity cases a judge can base his decision on what he thinks is right.

But what about a case that does not involve equity? More particularly, a case that can be determined by either of two competing legal principles? Can the outcome then depend on a judge making a choice based on his own values? I believe it can.

A case involving the Department of Environmental Protection and a land development company presents the classic conflict between two laws: a statute requiring the preservation of tidal wetlands and a constitutional provision prohibiting private property from being taken for public use without just compensation.

The company applied to the department to develop 277 acres of tidal wetlands into an industrial park. The department turned down the application. On appeal to the superior court, the judge ordered the department to receive a new application and decide it in a way that would not so restrict the company's use of its property as to amount to "practical confiscation." The company applied again, and when this application was also rejected, it appealed again to the superior court.

The company lawyer argues forcefully before me. "My client has spent over a million dollars making applications to the Department of Environmental Protection. The first one was made more than sixteen years ago. Every one has been rejected. Our proposals have always included saving some of the wetlands, but the department has never been satisfied. Refusing my client any use of its property for that length of time constitutes confiscation without compensation. Under the constitution the state must either permit my client to develop its land or pay fair value for it."

The evidence was that the land, if allowed to be converted to an industrial park, would be worth $60.5 million. There is no prospect that the state will pay that amount.

The assistant attorney general argues, "This land is the third largest tidal marsh in the state; it is an important source of nutrients to a variety of plant and animal life, and a beautiful recreational and aesthetic site. Although the company claims it is willing to save some of the wetlands, its development proposals are so extensive as to destroy all 277 acres. The department has acted reasonably in rejecting the last application, and this court should uphold the department's ruling."

What should my decision be? Has the department confiscated the land or regulated it reasonably? The precedents lay out general principles of what constitutes a taking by the state when it overly restricts a land owner's use of his property. The question is how to apply those general principles to the matter before me.

In *The Nature of the Judicial Process*, Justice Benjamin N. Cardozo describes judges researching the law to match the color of the case at hand against the colors of the cases in the law reports. He adds, "It is when the colors do not match, when the references in the index fail, when there is no decisive precedent, that the serious business of the judge begins."

I am engaged in that "serious business." On the one hand, the constitutional right of private property is important. It is particularly appropriate to vindicate that right in this case when a superior court judge has already warned the department that turning down the company's second application can constitute "practical confiscation," which will require the state to pay for the wetlands.

On the other hand, the state policy in favor of preserving the tidal wetlands is also important. Although sixteen years is a long time for the company to be deprived of the use of its land, the tidal marsh had been there for aeons. Once destroyed, it is destroyed forever.

My case is in the margin between state confiscation and state regulation. A decision can be justified either way. A judge who feels strongly about private property rights can properly decide for the company. I feel strongly about the environment and decide for the department. Values play the key role in my determination.

But I decide in a way that avoids direct conflict between the statute and the constitution. The problem, as I see it, is that the department has denied the company's applications entirely, without giving any indication of what it will approve. The company feels stonewalled. My decision orders the company to submit another application, with alternative proposals, and requires the department staff to guide the company in shaping a development plan that will be environmentally acceptable. It also orders that the evidence from previous hearings not be repeated, and that a strict schedule for processing the renewed application be adhered to so the company will not be unduly delayed. In that way, I hope to enable as much of the marsh as possible to be preserved, without denying the company its constitutional rights.

The decision has not yet achieved its objective. Two years later, the company and the department are still negotiating a plan that will allow some of the wetlands to be developed and will preserve the major portion of them forever.

Inevitably, in each trial as the evidence unfolds, I form a tentative notion of how the case should come out as a matter of common sense and simple fairness. That notion may change as the trial progresses, but at the end it usually gels. It stays in the back of my mind as the silent arbiter of my ultimate decision. If my decision does not coincide with my notion of fairness, there must be a good reason.

When the trial concludes, I must determine the facts of the case. This requires more than guessing at the credibility of witnesses; it requires resolving conflicts in testimony and making rational inferences from the evidence. I endeavor to do so objectively. Teleology plays no part in my determination of the facts. It would be flagrantly dishonest of me to choose to believe only those witnesses whose testimony supports a desired conclusion.

I research the law with an open mind. I do not let any preconceived notions set the direction or limit the scope of my pursuit of the relevant legal principles. I look beneath the words of prior court opinions for their meaning, beyond the letter of a rule for its purpose; I look to the history of a statute or constitutional provision for its intent, to contemporary society for its rational application.

Precedents and statutes lend themselves to more than one meaning, depending on the insight and intellectual prowess of the judge interpreting them. The unimaginative judge will search in law books for the fixed rule and apply that rule narrowly. In so doing, such a judge fails to heed the wisdom of Dean Roscoe Pound: "Yet the significant thing is not the fixed rule but the margin of discretion involved in the standard and its regard for the circumstances of the individual case."

When I discern a certain tensile tolerance in the law to meet the peculiar demands of the case before me, or I discover competing legal principles of equal validity, then I can legitimately bring into play my personal values, my own sense of justice. Such opportunities arise in only a few cases a year; but they are the cases that really matter.

Thus, donning the black robe does not require that I eradicate social concerns developed over a lifetime. But it does require that I permit those values to influence my decision making only within disciplined limits.

Yet the psychology of deciding is mysterious. Constitutional historian Charles A. Miller expressed it this way: "The three sources of decisions—values, rules, and facts—combine to focus on the mysterious 'act of deciding.' While the sources of decisions are rationally comprehensible, the act of deciding is not."

I am never satisfied with my determination of a case until it not only thinks right, but feels right. I imagined I was alone in that regard until I came across this passage by British political scientist Graham Wallas, quoted by Cardozo in *Paradoxes of Legal Science:*

When . . . I asked an American judge, who is widely admired both for his skill and impartiality, how he and his fellows formed their conclusions, he . . . laughed and said that he should be stoned in the street if it were known that, after listening with full consciousness to all the evidence and following as carefully as he could all the arguments, he waited until he "felt" one way or the other.

I once had a case in which I let how I felt about the result take over too much of my deciding, but it turned out all right in the end. A plaintiff had foreclosed a mortgage on the defendant's apartment building and sought a deficiency judgment against the defendant personally. A deficiency judgment is allowed for the difference between the amount of the mortgage debt owed by the defendant and the value of the property foreclosed upon and ordered transferred to the plaintiff. In this case the mortgage debt was $280,743 and the issue was the value of the property at the time of foreclosure. An appraiser called by the plaintiff testified that the property value was less than the amount of the other liens on the property, which, if I believed, meant the deficiency judgment should be for the full amount of the mortgage debt. An appraiser called by the defendant testified that the property value was higher than the other liens and the mortgage debt, which, if I believed, meant there should be no deficiency judgment.

My intuition was to come out somewhere in between. I found that by using the building's net operating income, estimated by one of the appraisers, and multiplying it by the capitalization rate of the other appraiser, I arrived at a deficiency judgment of $106,010. That figure felt just right. Delighted with the result, I wrote a brief opinion explaining how I reached my decision.

A few days later, plaintiff's counsel moved for reconsideration. At the argument on the motion, he pointed out first that I had erred in my multiplication. I had multiplied the net operating income of $96,116 by the cap rate of .1098 and come up with $1,055,354, instead of $10,553.54. Then he said gently, "Judge, when you use the income approach to determine a building's value, you don't multiply the cap rate; you *divide* the cap rate into the net operating income."

What a goof I had made! Wiping the egg off my face, I said to the lawyers, "Obviously both my arithmetic and appraisal method were dead wrong. But why don't you fellows step outside and try to settle this matter."

An hour later they came back into the courtroom with
a grin on their faces and said they had settled the case for
the figure that I had incorrectly calculated but felt was just
right.

After I think and feel what my decision should be, I must
arrange the facts and marshal the law in a written opinion.
Sometimes the facts and law do not fall into place; they assume a logic of their own and march off in a different direction. On several occasions I have started an opinion one way
and was forced by the writing process to reach an opposite
result.

My printed opinion in the bound case reports always
amaze me when I come upon them. They appear so positive
and certain, giving no hint of the doubt or vacillation that
went into their making, of the precarious choices I made on
credibility of witnesses, on weighing the facts, on selecting
the ruling principle of law. Any one of those close calls could
easily have tipped the case the other way.

A friend on the Connecticut Supreme Court often ex-
pounds to me on the impropriety of a judge "putting his
thumb on the scale of justice." He insists that a judge should
focus only on applying the law and not concern himself with
justice. It is easy for him to be detached. In the appeals court
the parties are faceless abstractions, the passions of the trial
muffled in the printed appeal record. But to me on the trial
bench the litigants have names I remember, personalities
that engage me, emotions that involve me. Clearly I do not
decide a case on the basis of my liking one party more than
the other. But I am keenly conscious of the impact of my
decision on the lives and fortunes of flesh-and-blood people.
The cases that stimulate me the most are not the ones that
are challenging intellectually, as much as I enjoy them, but
the ones about whose outcome I care very much.

My supreme court friend is only half-right. A judge must
apply the law. But if he is worthy of his office, he should
also strive for justice. In that regard he is like an artist as to

beauty. An artist does not paint beauty. He paints a picture and hopes to create beauty. A judge does not decide justice. He decides the cases before him and hopes to achieve justice. I do in every one of my cases.

6. CIVIL TRIAL
BY JURY

While civil court trials are events, civil jury trials are theater. Everyone in the courtroom responds to the presence of the panel of citizens in the mahogany-walled jury box. Bailiffs open court with greater flourish; lawyers, having an audience to play to, are more flamboyant; judges are more ceremonial.

The right to trial by jury was wrestled by the English barons from King John at Runnymeade and written into the Magna Carta. It arose out of a distrust of the king's magistrates and a demand that freemen be judged by their peers. More than an erosion of monarchical power, trial by jury represented a greater faith in the judgment of many than in the judgment of one. With every jury case I start, I am reminded of that proud Anglo-Saxon tradition.

In modern times, what the jury adds to a trial, more than

anything else, is the quality of unpredictability. Individual judges may decide differently from each other, but they do so within narrow ranges and on stated grounds that lawyers can understand. Jury verdicts are as random as lottery numbers; the reasons behind them are not disclosed and are often unfathomable. That uncertainty creates suspense and drama.

In most civil jury trials the plaintiff is seeking money compensation for personal injuries suffered as a result of a tort allegedly committed by the defendant. The wrong typically is negligence by a driver in the operation of an automobile, by a doctor in the treatment of a patient, or by a corporation in the manufacture of a product. Although the case is instituted against the tort-feasor, the real—although unnamed—defendant is an insurance company.

Plaintiffs choose jury trials because they hope they can induce sympathetic jurors to overlook weaknesses in the proof of the defendant's liability and to make large awards for the injuries they have suffered. Defendants (that is, insurance companies) choose juries at least in part because jury cases take longer than court cases to bring to trial. During the delay the companies earn interest on the reserves put aside for each claim.

Judge and jury try the case together, but each has a separate role. The judge presides over the courtroom and keeps the case moving in an orderly way. He rules on the admissibility of evidence. At the end of the testimony, he instructs the jury on the legal principles that govern the case. The jury, on the other hand, evaluates the credibility of the witnesses and determines from the evidence what the facts are. It applies to those facts the law given by the judge and renders a verdict for the plaintiff or for the defendant. If the verdict is for the plaintiff, it also awards a sum of money as damages.

The lawyers' battle of wits begins not with the calling of the first witness, but with the selection of the jury. In Con-

necticut, and to a lesser extent in most other states, the lawyers can question prospective jurors (called veniremen)
about their backgrounds, prior experiences, and general attitudes about the case to be tried. The main purpose of the
questioning (called the voir dire, French for to see and hear
the response to questions) is to reveal whether a venireman
should be disqualified for cause—that is, for an objective
reason like overt bias, personal knowledge of the facts of the
case, or acquaintance with the parties, attorneys, or witnesses. But lawyers have another purpose: to learn subtle
characteristics of prospective jurors that will enable them to
discern whether these persons, if selected, are likely to be
favorable or unfavorable to their case. Lawyers are allowed
to excuse a certain number of veniremen whom they do not
like, without having to give any reason for doing so. By
using these peremptory challenges, they hope to end up
with the jury they want.

The time and energy lawyers put into the selection process and their confidence in achieving their objective never
cease to surprise me. Typically, plaintiff attorneys try for
lovable Italian grandmothers and the like, who will respond
emotionally to their injured clients; defendant attorneys try
for accountant and engineer types who will stick to hard
facts. Both sets of attorneys rely on pop psychology and
superficial stereotyping of people. For all their cagey questioning and tortured analysis, in the end they act on
hunches.

Attorneys also use the voir dire to sell their case to jurors.
They frame their questions as statements designed to persuade. For example, plaintiff lawyers ask, "You understand,
of course, that our American justice system allows an injured
person like my client to recover compensation against a negligent person who caused his injuries?" Defendant lawyers
ask, "No matter how seriously a person is injured, he can't
just file a claim in court and recover money. Our law is that
he must first prove the defendant was at fault. You agree,
do you not, that that is only fair and proper?"

Although people may try to get out of being called for jury duty, once they are in the courthouse, they want to hear cases, and they feel hurt if they are not chosen for a panel. At the beginning of the voir dire, I always tell prospective jurors that if the lawyers reject them they should not take it personally. They need not go home that night and say to their spouses, "Gosh, honey, I hope you love me. I was just turned down as a juror." Lawyers cannot explain, even to themselves, why they pick one and not another. Those veniremen not accepted, I tell them, should rightfully assume that the lawyers made a mistake about them.

The Connecticut constitution provides that counsel shall have the "right to question each juror individually." This results in our jury selection dragging on for days, sometimes taking even longer than the trial itself. In the federal district court, across town, a judge interrogates a whole panel of veniremen all at once and gets a jury in an hour or so. Nobody has ever shown that our state juries are any fairer than the federal court juries. But that constitutional provision locks us into our system.

The practice used to be that judges supervised the voir dire in civil cases. It drove me crazy hearing the same questions asked by the lawyers over and over again. Now only a clerk is present; if either lawyer objects to a juror for cause, any judge available at the time rules on the objection.

When the selection is completed, I congratulate the jurors on being chosen. I explain our respective roles in the trial and state the issues of the case so they will be better able to follow the evidence in the context of what they must decide. Since there is likely to be conflicting testimony on these issues, I suggest that they turn on their credibility meters as the first witness approaches the stand.

I caution them on two more points. Because of our procedure of letting the plaintiff put on his evidence first, they should keep an open mind until they have heard the defendant's side. Also, they should not talk to anyone about the case during the trial, even among themselves.

In regard to my warning about discussing the case, I once tried an assault case involving a fight between two women. A witness testified how the women were rolling on the barroom floor pummeling each other. The defendant's lawyer, who was a tall, stout man, asked the witness to get off the stand and demonstrate what she saw.

"What," she said, "with whom? . . . You? . . . Not on your life."

The courtroom roared with laughter.

The next day my clerk told me a juror had told her that he had started chuckling in the middle of the night about the incident. His wife asked, "What in the world are you laughing about?"

He said, "Oops, the judge told us not to talk about the case."

By the time I conclude telling the jurors about the importance of their function and that we will be striving for justice together, the jurors are thirsting for the first piece of evidence.

.   .   .

The parents of a six-year-old child are suing a dentist and an anesthesiologist for malpractice. The sad-faced black woman on the stand testifies that the dentist decided to fill her daughter's many cavities all at once at a hospital while the child was under general anesthesia.

"When the dentist told you that, did you tell him anything about your daughter's blood condition?" asks the mother's lawyer.

"Yes, I told him she had a sickle-cell trait. We had found that out from school where Lori had been tested. I gave him the school medical report."

"Did the defendant say anything to you about that trait in connection with his plan to put your daughter under general anesthesia?"

"No, sir. He told us nothing about any risk involved."

"What happened next?"

"We thought filling Lori's teeth was routine. Both my husband and I went to work that day and had my mother bring Lori to the hospital."

"Later that morning did you hear from anyone?"

"I got a call from the hospital that Lori . . . Lori . . . Lori had died."

Tears streamed down the mother's face. After a pause her lawyer asked, "Did the defendant tell you what had happened?"

"He said Lori had a sickle-cell crisis, but I didn't understand at the time what he meant."

A photograph of the lovely, smiling girl is put into evidence. The plaintiffs' lawyer next calls a hematologist to the stand. "Blood cells," the doctor explains, "normally are oblong in shape and very malleable. They can squeeze into the smallest capillaries. The hospital record shows that when the dental work was done, and the anesthesiologist was bringing the child out of the anesthesia, she experienced a sickle-cell crisis. That means the blood cells of the patient suddenly assumed the shape of a sickle or crescent. In that shape they are no longer malleable enough to flow into her capillaries. Her blood backed up through her body and, in effect, drowned her."

"Doctor, is there a relationship between such a crisis and a general anesthesia?"

"Yes, studies of blacks in Africa with a sickle-cell condition indicate a substantial risk of a sickle-cell crisis during general anesthesia."

"Should the defendants have informed Lori's parents of that risk?"

"The risk is so well known it should have been explained to them so they could have decided whether it was worth taking."

The defendants put on equally qualified experts. They testify that the African studies are inconclusive, and sickle-cell patients run no special risk from general anesthesia.

While doctors differ and lawyers argue, the mother and

father sit stoically in the back of the courtroom. My eyes keep returning to the picture of the beautiful child. Her glowing image transcends the proceedings.

The jury renders a verdict for the dentist and anesthesiologist. The parents receive nothing.

.   .   .

This time the malpractice case is against a small-town hospital and two of its staff radiologists. The plaintiff is Dawn Spatta, a thirteen-year-old brain-damaged girl in a wheelchair, unable to walk or talk.

The evidence is that she had slumped to the floor unconscious and was rushed to the hospital, where blood was discovered in her brain. The next day the hospital searched for the location of the bleed.

An expert for the plaintiff explains the procedure. "The most likely cause was an aneurysm—that is, a spot where a blood vessel swells out like a balloon and often leaks. The medical chart reveals the hospital radiologist took several arteriograms of Dawn Spatta's brain to locate the source of the bleeding. He did this by inserting a catheter in an artery in her groin, passing it up through her heart and then guiding it into one of four arteries, each of which flows into a particular part of the brain. Then he injected dye into the catheter and took X-rays of the blood flow in the brain. He did this for the two arteries in the front of the neck, called the right and left carotid, and found no damage or leakage. Then he did it for one of the two arteries in the back of the neck, called the right vertebral, and found nothing. At that point he stopped. He never explored the left vertebral artery."

A few days later Dawn had another bleed. The hospital immediately sent her to Yale–New Haven Hospital. The radiologist's report accompanying the patient stated that *all* the arteries in her brain had been explored. Doctors at Yale–New Haven took two CAT scans of Dawn's brain but did nothing else for ten days. Finally they did an arteriogram of the left vertebral artery and found the aneurysm. Before they could operate, Dawn had a third bleed, which left her virtually a vegetable.

For four weeks the doctors on each side of the case clash over whether or not the defendant hospital and its radiologist met the prevailing standard of professional care and whether or not the erroneous report delayed Yale–New Haven's finding the aneurysm. All of us in court get an education about hematology and radiology of the brain. While the medical jargon and legal controversy swirl about Dawn, she sits unawares in her wheelchair.

Before the case goes to the jury, the parties reach a settlement. Dawn and her parents receive $1,310,000.

· · ·

The case involves the crash of a small plane. The only passenger, Charles Jubb, and the pilot were killed. The Jubb family sues the private airline company.

An expert in the reconstruction of airplane accidents, called by plaintiff's side, recounts all the evidence available about the crash: the recorded conversations between the pilot and control tower, the last known direction of the plane, the angle of its descent through the trees. His opinion is that the pilot's attempt to make a visual landing in a dense fog is the cause of the disaster. He says the pilot was negligent in making the flight when he was informed the route was covered with fog and he was not qualified to fly by instruments.

This being a death action, the damages the estate is entitled to recover is fair compensation for the loss of Jubb's earning power and of his capacity to enjoy life's activities. Under that standard virtually all information about Jubb becomes relevant. His son testifies to the kind of man his father was.

"Once when I was discouraged over flunking my CPA

exam, I talked to my father. In the middle of the conversation he went up to his bedroom and brought down a baseball. He said to me, 'This is my most prized possession. It is a baseball signed by the 1927 New York Yankees. They were the best team in all history. Here are the signatures of Lou Gehrig, Tony Lazzeri, Bill Dickey, and, of course, Babe Ruth. The Babe struck out more times than any other player in the game. But that never stopped him from hitting the most home runs. Learn from that, son. Never let past failure stop you from succeeding the next time you come to bat.' That was my father—always encouraging us and always facing up to the next challenge."

The defendant produces witnesses who give another picture of Jubb. Some eighteen years before the accident, they say, he was committed to a mental hospital where he tried to commit suicide. In more recent years he was convicted of drunken driving and his license was suspended. He went through bankruptcy; he lost his house by foreclosure; and his last bank checks bounced. His wife divorced him, and some of his children refuse to see him.

The jury renders a verdict in favor of the Jubb estate for $463,000.

.   .   .

The case arises out of an automobile accident but has an unusual twist. The plaintiff, John Prange, is a college student. While driving home from his part-time job, he was struck by a stolen car going ninety miles an hour the wrong way on a busy urban street. Prange's car was cracked in half by the crash, and his right foot was torn off, his left leg shattered, his neck fractured. It took him twenty months to recover. He appears in court wearing an artificial leg and using a cane. Gazing at him from the bench, I ponder the riddle of The Bridge of San Luis Rey: Why him? Why was this handsome twenty-five-year-old man placed in the path of that wild car?

The thief, who was killed in the accident, had no insurance. So Prange sued the police officers of the towns of Newington and Wethersfield for allegedly conducting a high-speed chase of the stolen car through a populated area. Witnesses on each side give irreconcilable accounts of the actions of the police just prior to the accident.

A witness called by the plaintiff testifies: "I was traveling north on Silas Deane Highway with my girlfriend. There was a lot of traffic on the road. Suddenly, just north of Welles Road, a white Thunderbird streaked by me, tailed by two police cars with their lights flashing and sirens blaring. I saw the Thunderbird swerve past a line of cars at a traffic light into the left lane and smash into Mr. Prange's car. The policemen were right behind the speeding car."

The witness's passenger confirms this version of the accident. If the jury believes it, the police violated their own pursuit policies by chasing a fleeing felon on a busy street, and thus were a contributing cause of the accident.

A witness called by the defendants testifies: "I was in a town ambulance at the Wethersfield police station, waiting to make a turn onto Silas Deane. I saw a white car speed by and a moment or two later heard a terrible crash. We raced to the scene, just two blocks away, arriving the same time as the police cars. It was lucky we got there so quickly because we saved the young man's life. I did not see any policemen tailing the stolen car."

Another occupant of the ambulance corroborated this account. If the jury believes it, the police were not at fault and did not cause the accident.

All the eyewitnesses are ordinary citizens with no interest in the outcome of the case. They appear to be accurately recounting what they honestly believe they saw. Cross-examination does not shake their stories.

The jury renders a verdict for the defendant police officers.

.   .   .

These are some of the many jury cases I have tried. Since the jury is the decision maker in such cases, my chief role is to generate the feeling in the courtroom that justice is being sought. But how to create that atmosphere? One way is to maintain dignity. If lawyers snarl at each other, I disengage them and get them back on the high road. I show them respect and demand that they respect the court. Another important way is to allow each side to present its case fully and, above all, to treat both sides evenhandedly. Since the eyes of the litigants, counsel, and jury are on me, and since I communicate to them not only by words, but by tone of voice, facial expression, and body language, I must always appear impartial. I never nod in affirmance of testimony I agree with or grimace at testimony I think is patently false.

I do try to lighten up the courtroom by starting each day with a "Good morning" to the lawyers, parties, and jurors. Occasionally I even attempt a bit of humor. Judicial humor is so unexpected that it brings forth more laughter in the courtroom than it deserves.

A woman approaches the witness stand. She is wearing a dark blue sweater on which is embroidered a bright green and yellow parrot. After she is sworn in, I say, "Shouldn't we also swear in the parrot?"

In a malpractice case against an ophthalmologist, the plaintiff's expert gives a fascinating explanation of how the human eye works. In an effort to undermine him, defendant's counsel asks him what he expects to be paid for testifying. He says his rates are $500 for the first hour and $350 for each succeeding hour. As the doctor is being excused after testifying for fifty-five minutes, I say, "Why don't we keep the doctor on the stand for another hour to take advantage of his reduced rates."

In about the third day of a jury trial, I say to the panel, "You notice when you enter the courtroom, the attorneys always rise. They mean to show their respect to you. The real trick, however, is to get your kids at home to stand when you come into the room."

Such feeble attempts may not earn me a reputation as a sit-down comic, but they do serve a purpose. They put people in the courtroom more at ease, and help dissipate the tension that builds up during a trial.

A funny incident once happened in the courtroom without the jury knowing of it. An orthopedic surgeon and frequent witness in my court approached the witness stand with both hands clutching large X-ray films to his body. The clerk said, "Raise your right hand." The doctor leaned across the witness chair and whispered to me, "I can't, Judge, my fly is open." Turning away from the jury, he zipped himself, while I tried to keep a straight face.

. . .

Passing upon the admissibility of evidence is one of the important responsibilities of a trial judge. The issue arises when one lawyer objects to a question asked of a witness by the other lawyer or objects to an exhibit being offered. The judge must determine whether the question or the exhibit complies with the rules of evidence. These rules are standards of reliability developed by courts over the years. Because they are designed to keep untrustworthy evidence from inexperienced triers of fact, judges feel more pressure to decide evidential issues correctly in jury cases than in court cases.

An example of objectionable evidence is hearsay. Although the everyday world operates on the basis of hearsay, it is excluded in court. When A testifies to what B said happened, there are too many chances for errors in the transmission. The law requires that A tell only what he himself saw or knows firsthand. If B has information, he must testify in court, so he can be cross-examined and so the triers can evaluate his credibility.

The rules of evidence are far from simple. The hearsay

rule itself has many exceptions. And applying the rules requires close judgment calls. At judicial seminars where hy-
pothetical questions are presented, experienced judges
disagree among themselves on the correct way to rule.

When an objection is made in court, the judge cannot
assume the role of Hamlet. The trial has stopped. He must
decide quickly and decisively whether to sustain or overrule
the objection. In such situations I rely on memory of the
rules, on experience and intuition. Often I cannot explain
my decision or justify it by any particular authority. It just
feels right. I hope I will remember to be consistent and rule
the same way when the same issue comes up again.

Once in a long, hotly contested trial, the lawyers made
constant objections to questions and exhibits. I admitted
over two hundred exhibits and excluded about half that
number. Late in the trial, over the defendant lawyer's objection, I allowed in a document under one of the exceptions to
the hearsay rule. The defendant's lawyer asked for a recess.
When we resumed he said, "Your Honor, our copy of the
transcript shows that two weeks ago you sustained an objection to the same document you just admitted."

Without blinking an eye, I said, "Well, Counselor, one of
my decisions must be right." That slightly cavalier attitude
is prevalent among judges. They want to be correct in their
rulings, and above all, they want to be fair to the parties. But
they know, at least in civil cases, appeals courts are very
unlikely to reverse them on evidential decisions, unless the
error is a real beaut.

There *are* judges who calculate early on in a trial which
side is most likely to lose the case and then decide each close
evidential question in favor of that side. Since the losing
party is the only one who can appeal and can only appeal
rulings against him, those judges are depriving that party of
any grounds for appeal. I never play that game.

Being forced to rule in the heat of a trial reminds me of the
story of a law professor, appellate judge, and trial judge
going duck hunting. They made a bet that the one who shot

the first duck would win ten dollars and the one who shot a
bird other than a duck would lose five dollars. By flip of a
coin, the professor went first. A winged creature flew over;
the professor took aim and hesitated: "It has the markings
of a water fowl; it may be a duck, but on the other hand
. . ." By then it had vanished. The appellate judge went
next. Spotting a flapping animal in the sky, he said, "It could
be our prey, but let me check this bird catalog." By then it
was gone. Now it was the trial judge's turn. As a fowl came
into sight, the judge shot and shouted, "It's a bird; I hope
it's a duck." I'm afraid on the bench I have shot many a
buzzard that way.

There are times when the evidential question is so important that the lawyers want to argue it before the judge. When
that happens I ask the jury to retire to the deliberating room.
I explain that during the argument the contested evidence is
likely to come out. If I rule it inadmissible and they hear it,
they may have difficulty removing it from their minds. Also
they may forget how I ruled and consider it in their deliberations.

After the lawyers argue, if the issue is crucial to the outcome and I am uncertain of the correct answer, I recess court
to research the point. But that is rare. Usually I rule decisively in order not to interrupt the pace and momentum of
the trial—and "hope it's a duck."

One of the glories of our system is that however vigorously the lawyers may have argued the evidential question
and however wrong they may think the judge's decision is,
once the ruling is made the lawyers may mutter, "Exception," to preserve their rights on appeal but they continue
on with the trial.

Sometimes the lawyers will argue an hour or more over
whether or not a question should be permitted to be asked
of a witness. Finally, I will rule that it complies with the rules
of evidence and may be asked. All turn to the witness and
expectantly await his answer. He says, "I don't know."

Throughout the trial I try to hear the case through the ears of the jurors and attempt to anticipate the questions they may want to ask. For example, when an orthopedic surgeon on the stand says he examined the plaintiff's "extremities," I always ask, "Do you mean, doctor, his arms and legs?" If a witness describes a car as going "down Main Street," I ask what compass direction he means. Or if the antecedent of a pronoun is unclear, I intercede with the old Harold Ross editorial comment, "Who he?"

In general, however, I let the lawyers elicit the testimony their way. Except to have technical terms defined or murky testimony clarified, I rarely ask questions until the attorneys on both sides have examined the witness fully. Then I do so in as neutral a tone as I can muster. The need to take the bite from my voice and the sharpness from my phrasing, so as to seem simply to be inquiring for the truth, hit me early on, when I was still adjusting to being a judge after years as a trial lawyer. When the attorneys in the first jury case over which I presided finished interrogating a key witness, I asked a few questions. After what I thought was my gentle inquiry, one of the lawyers vigorously objected that I had "cross-examined the witness." He was implying that I showed bias. His reaction took me by surprise, but it taught me a lesson I needed to learn.

When a judge intervenes in a jury trial, he should do so like a porcupine making love—gingerly. He does not know the case, only the evidence elicited up to that moment in the trial. Rashly thrusting himself into the trial can ruin the carefully prepared plan of one of the attorneys.

I am mindful of the story of the bumptious judge who took over a case and questioned the witnesses at length. Finally one of the lawyers could contain himself no longer and blurted out, "Judge, I don't mind your trying the case for me, but for God's sake don't lose it."

In some situations I intervene to correct an obvious mistake. An experienced lawyer questioned a doctor at length about his treatment of the plaintiff. When the lawyer finished, I noted that he had not asked the doctor the standard question—whether the doctor had an opinion, consistent with reasonable medical probability, that the plaintiff's injuries were caused by the accident. The defendant's lawyer cross-examined briefly and perfunctorily. I suspected that he knew that if the doctor did not testify to the causal connection between the accident and the injuries, the plaintiff could not recover damages.

Just as the plaintiff's lawyer was excusing the doctor from the stand, I called a recess and asked both counsel into my chambers. I told the plaintiff's attorney of his omission. He said, "Omigosh, my eye just skipped that question in my notes."

The defendant's lawyer looked disappointed. I said to him, "If you made a similar mistake, I would point it out to you. Trials are too important to be determined by an error like this." He accepted my explanation with good grace. When we returned to court, the plaintiff's lawyer asked the key question, and the doctor related the plaintiff's injuries to the accident. Defendant's lawyer cross-examined thoroughly. In the end the plaintiff got a deserving verdict.

One of the special joys a judge experiences on the bench is having a case tried before him by competent lawyers on both sides. Such lawyers rarely offer evidence that violates the rules, so few objections are made. They question witnesses so precisely and thoroughly that the judge has no reason to intervene. In such instances the adversarial system of trials fulfills its purpose: each lawyer vigorously presses his side of the case, and out of the conflict comes a full revelation of the facts and a complete exploration of the legal issues.

But when one of the lawyers is unprepared or incompetent, the adversarial system breaks down and the judge faces the dilemma of when and how to intervene.

Watching a second-rate lawyer struggle to phrase a question that will comply with the rules of evidence is particularly painful. Such a lawyer before me was interrogating his own investigator who had inspected a tenement house porch where his client fell.

"You examined the rear porch and found it defective, did you not?"

Other lawyer: "Objection, Your Honor, leading."

Me: "Sustained."

"What did you tell my associate about the condition of the porch?"

Other lawyer: "Objection, Your Honor, irrelevant."

Me: "Sustained."

After upholding a few more objections to the lawyer's futile attempts at wording questions, I suggested, "Why don't you just ask him to describe the condition of the porch?"

I can come to the rescue of a lawyer that way. But I cannot prepare the case of an inadequate lawyer, supply the witnesses he should call, organize his closing argument. I writhe silently on the bench as he mangles his client's case and loses.

If I do intervene in favor of the second-rater, I run the risk of the other party feeling that I tipped the scales of justice unfairly. Such a situation arose in a case in which Norman Caron sued Northeast Utilities Corporation for maliciously causing him to be arrested on the charge of stealing welding rods. Caron worked as an operating engineer for a contractor building a nuclear plant for Northeast, and one of his claims for damages was that the arrest caused him to lose his job. A Northeast officer vigorously denied that claim. He testified, "Mr. Caron was not our employee, so we could not have discharged him. Furthermore, we did not control the firing policies of the contractor Mr. Caron worked for."

Caron's lawyer did not cross-examine on the fact that Northeast issued identification badges to persons working at the nuclear plant and that when Northeast had Caron arrested, it pulled his badge.

I pondered: Should I bring up the point? Caron's lawyer

had confided to me that this was his first jury case, and his inexperience was apparent. I was convinced he had no trial strategy and would not raise the point later on. I hesitated. But the question was on the tip of my tongue, and I could not resist asking the corporate officer, "Can a worker without a Northeast badge get into the nuclear plant?"

"No, sir."

"When your company required the plaintiff to turn in his badge after he was arrested, what effect did that have on his job?"

"The contractor had to discharge him from that project, but it could have used him on another site."

"Do you know if the contractor had another project going in Connecticut?"

"I don't believe so, Your Honor."

Northeast's attorney asked that the jury be excused and then angrily moved for a mistrial on the grounds that my questions unduly favored the plaintiff. I denied the motion.

Caron's lawyer bumbled his way through the rest of the trial and won a jury verdict that his client merited. But for a long time afterward the charge against me of unfairness rankled. I thought I had not overstepped the line of impartiality. But it hurt that Northeast's lawyer, whom I respected, thought so.

Then there are times when appearances of incompetence can be deceiving. The stumbling lawyer may be carrying out a strategy to gain sympathy from the jury for his client, or he may deliberately not ask the obvious question so that the information comes out on cross-examination or through another witness at a time when its impact will be greater. In *Dianne DeMartino* v. *Parkview West Associates*, the defendant's lawyer simply assessed the trial situation a lot better than I did.

Dianne DeMartino sued the owners of her apartment house after she partially fell through the rotted floor of the balcony of her fourth-floor apartment. Although hospital emergency room doctors found only soft tissue strains of her low back and right shoulder, she complained of constant pain. Over the next six years she was in and out of hospitals, was treated by at least fifteen doctors and assorted health practitioners, and ran up medical bills of over $180,000. Among her diagnosed ailments were post-traumatic stress disorder and depressive neurosis.

After she testified, during the balance of the six-week trial, she sat beside her lawyer at the counsel table, faced toward the jury, clutched her back and shoulder, and grimaced in pain. Once in the middle of the trial she said in a loud, agonized voice, "Oh, God, the pain." At that point I called a recess and asked counsel to come into my chambers. I turned on the plaintiff's lawyer and said, "Dammit, your client can't carry on that way. She's testifying from the counsel table, for God's sake."

Before Dianne's lawyer could respond, the defendant's lawyer said, "I'm not objecting, Your Honor."

I looked at him in disbelief. "She's getting away with murder," I exploded.

"I'm not objecting, Your Honor," he repeated.

Well, if he was not going to object, I was not going to intervene. But I muttered to myself, "What a dope."

In the end, the jury returned a defendant's verdict. Although the landlord's negligence in failing to repair the rotted balcony floor seemed overwhelming, some of the jurors later told me that Dianne's grimacing during the trial (as one said, "It entitled her to an Oscar") made them disbelieve not only her testimony about her injuries, but also about how the accident happened. So the defendant's lawyer, who wanted Dianne to be allowed to put on her act, was a lot smarter than I had given him credit for.

7. BARGAINING OVER PAIN AND DISABILITY

Especially when trying jury cases, judges actively intervene to get the parties to settle. Although a judge is respected for conducting fair trials, he is even more valued for effecting compromises so trials do not have to be held at all.

The pressure to dispose of cases without trials is enormous. In this litigious age, courthouses are deluged with lawsuits filed by plaintiffs demanding compensation for every physical, mental, or emotional trauma that befalls them. If all of these cases had to be fully tried, each one would take ten years to be reached. The most expeditious way to move lawsuits through the pipeline is to settle them. In fact, over 90 percent of all personal injury cases claimed to a jury are disposed of that way.

When a judge negotiates settlements, he descends into a

strange marketplace. The merchandise transacted is plaintiffs' injuries, typically fractured bones, strained backs, post-
concussion headaches. The price bargained over is an
assessment of what the jury is likely to give. Since nobody
knows what that number is, the judge plays upon that uncertainty with both lawyers to induce agreements.

Each judge has his own style. One of my colleagues joshes
with the lawyers in his chambers, finds out what the plaintiff's lawyer really wants and what the defendant's lawyer
will really give, uses his charm to get them to agree to some
number in the middle, and never concerns himself with the
facts or law of the case. Another judge bludgeons settlements by implying retaliation in subsequent cases if the lawyers do not accept his figure. Still another judge has the rare
talent, derived from experience or intuition, to propose such
a fair value of a case that the lawyers accept it out of respect
for his judgment.

My style is to try to grasp the issues of the case and to
discuss the strengths and weaknesses of each side candidly
with each lawyer. When I suggest a figure I think the case
should be settled for, it is one I believe to be fair, as the case
then appears to me, and one I believe is in the interest of
both sides to accept. I never suggest to a plaintiff's lawyer
that he take an amount I think too low, nor to a defendant's
lawyer that he pay an amount I think too high. I want to feel
as good about a case I settle as one I decide myself.

·   ·   ·

In the case of Dawn Spatta, the thirteen-year-old brain-damaged girl in a wheelchair, the lawyers have just finished
picking the jury, and I call them into my chambers to inquire
about the chances of settling. They have already run the
gauntlet of several previous pretrial conferences with other
judges exploring settlement possibilities. But macho plaintiff
lawyers feel they cannot get the last dollar, and some insurance companies will not make their best offer until the trial
is about to start. Both sides have now tested each other's

determination to try the case to the limit. This is "fish or cut bait" time. Even though the lawyers have spent ten days picking the jury, a judge can often induce an agreement at just this point. At least I have to try.

My chambers are crowded with the lawyers. Dawn's attorney is tall, lean, handsome, very skillful, and very sure of himself. The three attorneys representing the hospital and the two radiologists are leading trial attorneys in large defense firms. They all have with them an assisting lawyer. This is a heavy money case, and everyone in the room knows it. The lawyers have spent four years taking depositions of each other's witnesses and exchanging medical reports, so they are familiar with each other's positions and the evidence likely to be adduced. I also have studied the file and think I understand the issues.

After some preliminary chatting, I look at Dawn's attorney and say, "All right, George, what do you want to settle this case?"

Negotiations always start with getting the plaintiff to state his demand first. Lawyers for defendants will not make an offer until they know what the plaintiff is asking for.

"Judge, my original figure on this case was five million dollars. The malpractice of the hospital and the doctors is clear as day, and you can see how seriously my client is injured. But to settle the case today, if we don't have to go to trial, I'll take three million."

"What do you fellows say?" I ask the defense lawyers.

"We've told George what we will pay his client for the case against all the defendants," says the lawyer representing the hospital. "We are authorized to pay one million dollars."

"Thanks, John. Your generosity overwhelms me. I've already rejected that offer twice."

"Applesauce, George. Your case isn't worth any more."

I ask the defendants' lawyers to step outside so I can talk to the plaintiff's lawyer alone.

"Do you want to settle the case, George?"

"Of course I do, Judge."

"Then what do you really want?"

"I think I can get my client to take 2.7 million. What do you think the case is worth, Judge?"

"I really don't have a handle on it yet. Is there any chance of settling any of the defendants separately?"

"No, Judge. The two radiologists are partners, so they can't be separated, and both are employees of the hospital, so their negligence is attributable to the hospital. They are all in it together. There's also another reason. All the defendants are insured by Aetna Surety and Casualty Company. Aetna's district claims manager, a guy named Targett, has been negotiating directly with me and keeping the defense lawyers out of our talks. He wants to wrap up the case in a single package."

"Has Aetna made any offer to you?" I asked.

"He's the one who finally offered me the million dollars the defendants' lawyers just mentioned."

"All right. Let me speak to the other side."

The plaintiff's lawyer leaves, and the defendants' lawyers enter my chambers. "What can you guys pay?" I ask.

"Not anything near what George wants," says the hospital's lawyer. "His case is not nearly as strong as he thinks it is. He's going to have real problems proving liability. The hospital and the doctors didn't do anything wrong."

"George says he'll take 2.7 million. Does that help elicit another offer from you guys?"

"It doesn't, Judge. We are firm at one million."

I call the plaintiff's lawyer back into my chambers. "The defendants can't give you more than a million if that will settle the case."

"No way, Judge. It's going to cost Dawn's parents seventy-five-thousand a year to maintain her in a convalescent hospital, and the doctors say there's no reason to believe Dawn won't live her life expectancy of sixty years."

"All right, let's try the case," I say.

The beginning of the typical tort trial can be thought of as an empty canvas upon which each witness is about to draw lines and add colors. A clear design will be sketched as the plaintiff and his witnesses tell how the accident happened. Bold colors will be splashed on the canvas as the plaintiff describes his injuries and his pain and suffering. Wavering lines may appear if he or his witnesses waffle on cross-examination. The canvas may be crosshatched in black if the defendant and his witnesses tell a different and more plausible story. As the trial proceeds and the picture on the canvas changes, a judge may call the attorneys into his chambers and inquire whether either wants to rethink his position.

After preliminary witnesses are called to get medical records into evidence, Dawn's father takes the stand. He describes Dawn before the bleed as being a bright, happy nine-year-old. Dawn's picture, introduced into evidence, shows her to be a blond, blue-eyed beauty. Dawn's father tells how his daughter came home from school that day excited and full of life. Suddenly, just before supper, she slumped along the side of the refrigerator to the floor in a coma. An ambulance arrived within minutes of a phone call, and Dawn was raced to the emergency room of the defendant hospital.

After some general medical testimony about angiograms —how they are taken and what they show—the plaintiff's lawyer calls the main defendant, the radiologist who performed the angiograms on Dawn. The doctor admits he explored only three of the four cerebral arteries. He also admits that his report was wrong when it said that he explored all the arteries. Under cross-examination by his own lawyer, the doctor explains that Dawn had been under anesthesia for four hours. At that point his judgment was that she could not take any more, and that is why he did not do the last artery. Moreover, he testifies that the probability of an aneurysm in the part of the brain fed by that artery is very small.

On redirect examination by the plaintiff's lawyer, the doctor cannot explain why he did not do the angiogram of that artery a few days later or why he made the mistake in his report.

We are now into the second week of the trial, and I think it propitious to talk settlement with the lawyers again. This time Mr. Targett of Aetna appears. I am used to settling with attorneys, but Targett insists on negotiating for the defendants. Since his company's money is at stake, I cannot find a reason to object. Again I ask Dawn's attorney what he will take.

"Two and a half million dollars. My case is going in well, and I've got the jury with me. This is my rock-bottom figure if we settle the case now. Otherwise, it's off the table."

"What do you say, Mr. Targett?"

"We won't pay that amount, Judge. But we will make a structured settlement: twenty-five thousand a year, guaranteed for ten years, whether or not Dawn lives that long, and if Dawn is still alive then, twenty-five thousand a year for the rest of her life."

"How much up front?" asks Dawn's lawyer.

"Seven hundred and twenty-five thousand, which should cover your attorney's fees, George."

"Don't be such a wise guy," snaps Dawn's lawyer. "But let me talk to my client."

The next day George rejects the offer, and the trial continues. Evidence comes in about Dawn's second bleed at the local hospital and her transfer to Yale–New Haven Hospital with her medical records, including the erroneous report of the radiologist. Yale does two CAT scans but nothing else for ten days. Finally the doctors there take an angiogram of the fourth artery and find the aneurysm that is the source of the bleed. They schedule an operation for four days later. In the interim Dawn has a third bleed, which renders her severely brain-damaged.

Again I call Dawn's attorney into my chambers. "George,

are you going to have testimony that Yale delayed the angio-gram because of the defendant's report?" I ask.

"I have a Yale nurse who will testify how confused the Yale doctors were about the medical records."

"Why the blazes didn't you sue Yale, too?"

"The Spattas didn't want to. They felt Yale saved Dawn's life."

"Well," I say, "that is the big hole in your case. Hell, the jury could find that Yale's failure to look for that aneurysm for ten whole days was the cause of the girl's condition, and they could give you nothing. Are you willing to lower your figure to settle?"

"What do you think the case is worth, Judge? You've heard enough of it now."

"I have, and at this point I do have a settlement figure to suggest to both of you. It is 2.3 million dollars. Would you take it?"

"I would recommend it to my client, Judge."

"That's all I can ask of you."

I get Targett into my chambers. "You're taking a heck of a risk in this case, Mr. Targett," I say. "If that jury comes in for Dawn, you're going to be whacked."

"We've offered him a good package. George should take it."

"I told him what I thought the case is worth: 2.3 million. George says he'll recommend it to his client. How about you?"

Targett says he'd like to propose another structured settle-ment. I call George in to hear the proposal firsthand. The discussion goes back and forth. I conclude that a payout over time will not work because each of them has a different assessment of how long Dawn will live. I urge them to get back to a lump-sum settlement.

Finally the case reaches the point where Dawn's attorney has to call his expert to give the key testimony that in his medical opinion the defendant doctors failed to meet the prevailing standard of medical treatment of radiologists. George confides in me that the expert wants $15,000 to come from St. Louis; the Spattas do not have the money, and his firm will have to advance it. I interpret that to mean he wants me to exert a final effort to settle the case.

I call Targett on the phone. "George wants the 2.3 million I suggested. I gather you will not pay that."

"That's right, Judge. It's too much. Don't forget, we haven't put on our defense yet."

"I know that. Look, George has not mentioned the figure I'm about to give you, but I think he will take it." Judges have to make an intuitive leap to a number they sense both parties will accept.

"What number do you have in mind, Judge?"

"One and a half million dollars."

Targett does not hesitate a moment. He says, "If George tells me he'll accept that figure, we can settle the case."

I tell Dawn's attorney the number I mentioned on my own initiative to Targett and what his response was. "You don't have to settle for that amount, but if you want to, I think Targett will pay it. Why don't you call Targett right now and discuss it with him."

Half an hour later George comes in and says the case is settled for $1,310,000.

"How come that amount? I thought Targett said one million five."

"The bastard nickel-and-dimed me," George says bitterly. "When I said I would take your figure, Judge, he knew he had me and that I wouldn't continue the trial. So I had to agree to 1.31 million. The Spattas are satisfied, but it's a comedown."

I am let down, too, because I feel Targett has deluded me. A lawyer never would have done that. I call all the attorneys into my chambers and ask, now that the case is settled, whether they want to enter a judgment in the agreed-upon amount on the record.

"No," says the hospital attorney. "We don't want to put anything on the record that admits the liability of the hospital and the doctors. We'll take a release from George, pay him the sum agreed to, and he can file a withdrawal of action."

"Okay," I say. "We'll just have the record show the case is settled. Thank you very much for disposing of the matter this way."

Everyone shakes hands and leaves, joshing about the next case they'll be trying against each other.

.   .   .

Oddly, the easiest cases to settle are those in which the defendant's liability is clear and the plaintiff is seriously injured, even totally disabled. When, for example, a young person is rendered a paraplegic in an accident caused by a drunken driver, the driver's insurance company will usually pay its entire policy by guaranteeing a fixed sum to the plaintiff over his lifetime. The major obstacle to such a settlement is negotiating enough cash up front to cover the fee of the plaintiff's lawyer.

Difficult cases to settle are those in which the plaintiff has only subjective complaints. Neither side's doctor can identify any signs of trauma, such as bruises, swelling, or spasm. But the plaintiff insists he hurts, usually in the back, neck, or head. The plaintiff's doctor relies on the history of the injury given to him by the plaintiff to connect the pain to the accident. The defendant's doctor, finding no objective signs, diagnoses no injury. Over the case hangs the question: Is the pain real or faked? The judge trying to compromise the case has to convince the lawyers what the jury is likely to believe.

Nuisance suits—cases brought in the hope not of winning at trial, but of getting something just for bringing them—are sometimes the hardest to settle. An example is an automobile accident suit in which the police report and the affidavits of several witnesses establish that the plaintiff ran a red light. The plaintiff's lawyer, either from pride, shame, or avarice, usually will not admit his case lacks merit and agree to withdraw it. Some insurance companies will pay something because they do not want to incur the cost of defense and the risk of a jury verdict. Other companies have the guts to refuse to pay a cent. Although I want to settle cases, I am always delighted with that position. Payment of any amount is a perversion of the civil justice system. It implies that the system is so inefficient (the cost of defending even a dog of a case is high) and so hazardous (the outcome even of such a case is unpredictable) that a price must be tendered. Payment is also submission to a form of extortion. Plaintiffs' lawyers know the burden they impose on defendants by bringing such cases, and they cynically demand a tribute to grant releases. Under such circumstances, in my view, payment is counterproductive. It only encourages marginal lawyers to bring more of such cases. In the long run the best course is to force plaintiffs' lawyers to go through the time and expense of trying their dogs and trust that juries will render the right verdict.

Cases impossible to settle are those that become a matter of principle for one or both parties. A plaintiff who has been libeled may not be satisfied with mere compensation but dearly want the vindication of a jury verdict to establish that the defamation is false. A defendant whose professional ethics have been attacked, such as an accountant accused of fraud or a banker charged with violating a trust, may likewise insist on the exoneration of a verdict to clear his reputation. I respect those matters of honor and never press for settlement in such cases.

Complicated cases, usually involving numerous parties and difficult questions of causation, require complicated settlement arrangements. For example, in the DES cases, in which it could not be proven which brand of antimiscarriage pill containing diethylstilbestrol caused birth defects in each plaintiff, all the drug companies producing the pills contributed to a settlement fund in proportion to each company's share of the market. I have settled malpractice cases involving several doctors and hospitals, and environmental cases involving a number of polluting companies, by similar, if not quite as complex, plans of proportional contributions by multiple defendants.

An experienced judge knows the lawyers and their susceptibility to settling. The timid lawyer settles as the trial starts. The cautious lawyer settles when the first problem develops in his case and he doesn't want to gamble. The realistic lawyer evaluates the case as it goes in and bails out if the odds tip against his success. The kamikaze lawyer ignores all signs that he is doing poorly and goes down in flames.

Even if the judge is able to get the lawyers to agree on a figure, the lawyers may not be able to convince their clients. Plaintiffs may have distorted telephone numbers in their heads from reading newspaper accounts of jury verdicts. Insurance companies go through shifts in settlement policies with changes in top management. Then there may be a hidden agenda: the doctor who balks at settling a malpractice suit at any price because he refuses to believe he did anything wrong: the company concerned that the settlement of a product liability action may generate more claims.

Rarely do judges discuss settlement directly with the parties. Once I broke that rule—to my chagrin. The attorneys had agreed to settle an automobile accident case for $30,000, but the plaintiff, who was a nurse, would not accept it. Both lawyers were convinced it was a fair amount, and the plaintiff's lawyer, in particular, felt the nurse was making a terrible mistake not to take it. They begged me to speak to her. I tried to put them off.

"Tell her I say it is a good settlement and she should take it," I said.

"I did, Judge," said the plaintiff's lawyer. "But she still rejects the figure."

Reluctantly, I agreed to see her. When she sat stern-faced

before me, I said, "You should listen to your attorney. He is very competent, and he is only thinking of your interests."

"I know, Judge, but I think my case is worth fifty thousand dollars."

"What do you base it on?"

"Well, after I pay my lawyer one-third, and some other bills, I will just have enough to put the down payment on the house I want."

"But the test is what the jury will give," I protested. "I'm sure you know your profession. Your lawyer knows his. I also hear a lot of cases, and I must say that thirty thousand is about what the jury is likely to award in this case."

"I want fifty thousand."

"You know there is no assurance the jury will give you even the thirty thousand the lawyers agreed to. The jury will not be told about that agreement. They may give you less than that amount or more. You are taking a real gamble."

"Judge," she said firmly, "I want fifty thousand."

The case was tried to a conclusion. The jury returned with a verdict of $51,250. The nurse gave me a gloating look and marched out of the courtroom triumphantly. I vowed to myself never to do that again.

When a settlement is reached during a trial, the jurors feel frustrated that they did not have a chance to decide the case, and the lawyers sometimes wonder how the case might have turned out. Once, when a case was settled after all the evidence was in, I suggested to the lawyers that we tell the jurors, they then make the closing arguments they would have made, I give my instructions of law, and we let the jury deliberate and tell us what it would have decided. Afterward they can ask the jurors what influenced their decision and what trial tactics were effective. The lawyers agreed, and so did the jurors when they were informed of the plan. When the mock verdict was announced, not only did the lawyers question the jurors, but the jurors questioned the lawyers and me about aspects of the trial. I thought the idea was

working out great and everyone was gaining from the ex-
changes until I noticed the lack of enthusiasm on the part of
the plaintiff's lawyer. The jury had indicated it would have
awarded $20,000, twice what he had settled for. Fortunately
his client had left before then. But I never did that again,
either.

Settlements are always compromises. Plaintiffs get less
than they hoped, and defendants give more than they ini-
tially intended. Neither wins or loses completely. Both
hedge against the unpredictability of juries. In the end, the
best settlement is one that leaves both parties a little dissatisfied with the result but completely satisfied with the judicial process that brought it about.

8. MORE ON CIVIL JURY TRIALS

When the last witness has testified and all the evidence is in, the attorneys get their chance to sum up to the jury. This is a climactic moment of the trial.

The story line of a trial develops like a mystery novel. Each witness tells what he knows about the event giving rise to the suit and then vanishes. Some matters are left hanging in midair; others, seemingly irrelevant, are pursued vigorously. The jury and judge are left wondering about the significance of a witness's answer extracted after vigorous cross-examination or a document introduced with a flourish. In closing arguments, the lawyers unravel the tangled strands, reveal the mystery of the clues, and proclaim, "You, ladies and gentlemen of the jury, will give the fitting end to this tale: a verdict for my client."

Good trial lawyers have a flair for the dramatic. A defendant's lawyer, in a case before me, gave his summation from the top of a stepladder that the plaintiff had claimed was defective. A plaintiff's lawyer, juggling a baseball as he summarized the evidence supporting his case, urged the jurors to keep their eyes on the ball and not be fooled by the curves thrown by the defense. Another lawyer made his point by singing a song from a Broadway musical.

Sometimes the high-blown rhetoric of the attorneys is unintentionally funny. A ponderous defense lawyer, seeking to diminish the complaints of the plaintiff that she suffered morning stiffness as a result of the injury sustained in the accident, said, "Heck, most of us wake up with some part of our body stiff."

In the case in which Charles Jubb was killed in the crash of a small plane, the attorney representing the defendant, Coastal Air Lines, put on no evidence to counter the testimony of the plaintiff's expert placing the blame on the pilot. But he made this argument to the jury.

"You remember, ladies and gentlemen, the evidence that the plane of my client had dual controls at the two front seats and these controls could not be decoupled. The pilot was in the left seat and Charles Jubb in the right. You also remember that the plane descended and hit the ground at a very steep angle.

"Now, the evidence also revealed that Charles Jubb was hospitalized in a mental institution as a manic-depressive some eighteen years ago and at the time slashed his wrists with a broken bottle. He continued in treatment with a psychiatrist for that same mental illness up to the time of the crash.

"The year before the accident, Jubb's woes, both emotional and financial, multiplied. His wife left him, some of his children rejected him, and he went into bankruptcy. Two months before the accident Jubb lost his job, the mortgage on his house was foreclosed, and his checks started bouncing. All this was reflected in his heavy drinking and losing his driving license as a result of it.

"The night of the accident Jubb had a manic episode. He

bought up half the merchandise in a Seven-Eleven convenience store, choosing items at random he clearly did not
need and euphorically shouting at customers. He called up
my client, the owner of Coastal Airlines, at midnight, and
demanded to be flown to Concord, New Hampshire, at
once. He announced that he himself was a pilot, which was
not true, and he shouted that the weather be damned.

"You remember the evidence that Jubb wanted desperately to get to Concord in order to pick up a customer's check
he desperately needed to cover his overdrawn bank balance.
When the plane reached Concord, the airport was socked in
by fog. Clearly the plane could not land. Jubb was thwarted.
By then his mania had subsided and he was in a depression.
All his family and financial troubles hit him at once. There
were the controls in front of him. He reached for them, and
in bleak despair . . ."

With these words, the attorney thrust his hands at the jury
and vigorously twisted both wrists downward. He walked
back to the counsel table and sat down. His unfinished sentence reverberated in the silent courtroom.

The plaintiff's lawyer leaped up. "Speculation," he
shouted, "all speculation. Charles Jubb would never commit
suicide—and murder, too. This is outrageous."

Plaintiff attorneys are especially clever arguing for damages, whether or not their clients are seriously hurt. One
lawyer, urging the jury to give a substantial verdict to the
plaintiff who had incurred a minor but nagging injury, effectively quoted Thackeray:

"The little ills of life are hardest to bear, as we all very well
know. But what would the possession of a hundred thousand pounds a year, or fame and applause of one's country-
men, or the loveliest and best-loved woman—or any glory
and happiness or good fortune—avail to a gentleman, for
instance, who is allowed to enjoy them only under the condition of wearing a shoe with a couple of nails or sharp
pebbles inside it. All fame and happiness would disappear

and plunge down that shoe. All life would rankle around those little nails."

He paused a moment and then closed with, "What my client seeks is just damages for a life which rankles around those little nails."

Connecticut once had a rigid rule that the plaintiff's lawyer could not suggest the specific dollar amount of the verdict the jury should return for his client. In the police chase case in which John Prange's right leg had been amputated and his left leg shattered, his lawyer argued this way:

"If this case involved the destruction of a thoroughbred horse having a market value of one million dollars, and if liability of the defendant were established to your satisfaction, you would have no trouble coming back with a verdict of one million dollars. If this case involved the destruction of a Ming vase having a market value of two million dollars, and liability was clear, you would have no trouble coming back with a verdict of two million dollars. If this case involved the destruction of a Van Gogh painting having a market value of three million dollars, and liability was clear, you would have no trouble coming back with a verdict of three million dollars. Now this case involves the destruction of my client's body, more valuable than a racehorse, a vase, or a painting. Consider that in deciding fair compensation for John Prange."

When the lawyers finish their closing arguments, the judge charges the jury—that is, instructs the jurors on the legal principles governing the case. I start by reminding them of my remarks at the beginning of the trial that they determine the facts on the basis of the evidence, giving what credence and what weight they deem appropriate to the testimony of witnesses. In reaching their verdict, however, they must apply to the facts of the law as I state it. I put it this way: "If by chance you should have a different idea of the law, or what you think it should be, you must disregard your personal notions and conscientiously apply the law as

I give it to you. Only in that way can justice be achieved under law."

The plaintiff, I explain, has the burden of proof. The defendant does not have to disprove anything. The standard in a civil suit is that the plaintiff must prove his case by a fair preponderance of the evidence—that is, by the better and weightier evidence. "Imagine in your mind's eye the scales of justice," I tell them, "on each side of which is placed the evidence on each controverted point. If the scales tip ever so slightly in favor of the plaintiff, he has met his burden of proof. If the scales are exactly even, or tip against the plaintiff, he has failed to meet his burden."

The nub of the charge is the judge's analysis of the legal elements of the plaintiff's cause of action. A simple automobile accident, for example, requires that the plaintiff prove (1) that the defendant was negligent; (2) that this negligence was the proximate cause of the accident; (3) that the plaintiff was injured; and (4) that based on his medical expenses, loss of wages, disability, and pain and suffering, the plaintiff is entitled to recover fair, just, and reasonable damages. The judge defines for the jury the legal concepts of "negligence," "proximate cause," and "fair, just, and reasonable compensation."

I struggled over my first jury instructions as if I were taking a law school exam. I borrowed sample charges from my colleagues, lifted them bodily from form books, extracted whole paragraphs from judicial opinions. In that simple negligence case I compiled a set of legal principles that summarized the encyclopedia of torts. Then I read my pedantry verbatim to the jury. It would have spun the head of a law professor.

In my early years, this was my standard charge for what conduct constitutes negligence:

One test in determining whether or not a person was negligent is to ask and answer whether or not, if a person of ordinary prudence had been in the same situation and possessed of the same knowledge, he would have foreseen or anticipated that someone might have been injured by or as a result of his action or inaction. If such a result from certain conduct would be foreseeable by a person of ordinary prudence with like knowledge and in like situation, and if the conduct reasonably could be avoided, then not to avoid it would be negligence.

My definition of proximate cause was similarly convoluted. Many, many cases later I started to notice the puzzled expressions on jurors' faces during my elaborate monologues. The whether-or-nots, the either-ors, the caveats and qualifying clauses, when read aloud to the jury, glazed their eyes and stupefied their minds. Being legally correct at the expense of clarity was tantamount to giving no instructions at all, so I simplified.

Negligence, I told the jury, meant "failing to use the care a reasonably prudent person would use under the circumstances. If the defendant failed to use that degree of care in this case, he was negligent." The defendant's negligence was the proximate cause of the plaintiff's injuries if it was "a substantial factor in producing the injuries."

That jurors are unfamiliar with even the most elemental legal terms was brought home to me when a juror raised his hand in the middle of one of my charges and said, "Judge, please don't say 'plaintiff' or 'defendant.' We know Mr. Gregory is suing Mr. Lebowitz, but we can't keep them straight if you keep referring to them as 'plaintiff' and 'defendant.' Just use the names of the parties."

Not all jury cases turn on well-established legal principles. Sometimes the applicable law is unsettled. In preparing the charge in the case of Lori Watson, the black child with the sickle-cell trait, I discovered that no Connecticut court had ruled on what constituted medical malpractice based on failure to obtain the informed consent of a patient for an operation. Other states had conflicting views. I had to devise a

Connecticut rule. Similarly, in the John Prange police chase case the Connecticut law was ambiguous as to the duty of reasonable care required of police pursuing a felon. Again I had to resolve the ambiguity.

But a charge does not state legal principles in the abstract. It relates the principles to the evidence, in order to give substance and meaning to them. The tradition in England is for judges freely to give their opinion of the worth of the evidence and, in so doing, strongly influence how a jury decides. The tradition in this country is for judges to marshal the evidence on each side of an issue and allow the jury to reach its own decision. When I discuss the evidence in my charge, I do so as fairly as I can and especially avoid intimating my belief or disbelief in the testimony of witnesses.

Instructing a jury to consider evidence against only one party and to disregard it as to other parties is particularly challenging. In a case against two defendants, for example, a witness may testify to what one defendant told him about how the accident happened. The testimony may indicate both defendants are at fault. It is admissible, however, only against the defendant who spoke to the witness, because it is an admission by that defendant. It cannot be considered against the other defendant, because, as regards him, it is hearsay.

Similarly difficult is the charge that the jury should consider evidence for one purpose and disregard it for all other purposes. Hearsay, when offered for the truth of the facts contained in an out-of-court statement, is inadmissible. But when offered to prove the state of mind of a party, it is allowed. In the case in which Norman Caron sued Northeast Utilities for maliciously causing his arrest on the charge of stealing welding rods, Northeast's investigator testified to conversations he had with several people about Caron taking the rods. Although these conversations were hearsay, they were admissible, not for the truth of the matters related, but to show Northeast had no malice when it had Caron arrested.

Explaining the distinction in both such instances to the jurors, and asking them to limit their consideration of the evidence to the proper party or purpose, is like throwing a skunk in the jury box and directing the jurors not to smell it.

In a complicated case a judge works long into the night on the instructions he will give the next morning. He has the benefit of suggestions by the lawyers of how he should charge, which are of varying help, depending on the competence of counsel. The judge can also confer informally with the lawyers in his chambers, test out his notions of the law with them, and get their objections beforehand. But in the end the judge must himself resolve the disputed and uncertain legal questions and make a positive assertion to the jury of what the law is. Any errors in his charge will be grounds for reversal by an appeals court. If, after a long case, the verdict is overturned because of his mistake, he must bear the full responsibility.

In contrast with court cases, in which a judge can set forth his reasoning in an opinion, a charge has no room for explanation or equivocation. In the Lori Watson case, I discussed with the jury the different rules of several states on informed consent and then gave what I thought the Connecticut rule should be. But explaining how I arrived at the law was probably a mistake.

The manner of delivering a charge is almost as important as its accuracy and clarity. As a neophyte judge I not only read my jury instructions; I pontificated them as if I were Moses. Eventually realizing that my duty was not role playing but communicating, I adopted a more conversational tone. After years of experience I learned to think through a charge until I had its concepts clearly in mind, and then I could express it with a few notes, while looking at the jurors and holding their attention.

Sensing that some jurors have little familiarity with group dynamics, I also include in my charge some suggestions on how to deliberate, encouraging them to keep an open mind until they have heard what the others have to say, and not to commit themselves too early, lest it become difficult for them later to change their minds. I remind them that the parties do not expect divine justice, only their conscientious best, and conclude by wishing them good luck in their deliberations.

When the jury retires, the tense wait begins for the lawyers and their clients. I know how they feel because I remember my days in practice pacing the floor outside the closed jury room door. As a judge, however, I turn to other tasks: empaneling a jury for the next case, starting a new court trial. I am curious about the verdict, but not emotionally involved.

From time to time I may be interrupted by the sheriff handing me a written question from the jurors. They may want to rehear the testimony of a witness or have a portion of my charge clarified. I call them back into court; the court reporter reads the requested testimony, or I try to explain more successfully the unclear legal principle. The questions are important clues about the way the jury is leaning. Based on them, lawyers on each side reassess their chances and renew their settlement negotiations.

In the John Prange police chase case, for example, the jury deliberated for five days and kept sending out questions relating to liability. The defendants had offered to settle for $250,000. In light of the jury's questions, I urged Prange's lawyers to take it. "The jury is hung up on liability," I said. "If they go against you on that, you won't get anything." But they insisted their client's case was worth at least $500,000 and chose to ignore the harbingers.

Sometimes the jury sends a message that it cannot reach a unanimous verdict. Then I have to give what we call in Connecticut the "Chip Smith charge," first used in 1881 in *State* v. *Smith*. Its substance is that while a verdict must be the conclusion of each member and not a mere acquiescence in the conclusion of fellow members, yet "in conferring together the jury ought to pay proper respect to each other's opinions, and listen with candor to each other's arguments.

If much the larger number of the panel are for a particular verdict, a dissenting juror should consider why his own conclusion is one which makes no impression upon the minds of the other jurors equally honest, equally intelligent with himself, who have heard the same evidence, with the same attention, and with equal desire to arrive at the truth, and under the sanction of the same oath."

When reading the Chip Smith charge, I add that the case has taken weeks to try at great expense to the parties; that if a mistrial is declared, another jury will have to hear the case all over again; that they are as competent as any other panel and should renew their efforts to reach a decision. So far it has worked; in the hundreds of jury cases I have tried, I have not yet had a hung jury.

When the jury informs the sheriff that it has reached a verdict, all involved return to the courtroom and I again ascend the bench. This is the magical moment. No matter how many times I have sat through it, my pulse quickens and my chest tightens. Will the parents of Lori Watson be compensated for her tragic death? Will Coastal Air's lawyer convince the jury that Charles Jubb committed suicide? Will John Prange get the million-dollar verdict his lawyer argued for?

The clerk calls the names of each juror, and each rises. The clerk asks, "Ladies and gentlemen of the jury, have you agreed upon a verdict?" The foreperson responds affirmatively. The sheriff takes the verdict forms from the foreperson and hands them to me. There is a form for a plaintiff's verdict and one for a defendant's verdict. The jury has filled out one of them. I read the verdict, keeping my face inscrutable, and pass the forms to the clerk. The lawyers are standing at the counsel table, their clients standing beside them. The clerk reads:

"Case number 12345, *Laura M. Watson, Administratrix of the Estate of Lori Watson* v. *Marvin Goodman, et al. Defendant's verdict.* The jury finds for the defendants. . . ."

"Case number 23456, *Barbara Jubb, et al., Administrators of the Estate of Charles Jubb* v. *Coastal Air Services, Inc. Plaintiff's verdict.* The jury finds for the plaintiff and finds the plaintiff shall recover against the defendant $463,000. . . ."

"Case number 34567, *John Prange* v. *Kenneth Tramadeo, et al. Defendant's verdict.* The jury finds for the defendants. . . ."

If I then say that the verdict is accepted and may be recorded, the clerk intones, "Ladies and gentlemen of the jury, hearken to your verdict as it is accepted and ordered recorded by the court." He then repeats the verdict and adds, "Is this your verdict and so say you all?" The jurors murmur their assent.

The losing lawyer can ask that the jury be polled. Each juror, as his name is called, must rise and indicate his agreement with the verdict. I have never had a juror disagree, but if one did, I would ask the jury to continue its deliberations until it reached, or found that it could not reach, a unanimous decision.

Several times I have not accepted the verdict. In those instances there was an obvious error on the face of the verdict form, such as the jury finding that the plaintiff's own negligence was a 30 percent contributing cause of the accident and not reducing the amount awarded to the plaintiff by that 30 percent; or in a contract action, the jury awarding the plaintiff interest on the debt owed and improperly computing the interest. In those cases I directed the jury to correct the error and return the verdict.

When the verdict is finally recorded, I thank the jurors for their service even if I disagreed with their verdict, because I know they did their best. Then I ask to see them informally in the deliberating room. My purpose is to answer whatever questions they may have about any aspects of the trial so their experience as jurors will be fulfilled. They, on the other hand, eagerly want assurance from me that their verdict was correct. Inevitably, without my asking directly, the conversation reveals clues about how they reached their decision.

This information is helpful to me in understanding how the jury system works.

Even when a verdict has been entered, all is not necessarily over. There may be an epilogue or even a series of epilogues. In the John Prange case, his lawyers came to my chambers to thank me for my handling of the trial and then added, "Judge, we sure should have taken your advice about settling for that two-hundred-fifty thousand dollars."

"You can't second-guess yourselves, fellows," I said. "You tried the case well. But you learned something. Next time you'll pay greater heed to the jurors' questions."

In the Lori Watson case, her parents' attorneys appealed to the state supreme court. They did not claim error on the substance of my charge on informed consent, because it was favorable to their client. But they did dispute the way I had explained to the jury how I had arrived at the rule by considering the decisions of several other states. The defendants were sufficiently concerned that the supreme court might reverse and order a new trial that they agreed to settle for their original offer to the plaintiff of $35,000.

In the Charles Jubb case, Coastal Air made a motion for me to set aside the verdict on two grounds: the amount of the verdict was excessive, and my charge improperly interpreted a regulation of the Federal Aviation Administration.

I have found jury verdicts excessive and ordered a remittitur—that is, either the plaintiff accept a lesser amount, or I will set the verdict aside. But in the Jubb case I thought the award of $463,000 for the death of a forty-five-year-old man was reasonable and refused to disturb it.

I have also set aside a verdict when I concluded my charge was erroneous. In one of my early cases a pharmacist was sued for having negligently initiated the arrest of a young schoolteacher whom he suspected of giving him a forged prescription for a controlled drug. The evidence at the trial revealed that the prescription was genuine. I instructed the jury that if it found the pharmacist was negligent, it could

find for the teacher. The jury returned a plaintiff's verdict
for $7,500. On the defendant's motion to set aside the ver-
dict, I reconsidered my charge. After much research and
thought, I concluded the pharmacist did not breach any duty
to exercise due care when he acted honestly, even if mistakenly, to prevent what he thought was an illegal drug purchase. To hold him responsible would have a chilling effect
on all citizens reporting to the police and thus stifle an important source of information about crime. On that basis I
set aside the verdict. But in the Jubb case I found no basis
for thinking my charge erroneous, so I denied Coastal Air's
motion.

One jury case I tried had a particularly poignant epilogue.
Two high school teammates, in the family car of one of them,
had sped to school for a varsity baseball game. The car
crossed the solid line on a two-lane road to pass another car
and crashed head on into a third car coming the other way.
Both boys were killed.

The parents of the deceased passenger, as administrators
of their son's estate, sued the parents of the deceased driver,
as owners of the car. Although there was insurance, the
lawyer for the plaintiffs attached the home of the defendants. The jury rendered a verdict of $390,000, which was
$90,000 in excess of the insurance. This meant the defen-
dants' home could be taken.

I called the attorneys into my chambers and said the accident had created enough anguish without destroying the
family of the boy who had driven the car. I urged the plaintiffs' lawyer to suggest to his clients that they forgo levying
on the defendants' house. They agreed.

That night it occurred to me that there was one thing more
the passenger's parents could do. The next day I wrote a
letter to them thanking them for their forbearance about the
house and adding: "You might also consider using some of
the jury verdict money to establish a college scholarship
fund at your son's high school. But to be meaningful it

should be a memorial to both your son and his friend. Both were fine boys. And but for the chance event of which family car was available that fateful day, their roles as driver and passenger could have been reversed."

They accepted my suggestion, and East Granby High School now has a scholarship in the names of Jeffrey F. Kurr and Frederick C. Joergensen. I have always felt good about that.

9. DOES THE
CIVIL JURY
SYSTEM WORK?

The tort liability model of fixing responsibility and allocating the costs of accidents and personal injuries is being fiercely fought over in this country today. The combatants are, on one side, trial lawyers championing the rights of injured accident victims and, on the other, insurance companies, manufacturers, and doctors decrying the $300 billion annual cost of tort liability and its consequences of keeping beneficial products and drugs off the market and forcing doctors to leave high-risk specialties. The battle is being waged generally out of the public view, but the public feels its heat in rising insurance rates and hears its sounds in legislative debates over tort reform.

Necessarily caught in the crossfire of the debate is the part that juries play in deciding tort cases. Questions about the efficacy of juries, however, arose long before the present crisis.

Dean Erwin N. Griswold, in his 1962–63 report to Harvard Law School, said, "The jury trial at best is the apotheosis of the amateur. Why should anyone think that twelve persons brought in from the street, selected in various ways for their lack of general ability, should have any special capacity for deciding controversies between persons?"

Justice Donald Alexander of the Maine Supreme Court, in a 1982 law review article, said, "It is highly unlikely that we would adopt the civil jury as a dispute resolution device if the system did not already exist. The very existence of the jury system has become the justification for its perpetuation. That justification is without merit."

On the other hand, Scott Baldwin, president of the Association of Trial Lawyers of America, said, as have all presidents of that association, "Juries are the greatest system for meting out justice that the world has ever devised."

The world, however, is not convinced. Only this country tries personal injury cases to a jury. England, which originated the jury, ceased making civil jury trials an absolute right in 1933 and since the mid-1960s has allowed civil jury trials in only a handful of actions: libel, slander, malicious prosecution, false imprisonment, and seduction. Conspicuously missing are personal injury cases. Other countries that inherited the English common law have similarly abandoned civil jury trials. The rest of the world is baffled by our adherence to the practice.

When I was a lawyer, I agreed with Baldwin. Then my answer to the question "Does the civil jury system work?" was an enthusiastic yes, because I won almost all of the jury cases I tried. (Of course, I settled the ones I probably would have lost.) After fourteen years on the bench, however, I no longer equate "work" with winning. The question now means:

1. Are trials conducted so as to enable juries to make accurate and reliable findings of fact?
2. Are the judge's instructions of law given in an under-

standable way so juries can comprehend and remember them?

3. Do juries deliberate in a rational way and arrive at conclusions based on the law?
4. Are jury verdicts just?

When I stated these criteria in a speech to a local bar association, a plaintiff's lawyer said candidly, "The last thing we want from juries is reason and the law. If we did, we'd try the case to a judge. What we want is for those six citizens to decide cases on the basis of their gut feelings."

"Maybe," I said, "but a system that is not based on reason and the law rests on a shaky foundation and is likely to topple."

Applying the above criteria, then, how does the civil jury fare in actual practice?

Are trials conducted in a way that juries can make accurate and reliable findings of fact? Hardly. Everything about a trial is designed to manipulate, confuse, and confound juries. Manipulation starts with the jury selection. Potential jurors are not aware of how carefully they have been analyzed before they are even summoned for selection. While in routine cases the voir dire is conducted by guesswork, in important cases sophisticated lawyers hire firms to sample community attitudes so they can identify juror types most likely to side with their clients. Moreover, lawyers question veniremen less in order to uncover ingrained biases than to inculcate biases in favor of their clients.

Jurors start off under tension in the unfamiliar setting of the courtroom. They do not know when to stand or sit or what to make of the sudden deference shown them by the lawyers and judges. The trial itself appears to them to be a shell game in which the truth is now revealed, now hidden, and often obfuscated. They hear the evidence being offered in no apparent logical order. Exhibits are introduced with no indication of their relevance. Things are left hanging, with connecting links furnished days later, if at all. Jurors, I am sure, would love to ask questions during the course of the trial to clear up their confusion, but that practice is not generally followed.

They also long to hear a witness give a straightforward narrative without interruption. But before a witness gets very far, an opposing lawyer objects. When the lawyers want to argue the evidential point, the jurors must leave. Sometimes a good part of the trial day is spent with the jurors marching out of and back into the courtroom.

After a witness finishes answering the questions of the lawyer who called him to the stand, the other side's lawyer starts to cross-examine. Cross-examination is intended to reveal falsehoods or clarify ambiguities, but jurors must often see it as an attempt to befuddle the witness and confuse the jury. Many times they are right. In one case before me, a housewife clearly described the visibility of oncoming traffic at the intersection where an accident had occurred. I knew her description to be accurate because I passed the intersection every day on my way to court. However, after the defendant's lawyer finished cross-examination, her testimony on that point was a total jumble. This happens over and over again.

Jurors strain to understand experts testifying on such specialized topics as the etiology of an arteriovenous malformation in the blood vessels of the brain or the mechanics of the spring suspension of an automobile. Their eyes glaze over when a doctor explains an X-ray or an engineer covers a blackboard with mathematical formulas.

Even more confusing to jurors is the diametrically opposing testimony of learned experts. Unable to evaluate such conflicting testimony on its substantive merits, they are likely to be influenced by the more authoritative manner or engaging personality of one of the experts.

During a trial, which may last weeks, jurors are generally not allowed to take notes. I scribble away on my yellow pad on the bench, but the jurors, whose duty is to determine the facts, are denied this obvious means of refreshing their recollection of the evidence.

Lawyers' closing arguments can baffle juries still more. Summations are supposed to assemble the evidence into a coherent picture. But in their passionate effort to sell their sides of the case, both lawyers sometimes sound more like snake oil salesmen. To the extent that they are equally persuasive, the jurors are even more confused.

Ideally, the judge's charge should lessen the confusion by relating the evidence to the legal principles the jury is to apply in making its decision. But I find that however hard I try to simplify, jurors have difficulty grasping legal concepts. An earnest juror once told me that she concentrated so hard on each principle, as I expressed it orally, that she could not retain the previous one. Moreover, instructions are given at the end of a trial when the jurors have to recollect the evidence against standards of relevance they did not know about when they were hearing the testimony.

Despite these handicaps, do juries deliberate in a rational way and arrive at conclusions based upon the law? We do not know. Jury deliberations are cloaked in secrecy, their verdicts given without explanation. The verdict ends the case, and that seems to satisfy us. It always amazes me that so much intellectual effort goes into a trial—lawyers researching the law and planning how to prove each material element of their cases, judges cogitating over evidential rulings and over jury instructions—and the process of decision making by the jury remains such a mystery.

Attempts have been made, however, to learn firsthand how juries decide. In the 1950s a group of legal scholars and social scientists at the University of Chicago undertook a comprehensive study of the workings of the American jury. Their methods included hiding microphones in jury rooms and recording actual jury deliberations. When a story about the recordings appeared in the newspapers, the storm of condemnation reached to the halls of Congress, and the project was abandoned. There have been other studies of jury behavior: *The American Jury* by Kalven and Zeisel (1966), based on questionnaires filled out by jurors and judges after the cases were over, and *Judging the Jury* by Hans and Vidmar (1986), based on trial simulations before persons acting as if they were jurors. Neither gives us any systematic knowledge of how juries reach decisions. Thus we have no solid basis for our faith in the jury system.

After one of my trials finishes, I usually chat with the jurors. Although my purpose is to help them more fully understand the experience they have just undergone, often they reveal how they arrived at their verdict. These revelations have been both surprisingly encouraging and profoundly discouraging.

The most competent jury I ever had was in the John Prange police chase case. One set of eyewitnesses had testified that the police cars had chased the stolen car up to the point of the crash. Another set of eyewitnesses had testified that the police cars had been much farther behind and traveling at moderate speeds. The jurors recognized that the testimony on this point went to the heart of the issue of liability. They told me that they resolved the conflicting stories by disbelieving the first set of witnesses because those witnesses had never mentioned the improper conduct of the police in statements they gave to investigating officers immediately after the accident. Evidence that the stolen car had been seen careening around corners at high speed before the police had located it convinced the jurors that the thief's reckless driving, rather than the police activity, caused the accident.

In fact, that jury did something remarkable. After five days of deliberation, they found they could convince one of their members to agree to a unanimous verdict only by writing out an explanation of their decision. They handed the paper to me with their verdict form. It said that they found three of the police officers negligent in violating the pursuit policies of their department, but their negligence was not the proximate cause of the accident. That was a model jury.

Other of my juries have not followed the law so rigorously but reached equally sound decisions. When I came on the bench in 1975, the law of contributory negligence required that juries render a defendant's verdict whenever they found that the plaintiff was the least bit negligent. I used to so charge the jury, although without much conviction. Jurors regularly ignored the law. When the plaintiff was careless in a minor way, they simply reduced the amount of damages they awarded. Their verdicts confirmed an observation of Dean Roscoe Pound: "Jury lawlessness is the great corrective of law in its actual administration." In time that common-sense approach resulted in the enactment of the law of comparative negligence that now legitimizes what jurors had been doing all along.

The worst jury I ever had was in a case in which an elderly woman sued the city of Hartford after she slipped and fell on a defective sidewalk. The city trial lawyer recognized that the woman had a good case and was willing to settle for the amount her lawyer demanded. But the lawyer could not convince her superior at City Hall who, for political reasons, did not want to seek approval of the settlement from the city council. The trial went forward. To the surprise of everyone, the jury returned a defendant's verdict for the city. When I spoke to the jury, the foreman told me that a photograph of the sidewalk, which showed a dangerous displacement of slabs, also showed the stoop of the woman's apartment house. The foreman said the jury figured the woman fell on that stoop rather than on the sidewalk. No evidence in the trial whatsoever justified that version of the accident.

These examples may reveal nothing more than the fact that there are good juries, bad juries, and in-between juries, just as there are good, bad, and indifferent judges. They also reveal that the jury system is fallible, not a new revelation.

Yet the two studies mentioned previously, Kalven and Zeisel and Hans and Vidmar, give high grades to the performance of juries. Kalven and Zeisel evaluated jury verdicts on the basis of whether judges who tried the cases would have decided the same way. They found judges would have reached the same decision as juries on the issue of the defendant's liability in 78 percent of the cases. My own rate of agreement with juries on that issue is even higher: probably 85 percent.

Moreover, juries are not responsible for one of the important criticisms leveled at the operation of our tort system, namely, the expansion of tort liability. Two entirely unrelated reasons account for that: one a matter of policy, the other of proof. The first is that legislatures by statutes or the courts by decisional law have eliminated the element of fault in product liability cases. Manufacturers and sellers are held strictly liable for an unreasonably dangerous product even though they exercised care in manufacturing and marketing it. The law is justified as a way of allocating the costs of accidents by deeming them an expense of doing business to be borne by the product purveyors. The second is the availability of doctors to testify against their colleagues in medical malpractice cases. Such cases were rarely successful as recently as 1975, when I left the practice. I represented a college sophomore who died as a result of insulin shock treatment in a private medical hospital. I could never get a psychiatrist to testify that the hospital did anything wrong. Today there exists a flourishing industry of medical experts who advertise in legal periodicals and offer to provide medical testimony on demand.

Some of the obvious defects in the way jury trials are conducted can be cured. For example, the judge should explain the governing legal principles at the beginning of the case, so jurors can listen to the evidence with a sense of relevance to the grounds upon which they will have to decide the case. Jurors should be allowed to take notes. They should be allowed to ask questions in the course of a trial by writing them out and submitting them to the judge for screening. The judge's instructions at the end of the trial should be in writing, so the jurors do not have to strain to understand them the first time they are heard but can study them more carefully while they are deliberating. I follow the first three of these procedures now, and all of them are followed in some state and federal courts.

What Winston Churchill said about democracy—that it "is the worst form of government except all those other forms that have been tried from time to time"—can be said about civil jury trials. For all the defects in the way jury trials are conducted, the only alternative is court trials. Judges have legal training and the experience of hearing many cases. But in other important aspects they are not clearly superior to juries. Most tort cases turn on the credibility to be accorded the witnesses. Six jurors from varied backgrounds are better at assessing the witnesses than a single judge from his limited one. Jurors are as able as the average jack-of-all-trades judges in our courts of general jurisdiction to understand technical and scientific testimony. Negligence, the primary legal principle in a tort case, is based on the community standard of reasonable conduct. Jurors, coming from the community, are especially qualified to apply that standard.

Tort trials are not logical theorems but slices of life, not line drawings but impressionistic paintings. They are determined not by abstract reasoning, but by understanding the common experience. In my opinion, when deciding the issue of liability, juries do a good job and reach just verdicts.

But having juries decide the *amount* of damages in personal injury cases is, I feel, the flawed feature of the tort system. It is not that jury awards are regularly too high. Multimillion-dollar verdicts get a good deal of publicity, but they are very rare—in Hartford Superior Court, not more than one or two in the last five years. Actually, in some of the cases I have heard, I would have given more than the jury did. The fundamental flaw is that jury damage awards are erratic. Although some are sensible, others are senseless and even irrational. Damage verdicts are damaging when they are as random as lottery numbers. That quality, more than any other, brings the system into disrepute.

As a judge I have, of course, observed the wide disparity in dollar amounts awarded for the same injury to similarly situated plaintiffs. A broken leg prompts $5,000 from one jury, $40,000 from another. Although grossly comparing awards is dangerous, because of the variables in each case, nevertheless such disparities often cannot be justified.

A patient whose double vision had been worsened by the operation of an eye surgeon, but cured by a second operation, won a verdict of $20,000. The lawyer who tried that case brought before me an action against another eye surgeon for the same type of injury; this time his client got $82,700.

In another case I heard, two middle-aged sisters, riding in the same car and involved in the same auto accident, claimed whiplash injuries. One had a 10 percent disability of the neck and $4,500 in medical bills. The jury awarded her $73,000. The other had a 5 percent disability of the neck and $3,000 in medical bills. The same jury in that case awarded her $108,000.

Judges can, to a limited extent, correct flagrant verdicts when motions are made after trial to set them aside. I did in the two sisters' case by ordering a reduction of the amount awarded the less seriously injured sister. In a case in which the jury granted a plaintiff $220,000 for only a 5 percent disability of her back, I also reduced the award. But judges are not supposed to act as superjurors, substituting their judgments for that of the juries. When they do, appellate courts are prone to reverse unless the verdict is so outrageous as to "shock the sense of justice."

The fundamental question remains: Why do juries render such capricious verdicts? The answer lies in three key characteristics of our jury system.

First, jurors are likely to decide only one case in their lives.

They are not only amateurs but neophytes when it comes to putting a value on injuries. With the blind leading the blind, I am convinced that during jury deliberations, when one juror assertively blurts out an amount, vague notions of what should be given suddenly crystallize into a definite number around which the others concentrate their thinking. The ultimate verdict is the product of that initial, off-the-top-of-the-head outburst.

Second, judges give jurors no meaningful help on the amount they should award. The standard charge tells jurors that the plaintiff may be reimbursed for his medical expenses and loss of earnings, and as for pain, suffering, and disability, now and into the future, the plaintiff is entitled to "fair, just, and reasonable compensation." There is no mathematical formula, jurors are told; they must use their best judgment in arriving at what in dollars represents "fair, just, and reasonable compensation."

I once had a jury really challenge me on that instruction. A plaintiff had sustained severe abrasions of her hands and a 10 percent permanent partial disability of her knee as a result of being pushed to the sidewalk by the defendant. The jury came in with the verdict for the plaintiff of only $496. I refused to accept it, told the jury it was too low in light of the plaintiff's injuries, and asked them to reconsider. An hour later the sheriff brought me a note from the jury. It read:

Your Honor,

In your charge to us you stated that there were no guidelines on which to determine the award.

By refusing the verdict, you have implied certain guidelines. If so, you need to make these clear before we can continue any deliberations.

If in fact your charge to us stands, i.e., we must use our best judgment, we respectfully stand upon our original award and verdict.

John Gleason, foreman

I called the jury back into court, gave them again my hackneyed instructions on damages, and directed them to rethink their verdict. They came back soon afterward with an award of $1,528. This time I accepted it, although I still thought it was inadequate. The incident illustrates that a judge repeating the phrase "fair, just, and reasonable compensation" provides no meaningful guidance to juries.

Third, jurors are never informed what the plaintiff really wants and what the defendant—usually an insurance company—is willing to pay. Thus, they are forced to act blindly, without the most obvious guidelines.

I actively elicit from the lawyers in my chambers during the trial the figures the parties are willing to settle for. In situations where the defendant's liability is clear, the plaintiff's demand and the defendant's offer define the parties' conceptions of the true worth of the case. But I am forbidden to reveal them to the jury because it is thought to inhibit settlements. Thus the jury unknowingly often renders verdicts outside those bounds.

In the eye surgeon case mentioned previously, with its $82,700 verdict, the plaintiff's lawyers had been willing to settle for the $20,000 he had received in his first case. In the trial involving the two sisters, with its $181,000 total award, their lawyer had sought to settle both claims for $40,000. I have had just as many cases in which the jury gave the plaintiff a fraction of what the defendant had agreed to pay. One of my superior court colleagues keeps a tabulation of the plaintiff's final demand, the defendant's final offer, and the jury verdict for each of the cases tried in his courthouse. From 1984 to 1988, for 101 cases in which the plaintiff prevailed, his records show that in 59 percent of the cases the verdict amount was either higher than the plaintiff's demand or lower than the defendant's offer. Such windfalls above what plaintiffs want and shortfalls below what defendants are willing to pay in over half the cases give tort trials the quality of games of chance and diminish their aura of justice.

But such results are inevitable when juries do not know the value the parties themselves put on their cases.

In light of these facts, how should the way juries determine damages in personal injury cases be reformed? Some state legislatures have passed laws limiting the maximum amount of compensation allowed for pain and suffering. Other serious thinkers suggest eliminating pain and suffering as an element of damages altogether or establishing a fixed schedule of payment for each category of injury, as under the workers' compensation law.

A better solution would require juries to operate under the method of "last best offer," used successfully in the arbitration of wage rate disputes. This could be effected without abandoning our basic system of juries deciding the full measure of plaintiffs' damages, including pain and suffering.

The trial would be divided into its two separable parts: the issue of liability and the issue of damages. The jury would first hear and decide whether or not the plaintiff proved the defendant was liable and, when the doctrine of comparative negligence was applied, the extent to which the defendant proved that the plaintiff's fault contributed to the accident. If the defendant won on liability, the case would be over: if the plaintiff won on that issue, the parties would be very likely to settle. My experience has been that in bifurcated trials when juries decide liability for plaintiffs, cases settle at least 90 percent of the time.

If, however, there were no settlement at that point, the trial would continue before the same jury on the matter of damages. After all that evidence was in, the judge would solicit in chambers—first from the plaintiff's attorney and then from the defendant's attorney—the amount of damages each believed the evidence established that the plaintiff was entitled to receive. Each lawyer could change his figure in light of the other's, until both arrived at final amounts they were willing to stand on. Those amounts would be submitted to the jury with the instruction that it could choose only one or the other. If the jury were allowed to pick a number in between, then the plaintiff's lawyer would have every incentive to submit a very high amount and the defendant's lawyer a very low amount. But when the jury must choose only one, each attorney would be motivated to submit a final amount that represented his notion of the fairest-possible award in order to earn the jury's vote.

The lawyers' submissions might not be the same as their settlement figures because they would not at that point be compromising between themselves. But their submissions would tend toward the middle ground because the plaintiff's attorney could not afford to state an amount too high or the defendant's attorney too low for fear the jury would pick the other's number. Thus, for lawyers experienced in evaluating their cases, reality and reason would govern.

A charge to the jurors on "fair, just, and reasonable compensation" would then have specific meaning. The judge would inform them of the amount each party believed that compensation should be and direct them to pick the one better supported by the evidence.

Both sides would gain from such a method. Both would be spared the jury's wild surmise. Damage awards would fulfill the reasonable expectation of one party and be close to that of the other. All would feel better about the trial.

As stated in the beginning of this chapter, strong forces are working to change the tort liability model of this country. One of the targets of this attack is the civil jury system. It is vulnerable primarily because of the erratic verdicts it spawns. We alone in the world allow juries free reign to fix the compensation of accident victims. If the jury system is worth preserving, restraints must be imposed. My suggestion reduces the capriciousness of juries and enhances the rationality of their awards. Its adoption will enable the system to work more effectively and, ultimately, to survive.

10. CRIMINAL CASES

When my assignment is changed from the civil to the criminal side of the superior court, I know I am in for a grim time.

Civil trials are relatively polite disputes between private litigants, mainly over money. Something good may happen to the plaintiff in the form of a substantial verdict, but, because of insurance, nothing really bad is going to happen to the defendant. The lawyers battle, but they also banter. In the course of the trial, I can even get in a joke from the bench that evokes more laughter than is warranted.

By contrast, criminal trials are bitter struggles. The state is seeking to convict and punish; the cornered accused fights back fiercely. Something bad has already happened to the victim of the crime, and something bad may happen to the accused. The lawyers scrap and snarl and rarely smile. Attempts at humor can be disastrous, as I learned in my first year on the bench.

I had before me a seventeen-year-old girl charged with possession of marijuana. Her mother stood beside her. Noting that the arrest report indicated that the family lived on Lox Lane, I could not resist asking, with a broad smile, whether that street intersected with Bagel Boulevard. The mother glowered at me. Later the prosecutor told me that the mother had wanted to impress her daughter with the seriousness of the matter, and my frivolity had struck the wrong note. It taught me a lesson I have never forgotten. The criminal court is no place for humor.

So I perform my duties seriously. And each role I play and each decision I make tests my mettle.

Despite the reality that the vast majority of defendants who appear in court are guilty as sin, the underlying premise of our criminal law is that each defendant is presumed innocent. An important responsibility of the judge is to give meaning and content to that presumption.

One way I do so is to say to all defendants the first time they appear in court that in the eyes of the law they are innocent until the state proves them guilty beyond a reasonable doubt. I then inform them of their constitutional rights: the rights to remain silent, to an attorney, to reasonable bail, to subpoena their own witnesses, to confront the state's witnesses, to trial by jury. By the tone of my voice I try to convey that those rights are important, and that I take them seriously. I also want to communicate that although I am an officer of the state, I am not a part of the prosecution by the state.

Another way I give content to the presumption of innocence is by treating each accused with respect. I always use a "Mr." or "Ms." before an accused's surname. A young man may have been called Willie or "boy" all his life, but in my court he is Mr. Jones.

If the accused cannot afford a lawyer, I immediately appoint a public defender to represent him. Public defenders are hired by the state on the basis of the same professional qualifications as prosecutors. Although overburdened by heavy caseloads, they defend their clients conscientiously and well. In many instances they are more skillful than private lawyers who charge high fees but have much less experience in the criminal courts.

The decision I make in setting bail will determine whether the defendant will remain free or languish in jail for from three to six months until his case reaches trial. Both the United States and the Connecticut constitutions expressly prohibit "excessive bail." The current Connecticut bail statute, which I drafted when I was in the legislature, provides that bail shall be set in an amount reasonably sufficient to assure the accused's appearance in court. Factors to be taken into account are the accused's ties to the community, his employment, his prior criminal record, and the seriousness of the crime charged.

A state official, called a bail commissioner, interviews the accused immediately after an arrest to ascertain these factors. At the accused's first court appearance, he recommends to the judge whether the accused should be freed on his own promise to appear or be required to post bail, and, if bail, in what amount.

Two cases illustrate the kinds of dilemmas faced when deciding on bail. Jack Weaver appeared before me on a larceny charge for purse snatching. He was a thin, black man with nervously darting eyes. The bail commissioner stated that he lived on and off in his girlfriend's apartment but had no steady address, that he had no job, a record of two previous larcenies, and was on parole. The commissioner recommended bail of $5,000. The prosecutor concurred; the public defender asked for a reduced amount. I recognized that the crime was not serious, but Weaver's tenuous ties to the community gave little assurance of his appearing for future court dates. With a silent sigh I set bail at $1,000, knowing that even that amount would keep Weaver in jail.

Robert White was charged with rape. He was a handsome, blond boy-man of about eighteen. His worried father and mother stood beside him. The bail commissioner reported that Robert lived at home, went to the local high school, had one previous assault charge nolled. He recommended bail of $25,000. The prosecutor disagreed vigorously. He said that White had picked up a high school classmate at an ice-cream parlor, taken her in his car to a deserted woods, threatened her with a knife, and raped her. He demanded bail of $100,000. White's private attorney argued passionately that because of the stable family situation, Robert should be released on his promise to appear.

What bail should I set? The alleged crime was serious, but the probability of the boy appearing was great. I fixed bail at $50,000, knowing White's family would pay a bail bondsman to secure his release.

Bail clearly discriminates against the poor, the homeless, the jobless. One Connecticut judge I know always requires bail in welfare fraud cases, choosing to ignore whether or not welfare mothers can raise it. I am at the other end of the spectrum. The ability of the defendant to make bail is always a factor in my decision. Giving the accused every reasonable opportunity to remain free until he is proven guilty best implements the presumption of innocence.

Being lenient, however, creates the lingering concern that an accused may commit another vicious crime after being let go on bail. The public has a right to be outraged when that occurs. I once released an accused who walked out of the courthouse and within an hour robbed an elderly lady, breaking her arm in the act. I always felt a special responsibility for that offense. Yet I have continued my practice of setting bail only high enough to assure the defendant's appearance in court, as the statute I wrote requires, and never as a means of preventive detention.

At the next court appearance the defendant is arraigned—that is, the charge lodged against him is read by the court clerk, who then asks: "How do you plead, guilty or not guilty?" The first time most defendants plead not guilty. But sometime later, usually after a plea bargain has been struck between the defense lawyer and the prosecutor, the defendant may change his plea to guilty. Then it is my job to be sure the defendant understands what he is doing and is making the plea voluntarily.

Canvasing a plea can take as long as an hour. First, I ask the prosecutor to recite the facts on which the charge is based, listening to be certain that each element of the crime is substantiated. For example, burglary in the second degree requires entry into a dwelling at night with the intent to commit a crime. If the facts stated by the prosecutor reveal entry into a commercial building, I do not accept the plea. If, however, the prosecutor's statement of the facts do sustain the crime charged, I ask the defendant to tell me in his own words what he did. If his version differs from the prosecutor's or does not contain an essential element of the crime, I tell him, "If what you say is true, you have not committed the crime for which you are charged. I advise you to consult with your lawyer about your guilty plea."

If the defendant admits facts that establish the crime, I inquire further:

"Are you satisfied with your attorney's advice and assistance?"

"Do you understand that you are giving up your privilege not to incriminate yourself, your right to confront your accusers, and your absolute right to a jury trial?"

"Have any threats or promises been made to induce you to plead guilty when you otherwise would not have done so?"

"Do you realize that I do not have to accept the plea bargain agreement reached between your attorney and the state's attorney; but if I do not accept it, you can withdraw your guilty plea and have a trial if you wish?"

"Has your attorney told you of the possible range of penalties for this offense?"

"Are you aware that if you are not a United States citizen, your guilty plea will constitute a conviction for a crime which could cause your deportation and denial of your admission to the United States or of naturalization?"

"Have you understood all of the questions which I have asked you?"

"Is there anything which I have said that you do not understand?"

"Do you still wish to plead guilty?"

On several occasions, after going through that litany, I was not satisfied with the defendant's answers, refused to accept the guilty plea, and set the case down for trial. However, most of the time I do receive adequate answers, order the plea recorded, and declare the defendant guilty of the crime charged.

Being certain that the defendant committed the crime and that his admission of guilt is knowingly and voluntarily made is not the only reason criminal judges canvas a plea carefully. Months later, when the defendant is in prison, reflecting on his fate, he may bring a habeas corpus proceeding to get out on the ground that the guilty plea was improperly accepted. Pains are taken to get his admissions of guilt and his understanding of the proceedings on the record to preclude him from disavowing his plea and prevailing in that subsequent proceeding.

If the defendant pleads not guilty, then the case is set down for trial. Before the trial date, defense counsel may make a motion to suppress incriminating evidence seized in a police search or to quash a confession made by the defendant to the police. These motions evoke two constitutional provisions: the Fourth Amendment to the United States Constitution, which prohibits "unreasonable searches and seizures" and requires that search warrants be issued only "upon probable cause . . . particularly describing the place to be searched and the persons or things to be seized"; and the Fifth Amendment, which provides that "[n]o person . . .

shall be compelled in any criminal case to be a witness against himself."

The courts have created a large and complex body of law interpreting and applying these amendments. The most important is the so-called exclusionary rule, which bars evidence obtained in violation of the Constitution from being used against the defendant in the trial. The purpose of the rule is to discourage the police from gathering evidence illegally. The consequence of the rule is that if the evidence is suppressed, there may be no other incriminating evidence to convict the defendant, and he may go free.

José Gomez was charged with illegal possession of drugs with the intent to sell. The police had obtained a warrant to search Gomez's pawn shop in Hartford for narcotics and drug paraphernalia. There they found quantities of cocaine and marijuana, along with water pipes, scales, and other devices used for weighing and packaging narcotics.

In my courtroom Gomez, a handsome Puerto Rican, listened intently as his lawyer moved to suppress as evidence all the items seized in the search. Although another superior court judge had signed the warrant authorizing the search, the motion required that I examine the warrant to determine whether or not it met a two-pronged test:

1. Did the warrant state facts establishing a reasonable basis for believing that property in Gomez's store constituted evidence of a crime?
2. Were those facts supplied to the police by credible and reliable informants?

The critical portion of the warrant read: "On 02-10-81 the undersigned Detective Sgt. Horilio did interview numerous persons ranging in age from middle teens to middle age. All of such persons interviewed indicated that a short Puerto Rican, whom they all identified as José Gomez, is and has been selling cocaine to many young residents on Park Street in Hartford."

Gomez's lawyer argued, "Judge, the warrant is insufficient. It does not identify the informants or give any basis on which to conclude they are believable and what they said is reliable."

He was right. The warrant did not name the informants or indicate that they had previously given accurate information to the police. I granted his motion to suppress the evidence.

In another case before me, the police report revealed that the police had responded to a burglar alarm going off in a discount store at two o'clock in the morning. Two blocks from the store they saw a young man running down the street. They pulled up beside him and shouted for him to get into the cruiser. One of the officers then said, "All right, kid, who else was with you when you broke into Two Guys?"

"Nobody, sir. I tried to get into the store myself, but the alarm went off."

When the young man, named Richard Shore, was charged with attempted burglary, his lawyer moved before me to quash the confession on the ground that it had been obtained in violation of the *Miranda* decision. (In the case of *Miranda* v. *Arizona*, the United States Supreme Court ruled that before questioning a person in custody, the police must inform him of his constitutional right to remain silent and to have an attorney.) The prosecutor argued that Shore admitted his involvement voluntarily, so there was no necessity to give the *Miranda* warnings. But it was clear to me that Shore was both in police custody and being questioned by the officer when he spoke, so the *Miranda* warnings were required. I granted the motion to quash the confession.

After my decision in each of these cases the state's attorney declined to prosecute, so Gomez and Shore went free. But in both instances the police work had been shoddy. The police themselves should have conducted a surveillance of

the Gomez store. Then their statements of what they observed in an affidavit accompanying the search warrant
would have provided a reliable basis for issuing the warrant.
In the Shore case, the police should have known when they
had Shore in the police car and questioned him that they had
first to advise him of his constitutional rights.

Such mistakes occur rarely. The police have learned that
to secure convictions they must comply with the law. Court
decisions have had the desired effect of raising the level of
police professionalism.

When faced with motions to suppress, I disregard the incriminating nature of the evidence being challenged and rigorously concentrate on the constitutional question of
whether or not the evidence was obtained legally. In deciding those motions, I feel like a true priest of the law. My
obligation is to uphold the Constitution, even if it means
letting an apparently guilty defendant go free.

Before the trial itself starts, the jury must be picked. In
contrast with civil cases, where the lawyers usually select
the jury with only a court clerk present, in criminal cases a
judge always presides over the voir dire. In a serious crime
the lawyers minutely question each venireman for hours,
zealously ferreting out any possible bias, and in Connecticut
the whole process can take from a week to as long as three
months. Presiding over jury selection in those cases is the
most tedious of judicial duties. In the beginning I make a
few rulings on the types of questions permitted, and then
the lawyers fall into a routine of asking the same questions
over and over again. After a few days of it, I am fit to climb
a wall. I feel like a prisoner on the bench and engage in any
kind of distraction, including surreptitiously scribbling chap-
ters of this book.

But when the first witness takes the stand, my interest is
rekindled. Because the accused's liberty is at stake, the tension is high. Often the main battle in criminal trials is over
procedure, particularly whether evidence damaging to the

defendant is to be let in. Although the law calls for the rules of evidence to be applied the same way in civil and criminal trials, in civil cases I tend to allow in evidence that may help the jury get the full picture. However, in criminal cases I apply the rules of evidence strictly. Defense counsel in particular are alert to raise every possible objection. When peppered with demands for evidential rulings, I sometimes feel like a linesman at a tennis match, calling each shot in, out, out, in. The pressure to be right is fueled by an awareness that every serious criminal case is going to be appealed; any of my rulings, if erroneous, can be the basis of a reversal of the trial's outcome.

Any inclination I may have to ask questions of witnesses during a criminal trial, even to have testimony clarified, is much more severely restrained than in a civil trial. Although I may intervene on behalf of an accused if his lawyer is inept and fails to ask an obvious question, I will never intervene on behalf of the state, such as to remind the prosecutor that he overlooked proving an essential element of the crime. Conceptually the two situations are the same. But because I am an officer of the state, I am fearful that if I help the state, the defendant will see it as my tipping the scales unfairly against him.

When the accused takes the stand, I am particularly cautious to refrain from indicating any doubt as to his credibility. Since the jurors glance constantly at the judge for his reactions to the testimony, I avoid any look, lifted eyebrow, or voice inflection that might reveal my feelings.

There are situations, however, in which I may not be allowed to remain serenely above the fray. The defense lawyer may adopt a tactic of deliberately seeking to induce me into incorrect rulings or improper conduct in order to have a ground for an appeal. My error is the defense counsel's hostage to fortune; if he loses the jury verdict, my error may enable him to get the case reversed by a higher court.

One such defense lawyer in a robbery case thought he

could enhance his chances by harassing me. When the prosecutor objected to one of his patently improper questions, he said sotto voce to the jury, "You see, the state is trying to keep the truth from you." I cautioned him, then upheld the objection. He took an exception in a tone that implied that I was in league with the prosecutor. Another time, after one of my rulings, he slapped a paper pad on the counsel table, turned his back to me, and, the sheriff told me, grimaced to the jury. Again I warned him. But his disrespectful conduct continued throughout the trial. At one point I found myself so furious at him that I angrily started to rule against one of his motions. But I checked myself in time. Looking at the troubled face of his client, I realized that he, not his lawyer, was on trial, and I should not take out my anger on him.

After the jury acquitted, I called the lawyer into my chambers and reprimanded him. He said brazenly, "It worked, didn't it?"

I said, "Maybe. But the next time you'll be held in contempt and go to jail, whether or not your client does."

Fortunately such conduct by lawyers is rare. Particularly in a small state like Connecticut, the relationship between bench and bar is one of mutual respect. Because there are so few judges, an active trial attorney cannot afford to alienate any one of them.

I always feel particularly tested by a case in which I learn before trial that the accused is surely guilty. The information may have come to me during a motion to suppress incriminating evidence, or to quash a confession, the truth of which was never questioned. Whether I granted either motion, so the prosecutor must attempt to convict the defendant by other evidence, or whether I denied either motion, so the evidence is overwhelming against the defendant, I resist any temptation to treat the trial as a charade.

For the trial itself serves an important cathartic purpose. If conducted fairly, it assuages the resentments of all who have a stake in the outcome: the accused, the victim and his family, the police, interested members of the public. The high barriers the state must overcome—such as the exclusionary rule barring illegally obtained evidence and proof of guilt beyond a reasonable doubt—give legitimacy to a conviction.

Criminal trials are didactic in their devotion to detail and sordid in their subject matter, yet they are the measure of a civilized society. By affording due process and basic dignity to the meanest, the courts assure them for everyone. When presiding over such trials, I feel that I am holding in check society's savage impulses for revenge while at the same time implementing its highest aspirations for fair play.

But the final decision in a criminal case lies with the jury. They evaluate the witnesses, weigh the evidence, and render the verdict of guilty or not guilty. Although I have some doubt about the efficacy of juries in civil personal injury cases, particularly in the awarding of damages, I have no doubt about the worth of juries in criminal trials. I rarely differ with their verdicts. When I do, I readily defer to their superior judgment as the collective conscience of the community.

From my vantage point, I see juries holding the state to a high burden of proof and tending to give the accused the benefit of the doubt. When American juries refuse to enforce the strict letter of the criminal law (a tradition that goes back to 1734 when a colonial jury acquitted John Peter Zenger of the charge of criminal libelling the British governor), even to the extent that they nullify the law (as a New York jury did in 1987 when it found Bernard Goetz, the admitted assailant of youths in a subway, guilty of only a minor gun possession offense), they represent a subtle distribution of political power, an arrangement by which equity and flexibility are built into the criminal justice system. And that is the kind of criminal justice system most of us want.

Today, however, there is a meaner tone and a deeper frustration in the criminal courts. The reason is the prevalence of drugs in the cities. Drugs spawn more violent crimes and account for close to 80 percent of all criminal cases. The police, responding to public demands for action, make more arrests and dump the avalanche of their arrests on the courts. Every morning, day after day, judges have pass before them a conveyor-belt line of persons accused of serious crimes. It takes all their mental strength and moral fiber to assure each of those persons the right to the presumption of innocence and to a fair trial. On such commitment rests the preservation of our constitutional values.

11. MURDER TRIAL

Murder is the ultimate crime, and murder trials stir the deepest emotions. Blood of the victim has been spilled, and blood of the accused, at least figuratively, is being sought by the state. Lawyers battle fiercely, jurors listen attentively, tension in the courtroom is palpable.

The case of *State* v. *Raffone* had its origin on November 10, 1977, when the body of Alfred Chisolm was found at the bottom of a laundry cart in the Connecticut state prison gym. Raw abrasions around the neck of the twenty-one-year-old inmate indicated that he had been strangled.

A grand jury indicted Salvatore Raffone and two other inmates for murder. The state decided to prosecute Raffone first. Two years later the case came to trial in the superior court in Rockville, a rural town about twenty miles from Hartford.

. . .

As I enter the courtroom from the door behind the bench, on the morning the trial begins, I glance at Raffone, who stands next to his attorney. He is a short, stocky man of about thirty-five. He looks up at me defiantly with his brown, piercing eyes, as the sheriff intones, "All rise. The Superior Court of Tolland County is now in session. Judge Robert Satter presiding." For that instant we stare at each other, until I, not he, look away.

I settle into my high-backed leather chair, and everyone else sits down. The jury, having already been selected under my supervision, now has to be sworn in. The clerk asks each to stand as his or her name and number are called. As they rise, I remember their occupations: first juror is a secretary; second, an engineer; third a bookkeeper; fourth an office manager; fifth a guidance counselor; sixth a housewife. The clerk then administers the oath:

You solemnly swear by the name of the ever-living God, that you will, without respect of favor of any man, well and truly try, and true deliverance make, between the state of Connecticut and the defendant, whom you shall have in charge, according to law and the evidence before you; your own counsel, and your fellows', you will duly observe and keep; you will speak nothing, to any one, of the business or matters you have in hand, but among yourselves, nor will you suffer anyone to speak to you about the same, but in court; so help you God.

There is a chorus of "I do's." The clerk then swears in the two alternate jurors.

Earlier, in a surprise move just before the start of jury selection, state's attorney Donald Caldwell reduced the charge against Raffone from murder to manslaughter first degree. The difference between the two crimes is significant. Under Connecticut law a person is guilty of murder "when with the intent to cause the death of another person, he causes the death of such person." In contrast, a person is guilty of manslaughter first degree "when with the intent to cause serious physical injury to another person, he causes the death of such person."

Caldwell felt that his evidence was more likely to prove the lesser crime and that by lowering the charge he was enhancing his chances of getting a conviction.

I briefly explain to the jury the concept of manslaughter first degree and the burden on the state of proving that the defendant committed the crime beyond a reasonable doubt. "When all the evidence is in, you, not I, will decide this case," I say. "You will render a verdict of guilty or not guilty. For some of you this will be the most important responsibility you will perform as a citizen of this state. Now, each of the attorneys will make opening remarks explaining his side of the case."

Caldwell ambles toward the jury box. He is a bulky, handsome man who exudes strength and dignity. In a straightforward manner he tells the jury that the state will prove that Raffone killed Chisolm. He admits that he will produce no eyewitnesses. But from the witnesses he will call and from the admissions Raffone himself made to other prisoners, he will establish to the jury's satisfaction that Raffone is guilty.

Attorney Leo Flaherty rises next. He is a lawyer in private practice, appointed by the court to defend Raffone. (The regular public defender was disqualified because he represented some inmates who will be called to testify against Raffone.) Flaherty is bald, florid-faced, and has a deserved reputation for tenacity and courage. He reminds the jury that the state has to prove that his client is guilty beyond a reasonable doubt. "By the end of the trial," he says, "you will doubt why the state has brought this case at all."

The lawyers' rhetoric out of the way, I nod to Caldwell to call his first witness. The jurors lean forward attentively. A thin, bespectacled man takes the stand. He identifies himself as a civil engineer and displays a large plan, drawn to scale, of the area of the prison where the homicide occurred. In precise, clipped fashion he points out the location of the gym, boxing ring, locker rooms, card room, and hobby shop. Flaherty concentrates his cross-examination on what a viewer could see by looking through a glass door into one of the locker rooms.

The next witness is a corrections officer. He testifies that he and a fellow officer were assigned to find Chisolm when Chisolm was reported missing at evening checkup.

Corrections Officer: "We went into the gym. I noticed a laundry cart under the boxing ring. It didn't seem right to me. I ducked under the ring and started pulling the cart toward me. It was very heavy. Somehow I felt as though he were in there."

Flaherty: "Objection, Your Honor. He can't testify to what he felt."

Me: "Sustained."

Caldwell: "Just tell what you saw and did."

Corrections Officer: "I kept the basket under the ring and said, 'I know you're in there, so get out.' I had my hand on the cart all the time and kept it under the ring just in case he was going to jump up or had something in his hand. I again said, 'Let's go; get out of there.' I also gave the canvas a kick and hit something hard. I started to pull the dirty towels and clothes out of the cart and spotted a right foot with the sock on it. I yelled to the other officer, 'I found him, and I think he's dead. Call the captain and tell them.' "

Caldwell: "What did you do next?"

Corrections Officer: "We removed the rest of the dirty laundry. He was fully clothed, but one sneaker was missing. His clothing was dirty and torn. It appeared he had been in a fight."

Caldwell: "I show you these photographs and ask whether you can identify them."

Corrections Officer: "Yeah, that's him. That's the inmate I found in the laundry cart."

The pictures are admitted as exhibits and passed among the jurors. Flaherty asks only a few cursory questions in his cross-examination.

The next witness is the acting chief medical examiner. In an objective voice, as if she were lecturing to medical students, she describes her autopsy of Chisolm's body.

Medical Examiner: "The body was that of an adult, black male clad in a long-sleeved, snap-front jacket. The right sleeve was torn at the shoulder seams. The white T-shirt was torn at both shoulder seams. There was irregular bloodstaining down the left half of the front of the shirt as well as the back of the shirt. His long tan trousers had the waist button and the top button of the fly recently torn off.

"The body had a measured length of five feet eight inches and estimated weight of 160 pounds. There was an abrasion one inch by three-eighths of an inch over the right eyebrow. The upper lip was split and the lower lip lacerated. The right cheek was swollen.

"A dried ligature furrow about the neck measured one-half inch in width and ten and seven-eighths inches in length, canting upward from left to right. There were also dried linear abrasions of the left thorax extending two inches to the left and one and one-half inches below the left nipple.

"An examination of the neck revealed considerable hemorrhaging of the mastoid and thyrohyoid muscles. There were fractures of the left superior horn of the thyroid cartilage and of the right arm of the hyoid bone with considerable surrounding hemorrhage."

Caldwell shows her photographs of Chisolm. She identifies them as fair representations of the injuries on the body she examined. One photo clearly shows the furrow abrasion around the neck. They are admitted into evidence and passed to the jurors, who look at them with much interest.

Caldwell: "Doctor, do you have an opinion of the cause of Chisolm's death?"

Medical Examiner: "Yes."

Caldwell: "What is the cause?"

Medical Examiner: "The cause of death is asphyxia by strangulation."

Caldwell: "Can you identify the kind of strangulation?"

Medical Examiner: "The strangulation was by canvas belt or rope around the neck."

Caldwell: "Is the physical evidence consistent with a hanging?"

Medical Examiner: "No. The ligature was applied horizontally to the body."

Flaherty asks on cross-examination what amount of force was necessary to cause a strangulation death. The medical examiner says it could be applied gradually and might or might not fracture bones.

Flaherty: "And how long would it take?"

Medical Examiner: "It would take two to five minutes. The force would have to be applied deliberately and intentionally."

Flaherty (in anger): "I move the doctor's last remark be stricken as not responsive to my question."

Me: "Granted. The jury is instructed to ignore it." I know there is a fat chance that they will.

Flaherty asks the doctor to estimate when Chisolm died. She says that the time can often be determined from knowing when the victim last ate and examining the contents of his stomach. But she conducted her autopsy two days after the death and so cannot fix the time of death.

Finally Flaherty shows the medical examiner a photograph of Chisolm with the top button of his trousers torn off and asks if she gave any significance to that. She responds that swabs were passed over Chisolm's mouth and anus to check for semen, and semen was present. On that note I adjourn the trial for the day.

The next morning the first witness is the prison recreational supervisor. He testifies that on November 10 the members of two all-star teams assembled in the locker room for football practice. Chisolm was one of the first to show up.

However, he does not recall seeing Chisolm on the field. After practice the recreation supervisor saw an inmate named Passalaqua push a laundry cart across the gym floor. He thought that odd but did not investigate further.

On cross-examination Flaherty asks the supervisor if he saw Raffone in the locker room that day. The answer is no.

At this point Caldwell says that his next witnesses are inmates. He moves to exclude the press from the courtroom when these prisoners identify themselves on the stand. These witnesses, he says, fear reprisals in prison if their names are mentioned in the newspaper. Flaherty immediately pops up to oppose the motion on the ground that his client has a constitutional right to a public trial. I deny the motion, but not without qualms over the consequences to the witnesses.

A few moments later the reality of terror in prison is dramatically revealed. Caldwell calls to the stand an inmate to whom the state offered complete immunity from prosecution for his testimony. Nevertheless the inmate refuses to testify. I tell him that if he continues to refuse, I will have to hold him in contempt. He says, "Judge, if I testify, my life won't be worth a plugged nickel in prison. That goes for any prison the state may send me to to finish out my term. My life is more important to me than immunity." I hold him in contempt.

The first inmate who does testify is a member of the football team. He says that on that day he started to go into the locker room when he heard a fight going on—"yelling, lockers banging, and that sort of thing." Not wanting to get involved, he left. Flaherty gets him to concede that he had not seen Raffone.

The next witness is Robert Walker, a former prisoner who has since been paroled. He speaks in a calm, self-assured manner.

"I saw Chisolm as I was going to the gym after the three o'clock count. He said he was going to football practice, too.

I was surprised. I didn't know he had made the all-star teams. I stopped in the gym to talk to one of the guards and then proceeded to the back locker room. As I approached, I heard loud banging. I looked through the window in the door. I saw Raffone with his arms around Chisolm, and they were struggling. McAlister and Passalaqua were also there. One of them swung at Chisolm. I'm not sure which. As soon as I saw what was going on, I knew it was none of my business. I turned around and walked out of the gym. About fifteen minutes later I went back and dressed for practice."

Caldwell: "Did you see Chisolm at practice?"

Walker: "No, sir."

Caldwell: "What else unusual did you see that afternoon?"

Walker: "After practice I was in the card room. Another inmate pointed to the gym. Passalaqua was pushing a laundry cart, and he left it under the boxing ring."

On cross, Flaherty vigorously tries to shake the witness's story, but Walker describes even more explicitly how he saw Raffone gripping Chisolm by the neck.

Flaherty: "Could Raffone have been trying to break up a fight?"

Walker: "Possibly."

Flaherty then tries to insinuate that Walker made a deal with the state police to testify falsely in order to get paroled. Walker bristles at this, denying it heatedly. That ends the second day of the trial.

The next morning Caldwell calls to the stand another inmate, who is serving a long term for escape. He was in segregation, he says, when shortly after Chisolm's death Raffone was brought into the next cell.

"Sal [Raffone] was top man in the prison for dope. He had a lot of pull, could get a lot done in the prison. I did things for him, mainly wrote his letters. Once I sent five one-hundred-dollar bills to his girlfriend in Colorado. He gave me grass.

"Then we were both moved to 'E' unit in the protective custody block. We were locked up next to each other a month or so, and Sal started to talk about the murder of Chisolm."

Caldwell: "What did Raffone say?"

Inmate: "He said that Chisolm found out that he was in charge of dope trafficking in the prison. Chisolm told Sal he wanted some of the dope action, or he would drop a dime on him."

Caldwell: "What did Raffone say to that?"

Inmate: "He said he got his men together, Willie Passalaqua, Mac McAlister, and Equllian Cruz. They got Chisolm down in the locker room so Cruz could talk sense to him and scare him. Willie, Mac, and Sal stationed themselves around the locker room to watch out for guards. Cruz talked to Chisolm, but Chisolm wouldn't listen. Cruz went crazy and killed him. Sal told me he was watching for the guards, and when he got in the shower room, Chisolm was dead. Sal and Mac then picked up the body, put it into a laundry cart, pushed it off to the side, and left."

Flaherty lets that story stand. He only asks the witness, "Whom did Raffone have influence with in the prison?"

Inmate: "Oh, with the administration, the staff."

The next inmate witness turns out to be the most incriminating against Raffone. He is a prison barber, who testifies that he collected the action each day for Raffone's gambling operation. Raffone complained to him that people were not paying him for dope. After Chisolm's death, when Raffone was placed in segregation, the barber went there to cut his hair. Raffone told him that Cruz had killed Chisolm. Later the barber arranged to get in a cell next to Raffone. They talked a lot; the barber told Raffone he did not believe the Cruz story.

Caldwell: "What did Raffone say?"

Barber: "He said, 'What the hell, it's your word against mine. I went down to the gym that day looking for Chisolm because he owed me money for smoke. I met Chisolm in front of the locker room, and he refused to pay for the smoke because he claimed it was garbage. McAlister and Passalaqua were with me. I whacked Chisolm with a pipe. Then we threw a rope around him and there was a struggle. Afterwards we put Chisolm into a laundry cart. Mac and Passalaqua went to practice, and I hid the pipe and rope in the hobby shop next to the locker room.' "

Caldwell: "Did Raffone tell you why he was in the locker room?"

Barber: "Yeah, to collect money from Chisolm. It was over marijuana."

Caldwell: "Why did Raffone tell you this?"

Barber: "I convinced him I was his friend. I really was his friend in segregation."

Flaherty gets the witness to admit that he never actually saw Raffone and Chisolm together. Then Flaherty zeroes in on his motivation for testifying.

Flaherty: "You arranged to get in the cell next to Raffone, didn't you?"

Barber: "Yeah, I already said that."

Flaherty: "And you arranged it because you wanted to be able to tell the police what you claimed Raffone told you?"

Barber: "Well, it wasn't like that."

Flaherty: "And you wanted to be an informer in order to get a break on your parole?"

Barber: "Well, I hoped it might help."

Flaherty: "So you made up this story to save your own skin?"

Barber: "No. What I said was true."

Flaherty (with disdain): "No further questions of this witness."

Caldwell's last inmate witness testifies that he had been a cellmate of Raffone a year or so after the murder. They spent hours talking "jail talk," mainly about things they had done in their lives. One day Raffone received a letter from his dying mother. He got very emotional. He said he vowed to his mother that he would never hurt anyone again. Then Raffone said, "About Chisolm, it was an accident. I and a couple of other guys were going to rough Chisolm up. I held him with my arms, and these other guys beat on Chisolm. Then I put Chisolm's body in the laundry basket."

With that the state rests. And I adjourn court.

The next day Flaherty puts on two witnesses. One testifies to a minor inconsistency in Robert Walker's testimony, the other to Walker's having told him he went to the police to get a break for himself. Then Flaherty rests.

That is the evidence the jury hears, with all its inconsistencies and glaring omissions. In the highest tradition of a prosecutor, Caldwell put on all the evidence he had, both that which was helpful to his case and that, such as the Cruz story, which was harmful. He could not call the men who were said to be in the locker room when Chisolm was killed —McAlister and Passalaqua, who were indicted with Raffone, or Cruz—because all of them had indicated they would plead the Fifth Amendment. Flaherty, on his part, did not call Raffone.

Caldwell sums up to the jury in his calm, deliberate way. He goes over the evidence from which the jury can reasonably find the following: Raffone conducted dope and gambling operations in the prison; Chisolm owed Raffone money; Raffone and his buddies cornered Chisolm in the locker room; Raffone grabbed Chisolm; his buddies struck Chisolm; Raffone hit him with a pipe; they threw a rope around Chisolm's neck; the struggle continued until Chisolm died; Raffone put him in the laundry cart; Chisolm was found that evening with a ligature furrow around his neck; the cause of his death was asphyxiation by strangulation. That evidence, Caldwell says, proves first-degree manslaughter. He closes, "The state has confidence in your good judgment and leaves it to you to decide."

Flaherty is more fiery. He reminds the jury that the state

did not produce one eyewitness to the homicide. Inmate Walker testified that he saw Raffone with his arms around Chisolm but admitted Raffone could have been breaking up a fight. All the other inmates testified to what Raffone supposedly told them. For an hour Flaherty dissects their testimony, showing that every one of them had an obvious motive to lie. By currying favor with the prison authorities and the state police, they were seeking to benefit themselves, he said.

"None of them," he thunders at the end, "are worthy of a shred of belief. You wouldn't believe them if you met them in your daily lives. You shouldn't believe them in this courtroom.

"Proof beyond a reasonable doubt! That's the standard the state must meet. There's enough doubt in this case to stretch to the moon. If you are going to follow the court's instructions and apply that standard to the evidence you have heard, you have to render a verdict of not guilty."

Caldwell closes with a few brief remarks. Again he expresses his confidence in the jury. With the arguments of counsel ringing in their ears, I release the jurors for the day.

That night I struggle over my charge. It is my first manslaughter case. I want to make my instructions accurate and clear. The elements of the crime are simple enough to explain. The jury has to find that Raffone intended to cause serious physical injury to Chisolm and as a result caused Chisolm's death. I particularly want to refine two aspects of my charge that I feel will be most critical to the jury's decision: the nature of the state's burden of proof and the significance of Raffone not having taken the stand. As to the latter, I know that the most likely conclusion for laypersons to reach about Raffone not testifying is that he is guilty. Otherwise, why would he not get on the stand, deny all the accusations against him, and declare his innocence?

But I know it is more complicated than that. Raffone has a long criminal record. If he testified, Caldwell would have led him through every one of his prior convictions for robbery, burglary, and assault, which would not only have shredded Raffone's credibility, but also have shown what a bad man he was and how likely he was to have committed the crime for which he was now charged. I have to fashion an instruction that directs the jury to recognize and respect Raffone's constitutional right to remain silent.

When court convenes in the morning, I say to the jury on the matter of the state's burden of proof:

"The law presumes the defendant innocent. The state has to prove him guilty of the crime for which he is charged; the defendant does not have to prove his own innocence.

"The state has to prove every element of manslaughter first degree and must prove every element beyond a reasonable doubt. What do I mean by proof beyond a reasonable doubt? You can understand the concept by placing emphasis on the word *reasonable*.

"A reasonable doubt is a doubt for which a reason can be assigned. It is something more than a guess, surmise, or conjecture. A reasonable doubt is not one raised by someone simply for the sake of raising doubts, nor suggested by the ingenuity of counsel or any juror, which is not justified by the evidence or lack of evidence. It is a doubt for which you can conscientiously give a reason. It is the kind of doubt which, in the serious affairs of your everyday life, you would heed and pay attention to.

"The state does not have to prove guilt beyond all doubt or to a mathematical or absolute certainty. What the law does require, however, is that after hearing all the evidence, if there is something in that evidence or lack of evidence which leaves in your minds, as reasonable men and women, a reasonable doubt about the guilt of Raffone, then Raffone must be given the benefit of that doubt, and you must return a verdict of not guilty. If there is no reasonable doubt in your minds, you must find the accused guilty."

Even as I read that portion of my charge to the jurors, I

wonder whether I have helped them much. The concept is
so vague. Yet it is the foundation upon which all criminal
law rests.

On the matter of Raffone not taking the stand, I tell the
jury:

"As you know, the accused did not testify in his own
behalf. He is not obligated to do so. In fact, he has the right
guaranteed in both the United States and the Connecticut
constitutions not to testify. You must not consider the
exercise of that right as evidence of guilt. The burden is
on the state to prove Raffone guilty beyond a reasonable
doubt. It is not incumbent on Raffone to prove his innocence. You are to draw no adverse inference or conclusion
from the fact he did not take the stand. There are many
valid reasons for his not testifying. He has that choice.
No taint or inference should be drawn from his choosing
not to testify."

The jury listens attentively, as they have throughout the
trial. When they retire to deliberate, I return to my chambers. Usually I start working on an unfinished opinion, but
not this time. The trial has gotten to me. I realize that I am
deeply involved.

As I stand alone by my window looking out at the gray
hills sloping toward the quiet town, I feel a deep sadness.
The trial revealed the brutality and lawlessness of life in
prison. Chisolm was violently killed. The garroting left sear-
ing bruises around his neck and broke two bones in his
throat. Semen was found in his mouth and anus. That was
never explained. Moreover, drugs were sold openly. Raffone
seemed to be the acknowledged head of the operation. Why
did the prison authorities allow it? Was it a way of control-
ling the inmates? During the trial a corrections officer, who
transported Raffone back and forth to the prison each day,
told me that Raffone complained that he had lost $20,000
when he was in segregation. Did the prison guards share in
those profits?

The case also revealed the qualities of friendship and loyalty among prisoners. The main evidence against Raffone was the testimony of fellow inmates reporting what Raffone confided to them. Maybe the informants were acting as good citizens. More likely they were eager to turn against Raffone for their own selfish interest.

I walk out to the corridor in front of the courtroom, in search of company. Knots of people are speaking in hushed tones. They drop their voices even lower when I approach. Flaherty paces up and down the hall, nervously smoking one cigarette after another. I can see that he cares. Having passionately defended his client, he now is suffering the agony of awaiting his client's fate. There is nobody for me to talk to, so I return to my chambers and resume gazing out the window.

The rest of the afternoon passes slowly. The feeling in the courthouse is that of people holding their breath. At five o'clock I excuse the jury.

Driving home in the cold December night, I ponder about the jury verdict. The state's case seems thin. I would not convict Raffone on that evidence. But what if the jury does? Should I set the verdict aside? No. There is enough evidence to support a conviction if the jury chooses to believe the witnesses. I make up my mind that if it is a guilty verdict I will let it stand.

Then I have another thought. If the verdict is guilty, I will have to sentence Raffone. Manslaughter first degree is a class B felony. The maximum punishment is twenty years. What should my sentence be? I put it out of my mind. That is a problem for another day.

The next morning the waiting begins again. But it does not last long. About midmorning the clerk pokes her head in my chambers to say the jury has a verdict. I ascend the bench. Raffone is brought up from the lockup and stands next to Flaherty. Caldwell hurries in from his office across the hall. The courtroom quickly fills with spectators. The jury files in, stern-faced and inscrutable. The clerk calls the roll of jurors. She then asks whether they have reached a verdict. A man in the jury box says that they have. The sheriff takes the paper from the foreman and hands it to me. I glance at it and pass it to the clerk. She hesitates a moment, I think for dramatic effect, then reads, "*State* versus *Salvatore Raffone*, case number 4325. *Defendant's verdict.* The jury finds the defendant, Salvatore Raffone, not guilty. Signed Alexander Jones, foreman."

Raffone breaks into a wide smile. Flaherty slaps him on the back. Caldwell reaches across the counsel table to shake Flaherty's hand. I congratulate the jury on their verdict and thank them for their service. As I rise at the bench and the sheriff announces that court is in recess, Raffone stares up at me triumphantly. This time our eyes do not lock. I faintly nod to him, then turn and walk through the door to my chambers.

So the system worked. The prosecutor presented the case fairly. Raffone was defended by a skillful, court-appointed lawyer. The trial was conducted according to the rules. The jury deliberated conscientiously. The issue they decided was not "Did Raffone kill Chisolm?" but rather "Did the state prove beyond a reasonable doubt that Raffone killed Chisolm?" They did not find Raffone innocent. They found him not guilty. The jury applied the law properly.

Raffone wins the case. But his triumph is short-lived. Soon after being released from prison, a year or so after the trial, he is convicted of another robbery in Florida, where he is serving a long sentence.

Yet although the system worked, the matter is left unresolved, the ending untidy. The stark fact is that Chisolm was brutally murdered. After the verdict Caldwell declines to try the two inmates indicted with Raffone because the case against them is even weaker. So no one is found responsible.

In the ancient Greek tragedies, souls of the unburied dead

roamed restlessly over the earth, haunting the living. Similarly, the unrequited soul of Alfred Chisolm hovers over Connecticut, taunting us for failing to bring his killer to justice.

12. DILEMMAS OF SENTENCING

I am never more conscious of striving to balance the scales of justice than when I am sentencing the convicted. On one scale is society, violated by a crime; on the other is the defendant, fallible but, nonetheless, human.

Originally the purpose of punishing criminals was retribution: an eye for an eye. Then it became incapacitation: remove criminals from society and confine them as dangerous persons. In the 1940s, when I was in law school, the dominant theory was deterrence. One of my professors used the phrase the deterrent efficacy of criminal punishment so often we called him "Mr. Deterrent Efficacy." For a long period after World War II, when faith in psychiatry and social engineering abounded, it was rehabilitation. In today's politically conservative times, with its emphasis on "law and order," the original theory has come almost full circle, but retribution is now called "just deserts": give the defendant what he deserves for the offense committed.

Yet however the pundits may differ about theories, as a trial judge I am faced with the insistent task of sentencing a particular defendant who never fails to assert his own individuality. I hear each cry out, in the words of Thomas Wolfe: "Does not this wonderful and unique I, that never was before and never will be again; this I of tender favor, beloved of the gods, come before the Eye of Judgment and always plead exception?"

In my early years on the bench, I presided mainly over misdemeanors, which are crimes punishable by a sentence of less than one year in jail. Because they are not so serious, I could be more creative, or even experimental, in sentencing. I almost always gave a first offender a free ride. The disposition was either accelerated rehabilitation, conditional discharge, or a suspended sentence. In accelerated rehabilitation, the accused does not even have to plead guilty or not guilty to the crime lodged against him. He is simply required to stay out of trouble with the law for a specified period of time (usually three to six months); if he does, the charge is erased. Accelerated rehabilitation was enacted when I was in the legislature to protect upper- and middle-class children from getting criminal records for their protest activities during the Vietnam War or for smoking pot. But as a judge I used the sentence equally for young black offenders and welfare mothers.

A conditional discharge means that after a defendant pleads or is found guilty, he is discharged without a jail sentence or probation. A suspended sentence means that after a defendant pleads or is found guilty, a jail sentence is imposed, but is not required to be served and the defendant is placed on probation.

When sparing a defendant from going to jail, I often imposed conditions related to the crime or the underlying cause of the crime. Young boys charged with destroying public property might be required to spend several Saturdays weeding the flower beds in the town green. A man charged with exposing himself in public might be required to obtain psychiatric treatment. If a husband was accused of beating his wife for the first time, I would get the court family relations officer to counsel the couple. When a crime stemmed from alcoholism, I would order that the offender attend Alcoholics Anonymous.

Once I had before me an eighteen-year-old man accused of larceny. The public defender mentioned, in passing, that his client was illiterate. The frustration of not being able to read, I thought, must be a major contributing cause of crime. I said to the youth, "Your offense is serious enough for me to send you to jail. But I'll put you on accelerated rehabilitation if you will enroll in the adult reading course at New London High School and complete it. What do you say?"

"Yeah, Judge, I'll do it. I want to learn to read."

"I warn you, the probation officer is going to check up on you. If you drop out, you'll be back before me, and I'll send you to jail."

"I understand, Judge. I'll do it," he assured me.

And he did. I know because I kept after the probation officer to keep me informed. But I never knew whether most of my sentences were effective or not. I always wanted to follow up on the offenders, but in those days, after three months in one town, I was assigned to another, so I never did.

While for minor crimes I usually gave a first offender a second chance, I did not so readily give a second offender a third chance. My attitude on that was molded by a story told to me by an inmate who was serving a fifteen-year prison sentence for bank robbery. Roger Burke was a clean-cut fellow with a winning Irish smile who had been permitted to participate in a conference on the Connecticut criminal justice system that I attended. When I asked him what had possessed him to commit that serious crime, he said:

"As a kid, the first time I was caught stealing a toy from a store the policeman patted me on the head and told me to run along. When I was a little older, the second time I was caught stealing, my father's lawyer made a deal with the prosecutor to have the charges dropped. The third time, I came before a judge and he warned me with a pleasant smile on his face. The fourth time, I was given a suspended jail sentence and placed on probation. By then I thought the law was a joke, and I would never go to jail no matter what I did. When I was twenty-five, I robbed a bank."

"Why a bank?" I interrupted.

"Because a bank isn't as dangerous as a liquor or corner grocery store. You can't tell when the owner of that kind of store may have a gun under the counter. Anyway I robbed the bank, was caught within minutes, and was socked with fifteen years. Fifteen years. If only a judge had punished me earlier," he added ruefully, "I never would have gotten into this mess."

That story stays in my mind when I sentence young people for second offenses.

A beautiful seventeen-year-old girl was before me for shoplifting a small television set from a department store. From the confident smile on her face as she pleaded guilty, I sensed that she felt her beauty would spare her any punishment. Noting in her record a prior conviction for shoplifting three months earlier, I sentenced her to thirty days, suspended after she spent three days in jail. She burst into tears as the sheriff led her from the courtroom.

To a high school boy from affluent Darien, who had stolen bicycles on two separate occasions, I gave the same sentence. The boy was dismayed, his self-assured parents furious.

My message to these youngsters was clear: "Stop it; stop it now." Fatherly advice from the bench was not likely to impress them. They had probably been lectured to ad nauseam. But I did not want them to leave the courtroom after a second offense without something happening to them. Hearing a jail door bang behind them, I hoped, might jolt them into realizing the consequences of breaking the law.

Once, after I sent a young black lad to jail for two days for his second offense of purse snatching, his mother waited in court all morning. When I was leaving for lunch, she came up to me and said, "Judge, I want to thank you for what you did to my boy. I haven't been able to control him. Maybe this will drive some sense into his head."

Yet I have no fixed pattern of sentencing young people. When they stand before me, I see them as vulnerable and fragile, teetering, as it were, on the edge of a cliff. My overwhelming desire is to pull them back from danger. But how? Shall I be lenient or shall I be harsh? Each choice has its risks.

Whether sentencing youths or adults, I found to my surprise, when later in my career I came to hear felony cases, that sentencing for minor crimes is more difficult than sentencing for serious ones. The decision for misdemeanors is whether or not to incarcerate; that is the hard one. The decision for felonies is the number of years in state prison; that is much easier. But sometimes even felony cases present the dilemma of whether to imprison or not to imprison.

George Edwards was tried before me for sexual assault first degree. The victim, Barbara Babson (name changed to hide identity), was a personable woman in her late twenties and a junior executive in an insurance company. She described on the stand what had happened to her:

"I was returning to my Hartford apartment with two armloads of groceries. As I entered the elevator, a man followed me. He seemed vaguely familiar, but I couldn't quite place him. When I reached my floor and started to open my door, I noticed him behind me. He offered to hold my bags. God, I knew right then I was making a mistake. He pushed me into the apartment and slammed the door. He said, 'Don't you know me? I work at Travelers with you.' Then I remembered seeing him in the cafeteria, and I remembered him once staring at me. Now I could feel his eyes roving over my body, and I heard him say, 'I want to screw you.' He said it so calmly at first, I didn't believe him. I tried to talk him out of it. When he grabbed my neck, I began to cry and then to scream. His grip tightened, and that really scared me. He forced me into the bedroom, made me take off my clothes. Then," she sobbed, "he pushed my legs apart and entered me."

"What happened next?" the state's attorney asked.

"He told me he was going to wait in the next room, and if I tried to leave, he would kill me. I found some cardboards, wrote HELP! on them, and put them in my window. But nobody came. Eventually I got up the courage to open the door, and he had left. I immediately called the police."

The "help" signs and police photos of bruises on her neck were admitted as exhibits. The woman continued, "The next day a policeman in plain clothes came with me to the insurance company. We waited in the cafeteria. Eventually the defendant here came in and I identified him to the police officer. He seemed in a daze, almost as if he expected to be arrested."

Edwards's lawyer cross-examined her vigorously, dragging her through the intimate details of her sex life. Then he tried to get her to admit that she had willingly participated in sex with the defendant. Through it all she maintained her poise. She left the stand with her version of the crime intact.

I so admired her. I knew how easily she could have spared herself that ordeal by simply dropping the whole rotten business. Many women in that position do.

Edwards took the stand in his own defense. A tall man with bushy hair, he was wearing baggy trousers and a rumpled shirt. In a low voice he testified that the woman had always smiled at him at work. He had learned her name and address and gone to her apartment house that day. When he offered to help her with her bundles, she invited him into her apartment. She was very nice and very willing to have sex. He denied using force.

I did not believe him. I could not conceive that Miss Babson would have called the police, pressed the charges, and relived the horrors of the experience on the stand if the crime had not been committed as she had testified. Even more significantly, the jury did not believe him, either. They readily returned a verdict of guilty of the crime charged.

Sexual assault first degree is a class B felony, punishable by a maximum of twenty years in the state prison. If I had sentenced Edwards then, I would have sent him to prison for many years. But sentencing could take place only after a presentence report had been prepared by a probation officer. This would take about a month, so I scheduled the sentencing for five weeks later. Because of the conviction, I raised Edwards's bail, but his family put up a bond to keep him out of jail.

The report was dropped off in my chambers a few days before the sentencing date. Unlike the trial, which had portrayed Edwards in the context of the crime, the presentence report portrayed the crime in the context of Edwards's life.

It revealed that Edwards was thirty-one years old, born of a black father and white mother. He had graduated from high school and had an associate's degree from a community college. He had served in Vietnam, where he had been decorated with the Purple Heart for wounds in action and the Bronze Star for bravery under fire. After the army Edwards had worked successfully as a coordinator of youth programs in the inner city of Hartford. Simultaneously he had taken computer courses. At the time of the crime he was a computer programmer at Travelers Insurance Company. Edwards was then separated from his wife and child, and fellow employees had noticed a personality change in him; he seemed withdrawn, depressed, and sometimes confused. His only criminal offense was a disorderly conduct charge three months before the crime, which had not been prosecuted.

The report described the impact of the crime on the victim. After the rape Miss Babson had been fearful of being alone in her apartment. She found herself constantly angry at men. Her work at the insurance company had deteriorated; she lost a promotion she was in line to get.

The report closed with the probation officer's recommendation: lengthy incarceration; need for psychiatric care.

I gazed out the window of my chambers and reflected. What should my sentence be?

When an accused has been found guilty of a serious crime, some Connecticut judges often give the maximum number of years set by statute. They reason that is what the legislature intended by fixing maximums. They also justify it on the ground that the defendant took a gamble when he forced the state to try him; if he loses, he should pay the full price.

I cannot let twenty years, fifteen years, ten years, trip off my tongue lightly. I know what state prison is like from the many times I visited clients there when I was a lawyer. Its terror and lawlessness were also revealed to me by trials like that of Salvatore Raffone. Each year of a sentence is 52 weeks, 365 days, 8,760 hours, behind bars. Moreover, in the United States the rate of incarceration (persons sentenced to more than one year in prison) is higher and sentences are longer than in any other Western country. Aware of that, and sensitive to the cruelty and waste of imprisonment, my tendency is toward the shortest sentence I can justify.

Furthermore, I do not accept the notion that an accused should be punished for exercising his constitutional right of requiring the state to prove its charges against him. But suppose the defendant lied on the stand, as I felt Edwards had about the use of force on the victim? Should I take that into account in sentencing him? Also, in the same way that I might view his admitting his guilt as the first step toward rehabilitation, should I view his putting up a false defense as an indication of a recalcitrant attitude?

I also had to consider the public reaction to my sentence, particularly the reaction of the women's groups that follow such cases. The public demands that the punishment be roughly proportional to the crime. This translates into pressure on a judge not to be too lenient; the public rarely growls when a judge is too harsh. I generally resist that pressure, but I cannot ignore it completely, lest I bring the courts into disrepute.

The effect of the crime on the victim and her attitude toward the punishment to be imposed also had to be taken into account. Miss Babson would be notified of the date of the sentencing and under Connecticut law was entitled to be heard. The presentence report gave me an indication of what her feelings were. Some judges give great weight to the comments of victims and their families. Although I listen to those comments carefully, I strain out the demands for revenge in my effort to reach a balanced decision.

My final consideration was the defendant himself. Edwards had no criminal record. The sudden change of personality noted in the presentence report might indicate psychiatric illness. But that would not excuse his use of force.

I reread the presentence report. What was fair? What was just? Then I wrestled with my decision for four more weeks, because the illness of Edwards's attorney postponed the sentencing.

Before the rescheduled date, I had weighed the factors, made up my mind, and lived with my decision for several days. In serious criminal cases I do not like to make a snap judgment from the bench. I may sometimes allow myself to be persuaded by the lawyers' arguments to reduce a preconceived sentence, but never to raise it.

·   ·   ·

Edwards rises next to his counsel as I enter the courtroom. This day he is wearing a blue suit, white shirt, and striped tie. Not only his dress, but his demeanor is entirely different from what it was at the trial. Then he had been disheveled and apathetic. Now he is neat and alert. I can feel his eyes intently boring into me as I slide into my chair.

I nod to the state's attorney to begin. He asks to have Miss Babson speak first. She comes forward to the counsel table. "That man," she says, pointing to Edwards, "did a terrible thing. He should be severely punished not only for what he did to me, but for what he could do to other women. I am furious at him. As far as I am concerned, Judge, I hope you lock him up and throw away the key."

She stops abruptly and sits down. The state's attorney deliberately pauses to let her words sink in before he stands up. Speaking with less emotion but equal determination, he says, "This was a vicious crime. There are not many more serious than rape. The defendant cynically tried to put the blame on the victim. But it didn't wash. She has been damaged in the most fundamental way. And the defendant doesn't show the slightest remorse. I urge the maximum punishment of twenty years in state prison."

Edwards's lawyer starts off by mentioning his client's splendid Vietnam War record and his lack of a criminal record. Then he goes on, "George and his wife have begun living together again with their child, and they are trying to pick up the pieces of their lives." I notice for the first time a taut-faced woman in the front row of the spectator section of the courtroom.

"More important," the lawyer continues, "George started seeing a psychiatrist six weeks ago."

He hands me a letter from Edwards's psychiatrist, whom I know to be reputable. It indicates that Edwards has been depressed by his wife's leaving him, confused by his war experiences, and very much in need of therapy.

The lawyer concludes: "If you will give George a suspended sentence, Your Honor, and make a condition of probation that he stay in treatment, he won't be before this court again. George Edwards is a good risk."

I look at Edwards. "Do you have anything you want to say, Mr. Edwards?"

The question takes him by surprise. Gathering his thoughts, he says with emotion, "I'm sorry for what I did,

Judge. I'm sorry for Barbara, and I understand how she feels. I'm sorry for my wife. I'm . . ." His voice trails off.

I gaze out the courtroom window, struggling for the words to express my sentence. I am always conscious that the same sentence can be given in a way that arouses grudging acceptance or deep hostility. An inmate once told me that he is still furious at a judge who had actually turned his back when sentencing him. "The bastard was a white-livered coward," the inmate said. "He didn't have the courage to look me in the face because he was ashamed of what he was doing."

I always speak directly to a defendant in a reasoned way, knowing that, whatever his outward bravado, he must feel terror as he awaits judgment from the black-robed menace on the bench.

But this time I realize that my problem is not *how* to sentence, but *what* to sentence. Before going on the bench I had decided to give Edwards eight years in prison. His reconciliation with his wife and his undertaking psychiatric treatment, however, were not factored into that decision. Nor was the sincere remorse he expressed. He no longer seems like a danger to anyone. What purpose would imprisonment serve?

I turn my eyes back to Edwards. He is standing beside his lawyer, waiting for my sentence. His hands grip the counsel table. The court reporter's fingers are poised over her machine. Silence. The hand of the clock on the wall makes its loud, one-minute leap. Dammit, I reflect, he committed rape, and for that he should pay a penalty.

It seems that my lips start to move before I am sure of what I am going to say:

"Mr. Edwards, you have committed a serious crime. I am not going to punish you to set an example for others, because you should not be held responsible for the incidence of crime in our society. I am going to punish you because, as a mature person, you must pay the price for your offense.

The state's attorney asks for twenty years because of the gravity of the crime. Your attorney asks for a suspended sentence because you are attempting to deal with whatever within you caused you to commit the crime. Both make valid arguments. I am partially adopting both recommendations. I herewith sentence you to state prison for six years."

Edwards wilts. His wife gasps. I continue, "However, I am suspending execution after four years. I am placing you on probation for the two-year balance of your term on the condition that you continue in psychiatric treatment until discharged by your doctor. The state is entitled to punish you for the crime you have committed and the harm you have done. You are entitled to leniency for what I discern to be the sincere effort you are making to help yourself."

Edwards turns to his wife, who rushes up to embrace him. Miss Babson nods to me, not angrily, I think; she walks out of the courtroom and back into her life. As I rise at the bench, a sheriff is leading Edwards down the stairwell to the lockup.

.   .   .

Once I give a sentence, I never second-guess myself. If I did, my life would be a nightmare. Judges acquire what a colleague calls a "bathtub mind." The drama, the dilemmas, the deliberations, drain away once a case is finished, and I am on to the next. With one exception.

A sentence I once imposed still haunts me. The defendant was charged with burglary and unlawful restraint. The victim, an elderly woman, testified that a man had entered her home at night, tied her to a chair, and robbed her of several hundred dollars. She had had difficulty identifying the defendant as the culprit from police photos but readily identified him in the courtroom. The defendant himself and four of his relatives testified that at the time of the crime he was at a family gathering. Yet after only a short deliberation, the jury returned a guilty verdict.

Because the jury could choose to believe the elderly woman rather than the defendant and his relatives, I had no basis to set the verdict aside. But I felt the victim's identification of the defendant had been shaky; courtroom identifications are notoriously unreliable. Furthermore, the defense witnesses sounded truthful to me. Now I had to sentence a man I did not believe guilty.

The presentence report increased my dilemma. It revealed that the defendant had been convicted twice before for robberies and had served three years in prison. That record did not increase the likelihood that he had committed the crime for which he had just been convicted, but it did require that I give him a long term for a third offense.

When, on a pretrial motion, I quash a confession that I believe to be true, I exercise all my professional discipline to assure the defendant a fair trial. Could I call upon that same professional discipline to sentence the defendant before me whom the jury had a right to find guilty but whom I believed to be not guilty? Could I suspend my own disbelief and pronounce the sanction of the state on such a man?

I did. I sent him to prison for twelve years. But there are still nights that sentence troubles me. My bathtub mind did not work on that case.

Fortunately I have never had to impose the death penalty. Although under Connecticut law that decision is made by the jury, the judge still has to pronounce the sentence. I could not utter the words. Consequently I would disqualify myself from a capital case.

Prosecutors play a significant role in sentencing. They are under such great pressure to move their huge load of cases, they frequently enter into plea bargains with defense counsel—a guilty plea, often of a lesser offense, in exchange for an agreed-upon sentence. The judge does not have to accept the bargain. If he does not, the guilty plea is withdrawn and the case will be tried. But the judge knows that his refusal will jam up the courts. I have turned down plea bargains, usually when I thought an inexperienced defense attorney had agreed to too harsh a sentence in light of all the facts.

Apart from plea bargains, prosecutors in Connecticut can recommend sentences to judges in the cases they handle. When doing so, they reflect their community attitudes about crime. In rural areas, like Litchfield County, burglaries are considered major offenses, and for them prosecutors are likely to recommend heavy sentences. In the cities, like Hartford, burglaries are so common that prosecutors are likely to recommend lighter sentences. Again, judges can follow or not follow the recommendations. I take them into account, while always exercising my own judgment. For in the end the decision is mine, and I alone must live with it.

Sentencing seminars, which judges attend from time to time, provide the opportunity for them to compare their sentencing patterns with those of their colleagues. Case studies are distributed, each stating the facts about a particular crime and defendant. Judges are asked to indicate the sentence they would impose. Mine are on the low side of the middle range.

These seminars reveal startling disparities among judges. On a given set of facts, the range of sentences can be from probation to ten years in prison. And this does not occur in a few instances. It occurs in nearly all the case studies.

In his book *Criminal Sentences: Law Without Order*, Judge Marvin Frankel said, "We boast that ours is a 'government of laws, not of men.' . . . [But] the almost wholly unchecked and sweeping powers we give judges in the fashioning of sentences are terrifying and intolerable for a society that professes devotion to the rule of law."

Recognition of this has led in recent years to reforms to limit those "sweeping powers." Connecticut has a Sentence Review Board, composed of three judges, which is charged with rationalizing different sentences for similar crimes. On the petition of a prisoner, it considers his sentence in light of all the factors in the case and the statewide average term for that crime and can reduce, or even increase, it. Other states require judges to make specific findings of facts relevant to their sentencing decision and to state on the record, in the presence of the defendant, the reasons for the particular sentence imposed. The most far-reaching reform has occurred in the federal court system. Authorized by Congress, the United States Sentencing Commission has established precise prison terms for each crime, with federal judges allowed only a narrow discretion to take into account specified aggravating and mitigating factors.

Requiring that reasons be expressed and identifying objective standards of sentencing are both desirable. But removing all judicial discretion would be intolerable. It would achieve uniformity at the expense of justice. Just as we want juries to leaven the inexorable operation of the law, we want judges to make individual judgments about each violator of the law.

In sentencing, more than in any other decision a judge makes, his life experiences, personal philosophy, and conception of human nature play a major part. I am sure mine do. I have no hang-ups about any particular crime. I have never been mugged; my home has never been burglarized; the female members of my family have never been sexually assaulted. If any of those terrible things did occur, I hope that I would not vent my anger on the next defendant who appeared before me. I agree with William James's resolution of the "dilemma of determinism": man has a choice, and, as a result, he is responsible for his actions. I believe that when people break the law, they should be punished. But I am not filled with moral outrage. Although a judge, I avoid being judgmental. I believe that people who do bad things are not necessarily bad. I can condemn a crime without being angry at the person committing it. I firmly believe people can change, and I would never give up on anyone.

Immanuel Kant's second categorical imperative is "Act so as to treat humanity both in your person and in that of every other man always as an end and never only as a means." I see the person before me as an individual human being, never as a statistic of crime in the city streets. I will not punish him severely solely in order to deter others. That would be using him as a means, not an end.

For me, the act of sentencing is an interpersonal experience between the convicted and me. He looks up at me, awaiting my judgment. I look down at him, conscious of my responsibility to be just to him as well as to the society I represent.

At the very moment that I exercise the great power of depriving another person of his liberty, I feel the deepest sense of humility. Who am I to make such a decision? Where do I get the wisdom? I cannot say I pray for divine guidance. But in attempting to balance the scales of justice, I strive for what is fair, what is right, what will help. Each time, I hope with all my heart that I achieve it. I am never sure that I do.

13. WHERE HAS LOVE GONE?

The cases in the family, juvenile, and housing parts of the superior court are tried by judges alone, without a jury. They present fairly simple legal questions and very puzzling human problems.

When I hear divorce actions all day long, day after day, in the family part, I try to imagine each couple before me as they were at the radiant moment of their wedding. Where has love gone? I wonder.

A red-haired, overweight, overly-made-up woman is on the stand. As tears streak through her rouge, she sobs, "All I wanted was to be held, to be hugged, to be loved. I don't have that anymore."

A man who ten years ago had gotten an eighteen-year-old high school senior pregnant, married her, and had three more children with her now testifies, "I never loved her from the beginning." The wife winces as if struck in the stomach.

A white woman married to a black man describes the venom contaminating their lives. "My husband taught the children to chant at the dinner table: 'Mommy is a dirty white dog, dirty white dog. Ha!' "

I am moved by these displays of raw emotion. How can I not be? This is not television. Real people two feet away from me are pouring out their hearts.

I am even more saddened by the casual way many people go about getting divorced, giving glib reasons like "We just stopped communicating" or "I now have different values." No real commitment had been made, it seems, no emotion invested.

When I practiced law, a divorce was granted only on proof of real fault on the part of one of the spouses, such as adultery, desertion, or intolerable cruelty. Although it is true that requirement led to hypocrisy, and even to distortions of the truth, it did slow down the march to the divorce court. It has always taken two to make a marriage, but under the current no-fault divorce law, one can dissolve it simply by declaring that in his or her opinion the marriage has broken down irretrievably. By making divorces so easy, we make them more prevalent.

I hear a case in which the couple has been married only a month before initiating the divorce action. I ask the young woman on the stand, "Don't you think you should give yourself more of a chance before breaking up so quickly?"

"Oh, Judge, we gave ourselves plenty of time," she responds. "We lived together for five years before we married."

"I see," I say. "The wedding caused the divorce."

"Not exactly . . . but . . . yes, in a way. We married in the hope of saving our relationship. It just didn't work."

The dissolution of very long marriages is another phenomenon I observe. In real puzzlement, I ask a seventy-year-old woman married for fifty-two years why she wants a divorce. "I've suffered enough at the hands of the old sot. I'm glad to be rid of him at last," she says. Half-facetiously, I ask a man who has been married forty-nine years why he cannot make it to fifty. "Not another year, Judge. Not another darn day," he says.

Under the no-fault law, the reason for the dissolution does not make any difference, so I rarely inquire about it. A few times, when I have asked, a spouse on the stand has broken down and said, "I don't want this divorce. Not at all. We can make it if he will really try." If I feel the witness is sincere, I stop the proceedings and tell the parties to seek counseling. If that does not succeed, their lawyers can claim the case for trial again. In two instances lawyers later told me that the parties did reconcile. That made me feel good.

Another time I have a happy surprise in court. An item on the calendar reads, "Motion re. separation." Under Connecticut law when a judgment of legal separation has been granted, either spouse, on proof that the parties have not cohabitated, can ask that the separation be changed to a divorce. When I call the motion, a middle-aged man and woman step forward. Neither is represented by a lawyer. The man starts to speak in a confusing manner. Not grasping what he is driving at, I ask, "Do you mean you want a divorce?"

"No, no," interposes the woman. "We want to stop the separation."

"That means you want a divorce."

"No, no," the woman persists. "We want to stay together."

"Oh"—it finally dawns on me—"you want to terminate the legal separation and resume your marriage."

"Yes, yes," they both exclaim.

"Well," I say, "I gladly grant your motion. But this also calls for a round of applause."

Everyone in the crowded courtroom claps. The beaming couple walk out the door arm in arm.

Lawyers are the main actors in divorce litigation. They determine whether there will be an agreement or a battle between the parties. Most are sensible and sensitive: they negotiate responsibly over alimony, property division, child support, visitation, and custody. In more than 90 percent of the cases they fashion agreements their clients can accept, so I simply enter judgment confirming the arrangement. Occasionally, however, I feel the agreement is not fair to one party or does not adequately provide for the children. In those instances I inform the attorneys of my thinking and offer them the opportunity to renegotiate. If they choose not to, I enter my own order. There is one type of settlement I scrutinize particularly carefully. Generally, the husband agrees to compensate the wife's attorney. If I find that the wife is to get a relatively paltry amount while her attorney is to be paid a large fee by the husband, I reject that arrangement out of hand.

When the parties do not agree, the lawyers must go to a court family relations officer for mediation before I will try the case. Using extraordinary skill and patience, these officers can often resolve the most bitter conflicts. They are the real heroes of the system.

Some lawyers, however, resist any attempts at settlement and want to battle over everything. They blame intransigence on their clients but often seem to me to be projecting their own inner demons. The worst are those who create adversity in order to justify huge fees. The victories they think they achieve for their clients are Pyrrhic; the harm they cause by deepening hostilities lives long after them.

When a divorce case goes to trial, the fight is not over the dissolution itself, but over money and the children. Although marital fault plays no part in the granting of the divorce, under Connecticut law a judge may take it into account in making alimony and property division awards. I give it little weight in deciding those issues. Yet lawyers persist in attempting to prove which spouse was more to blame: what insults were hurled, how much one spouse drank, when the other came home at night. I have the deepest sympathy for unhappy people unraveling themselves from unhappy marriages, but such petty details are irrelevant to the decision I will make. I simply stop listening.

Quarrels over specific pieces of property can become ridiculous. Once, after hearing what seemed like an eternity of evidence about who should get the marital bed, I finally said, "I'm adjourning this case for ten minutes. Either agree between yourselves, or I shall order the bed sawed in half—horizontally—and give each of you a half." A judicial colleague whose imagination I admired resolved a bitter contest over silverware by awarding the forks and teaspoons to the wife, the knives and soup spoons to the husband.

I once listened to a two-day wrangle about who had a right to certain living room furniture. In exasperation I said, "Don't you realize your lawyers are charging each of you $175 an hour, and you already have expended twice what the furniture is worth?"

Of course, I recognize that such fights are not really over the leather chair or brass lamp. Material possessions are symbols of the victory each spouse wants over the other. I just resent being asked to award the championship trophies.

There are, however, property disputes of substance, such as over division of the marital home. When one spouse is to get custody of school-age children, the couple will generally agree that that spouse should be allowed to continue in the house. But what should happen when the youngest child finishes school? As a result of the extraordinary rise in the value of residential real estate in the 1980s, the marital home, purchased by the young couple in 1970 for $45,000 with a $30,000 mortgage, can now be worth $250,000. The husband may claim that because he put up the original cash and made the mortgage payments, he is entitled to the full appreciation. I don't agree and usually order that that major asset of the marriage be divided equally.

Alimony creates its own emotional vibrations. Men hate to pay it, even when they know they should—particularly to a woman they have come to despise. A man I once ordered to pay a modest twenty dollars a week glowered at me with more animosity than criminals whom I have sent to prison for ten years.

Women also demand alimony with varying degrees of vengeance. But fundamentally they resent having to need it, feeling it diminishes them to take money from a man they have no use for.

Attitudes toward alimony have changed in recent years, largely as a result of the women's movement. Rarely is alimony asked for after a brief, childless marriage. In fact, some women will not request alimony even after long marriages. I have had several cases where the husband's income was in the $60,000–$70,000 range, the wife's in the $15,000–$20,000 range, and yet the wife refused alimony. One woman explained her position this way: "I'm able to stand on my own two feet. I don't want anything from him. All I want from this court is return of my maiden name, which I never should have given up in the first place."

Under Connecticut law, if alimony is not awarded at the time of the divorce, it can never be awarded. Consequently, despite a woman's assertion of independence, when I feel alimony is warranted, I sometimes grant a dollar a year to preserve her right to ask for more should she become ill, lose her job, or fall into real need.

When I do make an alimony award, it is rarely forever. I may not set a termination date for a woman in her fifties or older who stayed at home over a long marriage to care for her husband and the children. But for a woman in her forties or younger, I will order that alimony cease after a period of time sufficient for her to acquire skills and return to the job market—usually two to five years.

Occasionally a man will ask for alimony. If he cared for the children and the wife was the major wage earner, I have awarded it to him. In one case the wife was a bank executive who earned over $40,000 a year. The husband took the child to a baby-sitter and otherwise hung around the house. I gave him $100 a week for one year. His lawyer argued that if his client were a woman, I would have awarded much more. The lawyer was right. But since the man appeared to me to be sponging off of his wife and never intending to find a job, I thought I was more right.

Although ambiguous feelings surround support for an ex-spouse, the same is not true of support for the couple's children. Women do not hesitate to demand child support, and few men resist paying it, at least in concept. The hard question is how much. Often there is barely enough joint income to support one household, let alone two.

Typically, in a two-child family the husband earns at a blue-collar job $350 a week, the wife as a waitress $200 a week. If I award her $125 a week combined alimony and child support, she cannot support herself and two children on the $325, and he cannot support himself on the $225. Even for professional couples with much higher joint incomes, breakups cause financial hardships. The truth is that most families with children simply cannot afford to separate.

Almost always, however, it is the woman who feels more strapped after a divorce. Often I hear a mother complain, "It ain't fair. When he has the kids, he can buy them steak dinners and toys. I can't put hamburgers on the table or get them an ice-cream cone."

Issues related to child visitation and child custody are the more interesting and challenging to me. Spouses battling over property and money as tokens of triumph is understandable, but I cannot sympathize with children being used as symbols of vengeance.

Most women who are given custody want the father to see the children regularly. They understand the importance of the father continuing a relationship with the kids, and they also welcome being relieved of full-time responsibility. For them, the father's visitation is his obligation rather than his privilege. Some women, however, so reject their husbands that they want to push them not only out of their lives, but out of the lives of their children.

One woman, during a hearing, kept referring to the couple's daughter as "my child." She requested a weekly amount of child support but, with much more emotion, opposed her husband's motion for visitation. Suspecting that she was motivated by a compulsion to possess the child exclusively, I asked her, "Would you be satisfied with no child support from your husband if he had no right to see her?"

"Oh, yes. By all means. I can care for *my child* by myself. I don't need him."

"Well, Mrs. Slovak," I said, "you did not have that child by immaculate conception. She also has a father who is entitled to see her." I awarded him visitation rights twice weekly and every other weekend.

Another case presented a sharper dilemma. The evidence revealed that the father had had sexual relations with the couple's oldest daughter from age eleven to seventeen and with the second daughter from age twelve to fourteen. When he was discovered, the wife immediately put him out of the house and sued for divorce. The only question before me was the father's right to visit with the couple's third child, a ten-year-old son. On the stand the mother was livid in her opposition. "My husband's a monster," she shouted. "He molested our daughters for eight years. I never knew anything about it. Now he wants to see our son. Never. Never. The filthy, evil dog."

Her screams reverberated in the small courtroom. The father took the stand. He was a thin, meek man who spoke in a whispery voice. His lawyer asked, "Were you sexually abused by your father when you were a child?"

"Yes," he responded, "for many years."

God, I thought, how the sins of the one generation are perpetuated by the next.

"Have you ever had any sexual contact with your son?"

"No, sir."

"Why do you want this court to give you the right to continue to see your son?"

"The boy and I get along real well. We go fishing and do lots of things together."

What should I do? Often, when faced with this kind of decision, I sleep on it overnight. This time I followed my instincts. I said from the bench: "I understand how you feel, Mrs. Vreeland. You are repulsed by your husband's conduct and concerned about your children. I am making no order of visitation as to your husband seeing your fourteen-year-old daughter because none has been requested. But as to the boy, there has been no evidence of abuse. He still needs his father, and I am not going to deprive him of one. My order is that Mr. Vreeland shall have the right to have the boy every Saturday afternoon from one to six o'clock."

The mother whispered to her attorney who then said, "Your Honor, we would like that visitation supervised by a social worker."

"No," I replied. "There appears to be no reason for concern. I think the boy and his father should do things by themselves."

But the mother had the last word. She went to the state prosecutor and had her husband arrested for his sexual activities with the daughters. The father pleaded guilty. He was sentenced to prison for two years.

In another case, the father of a child born out of wedlock sought visitation rights with his daughter. He had been paying child support for five years under a court order. On the stand he admitted he had not seen the child since she was an infant but claimed the mother's family had kept him away. The mother had a different story.

"Joe came to the hospital after Sonia was born and denied he was the father. A few months later, when I was living with my mother, he wanted to see the child. We got into a fight, and he beat me up. He never came around again. He never sent the child gifts at Christmas or a card on her birthday. I was on welfare then, and the state brought a case for him to pay child support. I'm married now. My husband is like a real father to Sonia. I don't want Joe messing with her and getting her all confused."

Should I grant visitation rights? It would certainly complicate the child's life. But, I thought, the child's life was already complicated by the reality of her parentage. She might always wonder who her father was and why he had abandoned her. Better that she know him for what he is, reject him if he is a no-good, than spend her life searching for a fantasy father. I granted the motion.

Whatever the court order, visitation has a way of conforming itself to the actual relationship that develops between the parent and the children. A custody award has much more significance. For the children it determines where their home is, what local school they will attend, who their friends are. For the parents it determines who has primary responsibility and makes the important decisions.

Custody is no longer granted automatically to the mother, as it was when I practiced law. Now, more and more, fathers fight for custody of their children and succeed. In fact, with women working and pursuing careers, custody is often joint, with both parents sharing equally the responsibility of raising the children. Some women even agree to their husbands having sole custody without appearing to feel any sense of guilt or failure.

When custody is fought over, it is the fiercest of battles in the divorce court. The parties go at each other with talons bared. Again, family relations officers play an important role. In a nonadversarial setting, they interview the children, teachers, doctors, and other significant persons. Their studies give perspectives judges cannot glean from the evidence presented at the trial. I usually follow their recommendations on custody, but, in the end, the heart-wrenching decision is always mine.

•   •   •

Ross v. *Ross* is a divorce action that has devolved into a custody battle. I learn from the evidence that Mrs. Ross was in
a head-on automobile accident when her son was four. After
six months in the hospital and another year of treatment,
she was left with the left side of her body paralyzed. Before
the accident her marriage had been in trouble; after it, her
husband took delight in ridiculing her affliction in front of
the boy. Emulating his father, the boy too began taunting
his mother.

When the father started the divorce action, he took the
child, then seven, to live with him in another town, near his
girlfriend. He placed the child in school and showered him
with attention and gifts.

The mother says tearfully on the stand, "I lost my body in
an accident; I lost my husband to another woman. Am I now
also to lose my son by an order of the court?"

After a moment's silence, she adds with simple eloquence,
"I love that little boy."

The father's attorney urges that I talk to the boy before
deciding; the mother's attorney agrees. I recognize that my
seeing a young child places a great burden on him, making
him feel he has to make a choice between his parents. Also,
family relations officers and social workers are better trained
than judges to elicit a child's true feelings. Consequently I
am chary of complying with such a request. But in this case
I agree to see the boy.

Michael comes into my chambers without any show of
nervousness. After a few get-acquainted-type questions, I
ask him, "What are the things you like to do best with your
father?"

"Riding on the back of my dad's motorcycle and sailing
on his boat. Man, that's fun."

"How about with your mother?" I ask.

He pauses, and a frown comes over his face. "I can't do
anything with her. She can hardly walk."

A school psychologist's report helps me to understand the boy's answer. "Michael feels anxiety and resentment toward his crippled mother which he cannot verbalize. His mode of defense is one of denial. The father's hostility has contributed to Michael's rejection of his mother."

How should I decide? Clearly the boy at this time favors living with his father. Yet denying custody to the mother will not only devastate her; it may validate the boy's rejection of her. Michael seems to be under the undue influence of his father, who is both soliciting his affection and turning him against his mother. If Michael spends some time alone with her, he may respond to her deep love.

After much reflection, I award joint custody, allowing the boy to finish the school year with his father and requiring that he spend the summer with his mother. I order that another study be made by a family relations officer at the end of the summer, when the judge then sitting can decide with whom the boy should live for the next school year. Finally I order that the boy receive psychological counseling to help him resolve his conflicted feelings.

I have intervened in the lives of people I do not know. However well intentioned, my decision is based on little more than instinct and intuition. My solace is that the court retains jurisdiction of custody matters and if things turn out badly, the parties can return to court to have my order modified.

· · ·

The motion before me is for change of custody. The moving party is the mother, Susan Fletcher, an attractive brown-haired woman in her mid-twenties. As I listen to her testimony, I wonder whether I have tuned in to a midmorning television soap opera.

When a teenage college student working at a summer restaurant job, Susan became pregnant by Tim. Her mother promptly threw her out of the house. She went to live with Tim's family, where she slept on a living room couch. After the baby, Richard, was born, the couple moved into their own apartment. Both smoked marijuana, and they fought a good deal. Finally, in desperation, they got married. But the fights continued, and Susan went back to her mother, who allowed her home only on the condition that she leave Tim and abandon her son. At the divorce Susan consented to Tim's getting sole custody of Richard. For a whole year afterward she did not see the child, who was being raised by Tim and his extended family. Then she started to visit him once a week.

Four years passed. Susan became pregnant by another man. This time she had an abortion. However, within a year she married him. She and her husband moved into a beautiful home in a semirural town east of Hartford where he had a flourishing business. Susan, with Tim's consent, began having Richard stay over twice during the week and on every other weekend. Finally, when the boy was about to start school, she applied to have custody awarded to her.

Susan testifies, "I know I've made mistakes—smoking pot, abandoning my son, having an abortion. I'm not proud of any of that. But they happened. I quit dope because it wasn't getting me anyplace. I can't do anything about the abortion. I'd like to reclaim my boy."

I am impressed with her assuming full responsibility for her life. She places no blame on her mother, who seems to me to be the bête noire in the case. Susan continues, "When Richard visits us, he has his own room. My husband and I read to him every night. We are also teaching him to read. He has many friends in the neighborhood and will benefit from the excellent school in our town."

Tim is a stolid, black-haired man. He describes how he raised Richard with the help of his parents and aunts. He has a modest job as the manager of a fast-food restaurant and lives in a small Hartford apartment with his wife and a newly born baby. Just before the court hearing, Tim enrolled

Richard in an elementary Catholic school for the ensuing year.

On the stand he appears defensive about Susan's superior education and position. He testifies, "I may not be able to provide Richard with all the things Susan can. But I and my family cared for the boy from birth. He is happy with us and loves the new baby. He will start in our parish school next month. I don't want to lose him now when he is just turning five."

Tim's stubborn core of strength and stability also impresses me.

On the surface the issue appears to be over what school the child should go to and whether he should live in the city or a suburb. But I recognize that the real battle is over who should be the live-in parent and who the visiting parent. For Susan and Tim, that difference is all the difference in the world.

In custody cases the law creates no barrier between my heart and mind. The law is simple and clear: determine the issue on the basis of the best interest of the child. Applying that standard to the facts creates the dilemmas of judgment. Decision making in custody cases is both cerebral and visceral. A rational decision that does not feel right is just as wrong as an emotional decision that lacks logic. I am comfortable only when both my heart and mind concur.

The family relations officer's report says that both Tim and Susan are excellent parents and makes no recommendations of how I should decide. One evening at home, in the quiet of my study, I sketch an outline of my decision.

In civil court cases involving issues of law, I write out and have typed a full opinion so that it may be published as a precedent. But because custody decisions are based primarily on their facts and are of little precedential value, I usually deliver them orally to the parties in the courtroom. Moreover, a spoken decision has more impact when the judge can also communicate his concern for the parties by the tone of his voice. The next morning, looking directly at Susan and Tim, I say:

"I have thought long and hard about this decision. It is a very close call because both of you are loving parents. Both of you have a desire for the best interest of your child. To whomever I give custody, the other will have liberal rights of visitation to maintain a close relationship with the boy. I am struck with how Susan has surmounted her past mistakes and is a stronger person for her struggle to do so. I am also impressed with the way neither of you attempted to put down the other. That absence of recrimination is rare in this kind of case. It bodes well for both of you continuing as successful parents.

"The motion before me is for modification of a custody award made five years ago. Much has happened in that five years. Susan is clearly a different person than she was then. Tim, on the other hand, has remained the same steady, caring father. And most significantly, the boy has flourished. He is a happy, well-adjusted child. Under these circumstances, I see no reason for making a change. I deny the motion for modification and continue custody in the father."

I rise from the bench feeling I have done my best. Yet I wonder if it is good enough.

A few moments later the sheriff comes into my chambers. He tells me what happened when I left the courtroom. Susan and Tim turned to each other with tears in their eyes. They embraced. I interpret that to mean that Susan is relieved that my decision has lifted off her shoulders the responsibility of having voluntarily given up her son, and Tim is relieved that the decision went his way. Now both can accept my resolution, get on with their lives and with being the best-possible parents to the boy.

.   .   .

Each of the marital cases that parades before me represents a failure of the most beautiful and fragile of human relationships. At the end of a long day of listening to those sad, sometimes bitter, often moving stories, I am emotionally exhausted. I used to go home to my own loving wife and hug her tenderly.

14. PRISONERS OF
THEIR FUTURE

Presiding over juvenile matters always evokes in me the conflicting emotions of despair and hope: despair over the circumstances of children's lives, hope that intervention can bring about changes. Despair is frequently more intense than hope.

The juvenile court hears two kinds of cases involving children under the age of sixteen: cases in which the court must determine whether or not the child should be adjudged delinquent for having committed a crime and cases in which the court must determine whether or not the child was neglected, abused, or uncared for by his parents. In both, a child's future hangs in the balance, suspended like a teardrop on his cheek.

The first American juvenile court was established in Illinois in 1899. Until that time children who committed crimes were subjected to the same procedures and penalties as adults. Out of the humanitarian movement of the turn of the century came the concept of a separate court for children, operating under a separate set of rules and permitting a separate set of alternative dispositions. Hearings were to be informal and private; sanctions were to be remedial and rehabilitative rather than punitive. Over the first twenty years of the twentieth century, the Illinois experiment was replicated throughout the country.

The Norman Rockwell–like picture of the fatherly judge touching the heart of the errant child and by kindly admonition saving him from the downward fall did not, however, always comport with reality. Sometimes informal procedures denied constitutional rights and dispositions were not necessarily lenient. This was glaringly revealed in the 1967 United States Supreme Court case of *In re. Gault.*

Gerald Gault, fifteen years old, had been picked up by the Gila County, Arizona, police on a complaint that he was making lewd telephone calls. His parents were given one day's notice of the juvenile court hearing but were never apprised of the specifics of the charge. Moreover, they were not advised of their right to counsel for their son, nor was Gerald told that what he said in court could be used against him. Based on Gerald's admissions, the judge found him delinquent and sent him to the state industrial school for the balance of his minority—six years. If Gerald had been an adult, the maximum sentence for the offense would have been a $100 fine and thirty days in jail. On appeal, the Supreme Court reversed, ordered Gault's release and a new trial. It held, "The Bill of Rights is not for adults only."

As a result juvenile courts throughout the country began protecting the constitutional rights of children and allowing lawyers to participate in every phase of the proceedings. The courts themselves changed from quasi-social agencies to adjudicatory tribunals.

In the delinquency case I am hearing, José R. (the young-

ster's name is kept confidential in juvenile court proceedings) sits across the table from me, holding his slight, fifteen-
year-old body rigid. I try to look squarely into his soft, wary
eyes. (The bench of the juvenile court is not raised like the
bench of other courts. Adults are tall enough.) The petition
in the case alleges that José committed larceny in the fifth
degree by snatching a woman's purse.

Ranged on each side of José are the probation officer (who
signed the petition initiating the case), the court advocate
(who acts as the prosecutor), José's mother, and José's court-
appointed lawyer. Also in the courtroom are the court clerk,
the court monitor (who operates the recording machine),
and the sheriff—with me, a total of eight adults concentrating their attention on that young boy.

If José were to deny the allegations of the petition, a full-
fledged trial would follow. (Public defenders in the juvenile
court are more feisty and less likely to seek to cop a plea for
their clients than their counterparts in the adult court.) At a
trial the court advocate would have to prove that José committed the offense beyond a reasonable doubt. As judge I
would hear and decide the case without a jury.

The burden to be right about guilt or innocence weighs
heavily on me in the juvenile court. Although it is always
important not to convict an innocent defendant, it is equally
important in the juvenile court not to acquit a guilty child.
Adults are cynical about the criminal justice system and delight in beating it, but children do not understand how they
can be exonerated when they know they did something
wrong. There is the danger that the lesson they may learn
when that happens is that they can get away with anything.

At a previous hearing, however, José has admitted responsibility. My task now is to determine what should happen to him.

The probation officer's social study and a psychologist's
evaluation reveal that José is the sixth of nine children. His
father is in Puerto Rico and has had little contact with the

family for many years. His mother is a passive, depressed person, prone to excessive drinking. The family lives in a crowded Hartford apartment. José is a sophomore at Bulkeley High School, reading at the fifth-grade level but getting good grades in mechanical drawing and industrial arts. On intelligence tests he scores low in vocabulary and high in block design and object assembly. His attendance is good, and he frequently stays after school to work in the shop. He is liked by his classmates, but in his neighborhood he associates with teens who abuse alcohol and drugs. So far José has avoided these. He has a record of two previous offenses in this court, one for trespassing and another for shoplifting, for which he is on probation.

The psychologist emphasizes José's chaotic home life, low self-esteem, and lack of internalized values. His diagnosis: "Definite defects of character formation as a result of family and social environment." These studies all seem to end up with the same diagnosis. I have read scores of them. How is the court to deal with such children?

Before deciding on the disposition of a case in the juvenile court, I discuss it informally with the lawyers and probation officer in my chambers. In José's case the alternatives are (1) place him on vocational parole and allow him to go to work; (2) continue him on probation with more stringent conditions; (3) commit him to the Department of Children and Youth Services for placement in a private treatment home or training school; or, as a last resort, (4) commit him to DCYS for placement in Long Lane School, the state juvenile detention facility.

"Mrs. R—— can't control the boy," the probation officer said at our conference. "She is defeated by struggling to make ends meet on welfare and trying to raise her other children. We can't expect any help from her."

"I don't see any choice but Long Lane for José," the court advocate said. "This is his third offense. He can't continue to get away with that conduct."

"He's certainly going to get into even worse trouble if he stays in Hartford," added the probation officer.

José's lawyer agreed. "I know the guys he runs around with. I've represented some of them in this court. They're toughs, and they are going to pull him down."

But for me hope struggled against despair. "How about his shop skill?" I asked. "Can we build on that?"

"If the state is willing to pay twenty thousand a year, we can send him to the Connecticut Junior Republic," the probation officer mentioned. The Junior Republic is a home for delinquent youngsters in the Litchfield hills where the boys and girls govern themselves by electing their own "town council" and "mayor." It has fully equipped carpentry and motor shops and provides excellent vocational training. The probation officer thought that José might benefit from the program.

"Good Lord," exploded the court advocate, "we can't spend that kind of money to send every kid who gets into trouble to a private school. We'll bankrupt the state."

They all turned to me. I leaned back in my chair, hands behind my head, and looked up at the ceiling. Finally I said, "I think it's worth it. If José can use his skill not only to learn a trade, but to gain self-esteem, we have a chance of saving him. Let's do it."

I smile at José in the courtroom, who averts his eyes even though this is the third time he has been before me. "Because you admitted taking the woman's pocketbook, José, I have already found you delinquent. I could send you to Long Lane, where undoubtedly many of your neighborhood friends are. But because of your ability with shop tools and because I think you are a good kid, I'm going to give you a break. I commit you to DCYS for placement at Connecticut Junior Republic. There you can develop your skills and learn a trade. I hope you will take advantage of this chance. Good luck, son."

I nod to him and stand up. For the first time he smiles

back at me. That smile inspires me to keep tabs on José. A probation officer informs me that José succeeds at the Junior Republic. On graduation he gets a job as an apprentice cabinet maker. Three years later he has progressed in his work and has had no brushes with the law.

Other children who come before me are from the same background as José, but they are turned off by school, involved with alcohol and drugs, already imbued with the lawless culture of the street. They are charged with serious crimes like armed robbery, burglary, even murder. Emulating their fathers and older brothers, they are sullen, defiant, and hardened. The despair they stir in me is that their future is already predictable, and it extends from Long Lane to reformatory to state prison.

Yet in dealing with even these children there is always the hope that, being so young, they can change or that a teacher, community counselor, or probation officer will reach them and steer them in the right direction. Youth workers have plenty of success stories. José is not the only one.

Even more challenging than the delinquency cases, in which children commit crimes against society, are the neglect cases in which parents commit crimes against their children.

The petition reads: "Your Petitioner Mark J. Marcus, Commissioner, Department of Children & Youth Services, respectfully represents unto the Court as follows: Roger T., male, 10 years, 10 mos., birthdate 9-7-72, is abused in that he has been deprived of necessities. In January 1983 his father Douglas T. punished Roger by denying him food for three days; he also punished Roger by making him sit up in a chair all night and pointed a gun at his head."

My task is to determine whether or not the boy should be committed to DCYS. A court-appointed clinical psychologist testifies to the truth of the petition's allegations and adds: "Roger is fearful of his father because of the punishment he has received and at the same time desperately wants his approval. The tragedy of his life is that his father withholds that approval."

Roger's father takes the stand. He is a short, square Japanese man with fierce beetle brows. His lawyer's questions elicit his background. At the beginning of World War II, when he was seven and living with his family on the West Coast, he had been interned in an American camp for three years, an experience he recalls with anger. Later, in his teens, he was drafted into the navy and assigned to wait on naval officers aboard ship. He recalls that also with anger. After being educated as an engineer, he married his first wife, Roger's mother. She became psychotic after the boy's birth, and the father took her back to Japan and had her put into a mental hospital. He then returned to this country, divorced her, and tried to raise Roger by himself. To give the boy a mother, he married another woman, but that marriage failed also.

He testifies how he treated Roger for getting poor grades in school. "I insisted he come home in the afternoon and study. Sometimes I stood over him when he was doing his homework and urged him to think faster."

He is also angry at Roger over an incident of coins being stolen from his collection. "When Roger lied about it, I denied him food and made him sit up all night in a chair. That is a Japanese way of disciplining children. I also pointed a gun at his head because American guards pointed guns at me when I was his age in an American concentration camp. Let me raise my son my way. I don't want him to be a banana—yellow on the outside, white on the inside."

To rebut Mr. T.'s demand that he be judged by the child-care standards of his country, Roger's court-appointed attorney produces a Yale sociology professor—himself a third-generation Japanese-American—who specializes in contemporary Japanese society. The professor testifies that the mother provides the warmth and love in a Japanese family. The father is the authoritarian who discourages intimacy.

When there is no mother around, the home is cold, rigid, unloving. Under those circumstances the father-son relationship is volatile and dangerous.

"In Japan and among first-generation Japanese-Americans, punishment of an errant child is by shaming him," he explains. "It is standard to lock the child up in a dark room and deprive him of food. Second-generation Japanese-Americans, like Roger's father, will shame a child but not deny him food. Also it is not normal for second-generation Japanese-Americans to require that a boy sit up in a chair all night and to point a gun at him."

This court proceeding is a great loss of face to a Japanese father, the professor says, because it shows he cannot solve his own family problems.

I ask him about the Japanese attitude toward psychological counseling. The professor answers, "In Japan, communication of emotions is nonverbal; it is by face-to-face contact and body language. If Japanese have to talk between themselves, there is already a breakdown of the relationship. Psychotherapy is rare in Japan because it is verbal. Second-generation Japanese-Americans may accept it for their children, but find it too threatening for themselves."

On another day I meet with Roger. My purpose is to communicate to him that however his fate is decided, it will be not by an unseen force, but by a judge concerned about him. Roger is a small, withdrawn boy who peers through horn-rim glasses with a wan look. At one point he says to me in bleak despair, "If I go back to my father, it will be the end of me."

To establish some temporary space between the boy and his father, I commit Roger to DCYS for placement in a residential treatment facility that provides excellent education and therapy. I urge Mr. T. to see his boy regularly and repair their relationship.

But on the father's first visit to the school, he gets into a fierce argument with the administrator and has to be forcibly removed by the police. On the next visit, the day before Christmas, Mr. T. hurls the presents he brought for Roger against a wall, shouts obscenities, and leaves. On another visit at a restaurant with a DCYS worker present, Mr. T. says to Roger, "Look hard at me because you will not see me again. I am going to commit suicide." That is the ultimate Japanese threat. Roger is terribly agitated.

When this is reported to me, on the motion of DCYS, I terminate visitation until the father agrees to undertake psychological counseling. As the Yale professor predicted, he refuses. Mr. T.'s sister in San Francisco, contacted by DCYS, agrees to have Roger live with her and her family. I authorize that arrangement.

Mr. T. does symbolically commit suicide as to his son. He writes to me declaring that he no longer considers himself Roger's father and will have no further contact with the boy.

Four years later, I learn from looking at the file, Roger is still living with his aunt, doing well in school, but showing a disturbing tendency to steal things and to lie. His aunt and her husband do not want to adopt him. His status is in limbo; his future . . .

Would things have gone better if I had somehow enabled the father to save face? I ask myself that often. But when I remember Mr. T.'s fierce beetle brows and uncontrollable rage, I realize nothing would have prevented his destroying himself and his relationship with his son.

A more typical case of child abuse comes before me on another day. Florence is a teenage mother, her lackluster eyes already showing the ravages of drugs. The DCYS petition alleges that her six-month-old baby has had one arm and several ribs broken. The physical abuse is mild compared with some I hear: babies shaken so violently as to cause permanent brain damage, bodily paralysis, even blindness; babies whose bodies are covered with burns from lighted cigarettes; babies infected with gonorrhea of the mouth and anus; young girls sexually molested by fathers, young boys by mothers. A litany of parents' inhumanity to children.

My experience in court is confirmed by the 1988 report of the National Commission on the Constitutional Rights of Children: "No society in the world has allowed such a vast and extensive brutalization of its children, physically, sexually, mentally, and socially, as ours. An American psychologist observed that if the emotional damage done to children could be seen on the exterior of their bodies, we would have to cringe and look away from such a hideous sight."

Florence claims her child fell out of the crib, but a hospital doctor testifies the injuries could only have been caused by the baby being violently squeezed. I have no difficulty finding abuse.

The report of a court-appointed psychologist states: "Florence's childhood was traumatic. She was abandoned by an alcoholic father, and was herself a victim of neglect. She regularly takes drugs and has men stay overnight. Florence loves her child but cannot control her temper."

These findings are echoed by psychiatrist Alice Miller in her book *For Your Own Good:* "Human destructiveness is a reactive, not innate phenomenon. . . . We punish our children for the arbitrary action of our parents that we were not able to defend ourselves against."

The case before me illustrates the lethal combination of poverty, drug use, and teenage pregnancy. Child abuse, of course, is not confined to the poor. It also occurs among the middle class and the affluent. But it is most prevalent where everyday living is harsh, and frustrations are taken out on defenseless children.

What should my disposition be? Letting the child remain with Florence runs the risk of future physical abuse. Taking him from her when she loves him creates the risk of emotional deprivation.

Because my priority must be to assure the child's physical well-being, I commit him to DCYS for placement in a foster home. I specify to Florence what is expected of her to get her child back: visit him once a week, participate in a class in parenting skills, undertake psychological counseling, and keep in touch with DCYS.

Again there is the mixture of despair and hope: despair that Florence will not follow through and her child will bounce around foster homes for years; hope that she will rehabilitate herself and reunite with the boy.

Sitting on the juvenile court, however, does give me an appreciation of foster parents who take in unwanted, abused, and even severely handicapped children and give them consistent, loving care. Without them, the alternative is institutionalization of these children, a prospect too dismal to contemplate.

In Connecticut, a private organization of volunteers, known as Children In Placement, follows up on children placed with DCYS. If the mother does not meet the court's expectations of her, Children In Placement alerts the court and urges DCYS to bring a proceeding to terminate the mother's parental rights, so that the child can be permanently placed in a foster home and, hopefully, adopted.

When a court terminates parental rights, it decrees that the father and mother are legally no longer the child's parents. Since in most cases the child is illegitimate and the father has vanished, the mother is the one in court fighting to keep her child.

Joyce is such a mother in a termination proceeding brought by DCYS. She is a brown-skinned woman wearing a thin cotton dress this winter morning. The DCYS social worker presents the following evidence: Joyce was sixteen when she gave birth to Mary Ann out of wedlock. Over the next four years she had three more children by different men. The last child so crowded the apartment in which she was living with the father that she left Mary Ann with a friend. The juvenile court committed the girl to DCYS for placement in a foster home. Over the next two years Joyce met none of the expectations specified by the court. She made no visits to Mary Ann, did not find an apartment large enough to take Mary Ann back to live with her other children, and did not keep in contact with DCYS. During that time Mary Ann flourished with the foster parents, who now desire to adopt her.

On the stand Joyce explains her failure to see her daughter for two years: "I had no car, and none of my boyfriends would drive me."

"Don't Mary Ann's foster parents live on a city bus line that runs past your apartment?" asks the DCYS lawyer.

"I had other problems troubling me, too," Joyce says. "But I'll see her every week from now on, I promise."

"You still don't have an apartment with enough room for Mary Ann, do you?" persists the DCYS lawyer.

"I'll find a way to care for her. Please, Judge," she adds, turning to me, "don't take my baby away from me. Give me one more chance."

Again the standard to apply is the best interest of the child. Joyce expresses love for Mary Ann, which is something to build on. But her failure even to see her daughter for two full years bodes poorly for her fulfilling her promises. The DCYS social worker reports that Mary Ann thrives beautifully with the foster parents and strongly recommends terminating Joyce's parental rights. What should my decision be?

After reflecting at length about the case, I find clear and convincing proof that Joyce has abandoned Mary Ann in that she has (in the words of the Connecticut statute) "failed to maintain a reasonable interest, concern, or responsibility as to the welfare of the child." Mary Ann's best interests, I conclude, will be served by ending any possibility of her returning to her mother and by opening the possibility of her being adopted by her foster parents.

In my view, the three most difficult decisions a judge has to make, because they involve the exercise of the most awesome power over people's lives, are: (1) sentencing the convicted, (2) awarding custody of children, and (3) terminating the relationship between parent and child. Of the three, terminating parental rights comes closest to playing God. Prison sentences come to an end, criminals often being released well before the imposed term. Custody can be modified if a change in circumstances warrants. But a judge's decision declaring a woman is no longer the mother of her child is forever.

A line in *The Prince of Tides* haunts me: "There is no fixing a damaged childhood." It affirms the persistent vision I have from the juvenile court bench not only of parents as prisoners of their past, but also of children as prisoners of their future. Often I am tempted to give a hug more than a judgment.

15. THE FACE OF POVERTY

When I sit on the bench of the housing session of the superior court in Hartford, I look squarely into the face of poverty. That face is often black or brown, and frequently female, accompanied in court by small children. Sometimes the face is submissive, defeated by the battle; at the moment of my decision ordering an eviction, it may dissolve into tears. Once a woman crumpled in a dead faint on the courtroom floor. Other times the face is angry, fiercely angry at the cruelty of the situation: eyes blazing, lips curling, voice snarling with rage. Emotions are near the surface when what is at stake is a life necessity like housing.

People come before the housing court mainly because they are poor: tenants being evicted because they are too poor to pay rent; landlords being accused of housing code violations because they do not have the money to repair old buildings.

In contrast with criminal court cases, which usually involve some form of wrongdoing, housing court cases rarely involve moral fault. Both tenants and landlords are victims of underlying inequities in our society.

At the end of one eviction case, a woman screams at me, "Where can I go with my two children? You find me a place, Mister Judge." I have no answer.

And I have no answer to the lament of landlords, either. An apartment house owner rents a two-bedroom flat to a family of four. Within a month relatives of the tenants move in with three more children. Soon holes are punched in walls, windows are broken, overused appliances fail. Then the tenants fall behind on their rent. At the eviction proceeding before me, the landlord rants, "The nine people living in those four rooms are wrecking the place. On top of it, they don't pay the rent, so I can't pay my mortgages, taxes, and fuel bills. That's not fair, Your Honor."

Case after case reveals the struggle for existence going on in the city: gas stove burners left on all day to heat cold flats; welfare mothers slowly losing their tenuous foothold on life's slippery stairway; above all, desperate people scrambling for any affordable accommodation. One tenant slams on the counsel table a bottle containing a large rat he claimed he killed in his apartment; another displays a plastic bag with two cockroaches she claims the doctor took out of her child's ears. The suffering comes to light in the context of law cases, but the dilemmas presented in the housing court are easier to decide legally than to solve fundamentally.

An owner contracts to sell a four-unit apartment house to a person forced to get around by wheelchair. A condition of the sale is that the handicapped buyer gets possession of the first-floor apartment. The tenants of that apartment are a couple with four school-age children. At the action brought by the owner to evict them, they point to the impossibility of finding other affordable housing. Since they have paid their rent regularly, they ask for a delay of eviction for six months, the maximum allowed under the law. "You can't do that, Judge," the landlord argues. "My buyer won't wait that long, and I'll lose the sale."

How should I decide? Both have valid claims on my conscience. I compromise. I allow the tenants to stay three months, hoping that decision will save the sale and give the tenants sufficient time to find another affordable home. But there lingers in my mind, what if the tenants cannot?

Another woman, destitute and with three small children, is explicit about what she will do if ordered out of her apartment. Having failed to pay her rent for several months, she is legally entitled only to a three-day delay of her eviction. I ask from the bench, "How are you going to find a new place, pay the first month's rent, security deposit, and moving expenses?"

"I don't know. I'm looking for a job."

"Suppose you can't swing it?"

"Well, then we'll live in the back of my car," she says.

"With your three children?"

"We'll manage," she says as her outward show of confidence ebbs.

The housing session of the superior court was established as a pilot project in Hartford in 1978. Before then housing matters, such as summary process actions in which landlords sought to evict tenants, and criminal proceedings against landlords for violating housing codes, were heard on the regular civil and criminal calendars of the court. Considered to be relatively minor cases, they were taken up and decided when a court got around to them. Citizen advocacy groups became dissatisfied with this method of dealing with cases that not only required quick decisions, but also were of major social significance. They lobbied the legislature to create a separate docket of the superior court, euphemistically called the housing court, to focus judicial and social resources on housing matters. The success of the Hartford experiment led to its adoption in the other major cities of Connecticut.

The housing court statute provides: "Any judge assigned to hear housing matters should have a commitment to the maintenance of decent, safe, and sanitary housing." It also created a citizen advisory committee to oversee the workings of the court and to recommend to the chief court administrator suitable superior court judges to be assigned to it. When the committee recruited me, I readily agreed. Several other judges had turned down the committee because they felt the court had too little prestige. At the time I was sitting in rural Rockville and thirsted to return to Hartford and wrestle with the real problems of the poor. Little did I realize how intense those problems had become since my earlier involvement, as a lawyer, with Hartford's antipoverty agency.

The housing court was then located in a small white building in the middle of a state parking lot. Everything about the building was undersize: ceilings low, halls narrow, offices tiny, courtroom cramped. The sense that justice was being sought had to be generated not by the physical trappings, but by the dedication of the court personnel.

The first morning I arrived (and it was to be so every morning), the anteroom of the housing court was jammed with the People—mothers with babies in arms or small children hanging onto their skirts, unemployed workers with care-creased faces, young people with straggly hair, old people in ragged clothes. The resigned expressions on their faces were the same I imagined they wore outside of welfare offices, waiting for a faceless clerk to apply a senseless regulation to them. As I slid through the crowd, I wondered what was I getting myself into, how I could deal with their problems.

Fortunately I was assisted by an amazing court staff. Housing court clerks are besieged all day long by tenants and landlords trying to act as their own lawyers. The clerks patiently explain the procedures to these confused "pro se" litigants and help them fill out the proper forms. Their courteous assistance sets the tone of the court.

Housing specialists perform a role similar to family relations officers in the divorce court but have a greater range of responsibilities. They help tenants find temporary shelters and clear away bureaucratic welfare department red tape to get housing allotments released. (In the case of the mother with the three children who contemplated living in the back of a car, they expedited her getting on welfare to enable her to pay for an apartment.) They monitor compliance with court orders requiring corrections of housing code violations and direct landlords to sources of funds to finance repairs. Their most important function, however, is to mediate disputes between feuding landlords and tenants and help them reach an agreed-upon resolution of the cases scheduled to come before the judge.

Frances Caliafiore and Linda Bantell have been the housing specialists at the housing court in Hartford since its inception. Frances graduated at the top of her law school class. Linda has a master's degree in public health. Both in their early thirties, they are personable and knowledgeable. Their charm takes the steam out of the most bitter conflicts, and their expertise in the law gives credibility to their assessment of the relative merits of the parties' claims. They are especially skillful at mixing the ingredients of compromise: the desire of landlords for possession of the apartment and payment of back rent and the desire of tenants for more time to pay arrearages or to relocate.

A large black woman with two children clinging to her dress is before me. It is a typical eviction case. The landlord's complaint alleges that she has not paid her rent for three months. In a deep, sad voice she explains that the welfare money has gone to bury her father. Frances has worked out a compromise for the parties and reads it into the record. The landlord will allow the tenant to stay in the apartment if she will from now on keep her monthly rent current and pay ten dollars a week on the arrearage until it is fully paid. I enter an order confirming the settlement.

In another case the landlord impassionately describes the unsanitary condition of the apartment of an elderly woman he is seeking to evict: "Neighboring tenants told me of a strange odor coming from the apartment, so I investigated. Such a mess, Judge. The kitchen sink is filled with food-encrusted dishes, the bathroom toilet stuffed and overflowing, the bedroom and living rooms stacked to the ceiling with boxes and clothes. I don't know how anyone can live in such a pigsty."

The silent, bewildered woman has no lawyer. I refer the case to Linda for mediation. She returns to say, "Mrs. Washington just lost her son, and she is depressed. I have convinced the landlord to postpone the matter for a few weeks while I see what can be done."

Linda does plenty. She arranges for the woman to start seeing a social worker to deal with her depression and for a home care worker to help clean the apartment. Three months later the case comes before me again. Linda announces that the apartment is back to normal and the landlord has given the tenant a new lease. "You can close the case, Judge," she says airily.

If those matters had been tried before me, and I had been required to apply the law strictly, I could not have reached such desirable results. Over and over I say under my breath, "Thank you, Frances; thank you, Linda."

Even housing court sheriffs are surprising sources of help. When I enter an order evicting a family, they will sometimes delay enforcing it until the family can find another place; occasionally they even contribute to the moving expenses out of their own pockets.

Legal aid and neighborhood antipoverty lawyers are the knights in shining armor of the poor. They know landlord-tenant law inside and out and are adept at turning any one of its provisions into a shield for their impoverished clients. Fair game for them are the attorneys from downtown firms who only occasionally venture into the housing court to represent the few affluent landlords with cases there. When one of these high-tone attorneys, in his inevitable three-piece suit, finishes presenting his case and confidently asks for a judgment of eviction, a legal aid lawyer may respond, "Your Honor, I move to dismiss the complaint under section 47a-23a of the General Statutes."

Smiling inwardly, knowing the hotshot attorney has already had his head handed to him and doesn't know it yet, I say, "Would you mind explaining the basis for your motion more fully for the benefit of plaintiff's counsel?"

"As Your Honor knows, that statute requires that the landlord must serve on my client a notice to quit the premise eight days before a summary process action can be started. In this case this landlord started the action seven days after serving the notice to quit."

"Well," blusters Mr. Three-Piece Suit, "what difference does it make if we started the action a day early? No public policy purpose will be served by dismissing the complaint on that basis."

I lean over the bench and say, "Summary process is a statutory remedy. It provides relief to landlords much more quickly than an ordinary civil suit. For that reason the requirements of the statute must be strictly complied with. Since your client failed to give the required number of days notice, the tenant's motion to dismiss is granted."

When a tenant, who is under an oral month-to-month lease, is served an eviction notice during the first ten days of the month for failure to pay rent, the situation is also a setup for the legal aid lawyer. This is a common mistake of a downtown attorney inexperienced in landlord-tenant law. With lip-smacking relish, the legal aid attorney moves to dismiss. "The statute is very clear," he explains. "It provides for a ten-day grace period to pay rent under an oral lease. In this case the notice to quit was served on the ninth day of the month. Consequently, it is too early for the current month. It is also too late for the preceding month, because such

notice must be served during the month in which the rent
was not paid."

He is dead right. I throw the case out and again send Mr.
Three-Piece Suit packing. I must confess a secret delight in
seeing the rich, who so often use legal technicalities to their
advantage, being outclassed in their own game by the skillful representatives of the poor.

But such victories in cases in which tenants fail to pay the
rent are short-lived. Tenants may get another month or so
of free occupancy, but the landlord starts the action over
again, doing it right the second time. In the end he wins.

However, tenant lawyers need not rely only on technicalities to protect their clients. The Anglo-Saxon common law
that conferred absolute dominion over private property on
land owners has changed substantially over the years. In the
1960s and 1970s in particular, many state legislatures enacted
comprehensive landlord-tenant acts governing the relationships of lessors and lessees. These acts provide tenants with
defenses of substance. For example, a landlord can no longer
bring an eviction action in retaliation for a tenant's attempting, by lawful means, to correct a condition that breaches a
state statute. When a landlord tries to remove a tenant for
complaining to local authorities that the apartment house
violates housing code provisions, I uphold the defense of
retaliatory eviction. On the other hand, when a landlord
once sought to evict a tenant whose homosexual activities
disturbed other tenants, I denied the defense, on the
grounds that no state statute prohibits discrimination based
on sexual orientation.

State statute also now bars a landlord from terminating
the lease of a tenant who is physically disabled or over sixty-
two years of age and has an annual income of not more than
$21,000. When a neighborhood legal services lawyer as-
serted that defense in an eviction action, a landlord attorney
argued before me, "It doesn't apply here, Your Honor. That
provision was in a legislative bill entitled 'An Act Concern-

ing Condominium Conversions.' This case involves an ordinary rental situation."

It was the first case under that section, and I looked up the legislative history. The provision *was* part of a bill relating to condominium conversions. But the debate on the floors of both the house and senate was over whether that protection to disabled, elderly, and low-income tenants applied independent of conversion situations. The import of those remarks was that it did. In fact, an amendment offered on the bill to limit the protection only to condominium conversions was defeated. Thus I held that the legislative intent was that the defense was available generally; since the tenants before me were over sixty-two and had annual incomes of less than $21,000, I dismissed the summary process action against them. That interpretation of the law has prevailed.

The landlord-tenant act, however, is not a one-edged sword directed only against landlords. It also imposes responsibilities on tenants, such as requiring them to keep their premises safe and clean, to use apartment facilities and appliances in a reasonable manner, and to conduct themselves so as not to disturb their neighbors. When tenants violate these requirements, I enforce the law against them and in favor of landlords.

When criminal proceedings are instituted against landlords for violating housing codes, if I find them guilty, I can impose a fine or jail sentence. I came on the bench of the housing court with a missionary zeal to enforce housing codes and eradicate deplorable housing. The notion of slumlords profiting from such housing seemed outrageous to me. I quickly discovered that there are few slumlords, because no profits can be skimmed from dilapidated buildings. The typical landlords coming before the court are small-property owners struggling to realize enough from their rents to pay expenses.

When I find a code violation, the alternative of sending the landlord to jail rarely crosses my mind. (I did agree, though, with the decision of a housing court judge who incarcerated a landlord for failing to install fire detectors in his apartment house.) My usual resolution is to impose a fine high enough to discourage repetition but not so high as to preclude the ability to repair. Often I rely on the housing specialist to help the landlord key into state programs that will qualify him for funds to make necessary renovations. My missionary zeal gives way to a realization that too strict code enforcement takes housing off the market and increases the scarcity.

In contrast with civil court cases, which require grappling with a wide variety of statutes and legal principles, when I am sitting on the housing court, I apply over and over again familiar provisions of the landlord-tenant act. Although housing matters are not confined to apartment evictions and sometimes require construing complicated commercial leases, still the focus of the legal issues is relatively narrow. For the first time on the bench, I master a specific area of the law. I also contribute to its development. Prior to the establishment of the housing court, few cases on landlord-tenant matters were published in the law reports. The first housing court judge wrote many opinions clarifying the law and interpreting the statutes, and I, as the second one, continue that practice.

That mastery makes me more creative in achieving just results in individual cases. But it does not invest me with the power to ameliorate generally the harsh consequences of the housing situation of the poor.

The nub of that situation is scarcity of affordable accommodations. Two parallel movements enhance that scarcity. On the one hand, old apartment buildings in the cities are being rehabilitated and converted to condominiums for the affluent; on the other, no new public housing is being built, federal and state assistance necessary to build private low-income housing is drying up, and rent subsidies to enable underincome tenants to live in existing apartment houses have been slashed. The result: more and more poor people chasing after fewer and fewer apartments; and those apartments, because of overuse, are becoming more and more dilapidated.

The housing court staff likens itself to a M.A.S.H. unit. Society's wounded keep coming in to be bandaged and sent back out to battle. Or they refer to the process of one tenant getting evicted and another moving in as a game of musical chairs. When the song ends, someone loses the scramble for a chair and falls out of the system. In real life even people with jobs are unable to find affordable accommodations and join the ranks of the homeless.

Under those circumstances, as a housing court judge, I feel I am pulling chestnuts out of fires fueled by the failures of other branches of government. And those failures are massive. Inadequate and insufficient shelter for the poor results in a growing army of homeless and a depressed and degraded population of children that threatens the stability of our cities and the future of our country.

To legislators and executive department officials, housing problems are matters of abstract public policy, but to me on the housing court bench they are matters of immediate human anguish. I cannot stuff my ears or blind my eyes to desperate people before me crying out, "Where am I to go? What am I to do?"

By the end of a year on that court, I am

- more touched than I can bear by the plight of the poor;

- more furious than I can control at the federal government funding missiles in space ahead of housing in the cities;

- more concerned than I can express about the buildup of social tensions around the housing crisis;

- burned out.

I ask for a new assignment. On my last day I feel like a traitor leaving the valiant staff of the housing court. And on that day, as I look at the People in the courtroom, I know they cannot escape.

16. ON BEING REVERSED AND SITTING ON THE SUPREME COURT

Do I wince when a decision of mine is reversed by an appeals court? You bet I do. Sometimes I am embarrassed by my stupidity being glaringly revealed; sometimes I am angry at the stupidity of the appellate judges; and sometimes I am resigned to the vagaries of appellate review that all trial judges must suffer. But always a bit of my pride is bruised.

Every Tuesday I run down the index of appellate and supreme court cases in the *Connecticut Law Journal* in much the same way humorist Robert Benchley used to scan the morning obituary page after a hard night to see if his name was there. If one of my decisions has been ruled upon, I anxiously leaf through the pages to it. If it has been upheld, I sigh with satisfaction. If it has been overturned, I just sigh. Connecticut high courts indicate reversal of a lower court decision by "Error" and affirmance by "No Error." To paraphrase John Whittier: Of all sad words of tongue and pen, the saddest are "There is error"—again.

There is a difference between lawyers losing a case and judges being reversed. Lawyers try the cases that come their way. They are stuck with whatever the facts are on their side of the dispute. Moreover, they have to contend with unreliable witnesses, opposing counsel, and intractable law. They have plenty of legitimate excuses for not winning. A trial judge, however, has no place to hide. He determines the facts from the evidence, chooses the legal principles to apply, and makes a decision that is his own and for which he must take complete responsibility. His professional pride always rides heavily on how he fares under appellate court scrutiny.

When I came on the bench, I vowed that I would never be reversed. For three years I ran up a string of affirmances. I did have a near miss. An opinion of mine was affirmed but on other grounds than I had stated. This was an assault on my reasoning, but still it was not a reversal. I came to feel immune from the rapier of the higher courts. Then one day, turning to one of my decisions in the law journal, there appeared the dreaded words: "Error in part; judgment directed."

The ruling surprised me because *Arterburn Convalescent Home, Inc., et al.* v. *Committee on State Payment to Hospitals* raised no difficult questions. The Committee had denied a group of licensed convalescent hospitals the right to intervene in an administrative proceeding it was conducting to set Medicaid reimbursement rates. The hospitals applied to superior court to be allowed to be parties in that proceeding. I granted them the right and also directed the Committee to set the same rate for the plaintiffs as it had for other hospitals, under a statute that required a uniform rate. On appeal of my decision, the supreme court affirmed the part that allowed the intervention but found I had erred in directing what action should be taken by the administrative agency.

That, the supreme court said, "would be an impermissible judicial usurpation of the administrative function."

The world did not come to an end. The adage is not true that when a judge is affirmed, nobody remembers; when he is reversed, nobody forgets. None of my colleagues gibed me about the reversal. Judges are sensitive to each other's feelings on that score, I realized. They know that next time it could happen to them.

Reversals go with the territory. Almost every significant trial court case is appealed. Why shouldn't the losing party take a second bite at the apple? Appeals to Connecticut's intermediate appellate court are simple and inexpensive. They can be taken merely by filing a notice, and the record and briefs need only be typewritten. (Appeals to the supreme court, however, are only by permission of that court, and the record and briefs must be printed.) Further, for trial judges to err is not only human but understandable. In jury cases, they rule on evidence and give instructions to juries in the heat of a trial. In court cases, they research complicated legal questions when they get a free moment between trials and most often at night and over weekends. They decide in lonely isolation. As conscientious as they try to be, they cannot be as reflective and thorough as the justices of the upper courts, who deliberate together and spend their entire working day on research and opinion writing.

Trial judges are also at the mercy of the lawyer who defends their opinions in the higher court. If the lawyer writes a second-rate brief, the risk of reversal increases. The clerk of the appeals court sends both sides' briefs to the trial judge. When the appellee attorney advances poor arguments, I am sometimes tempted to instruct him how to sustain the victory won before me. But the ethic is for the trial judge not to intervene. My role at that stage is to remain silent and bear it.

Trial courts, however, are not the only ones reversed. The appellate court is reversed by the state supreme court and the state supreme court by the United States Supreme Court. With that hierarchical review, it is inevitable that from time to time higher courts will see cases differently from lower courts. How else can they justify their existence?

In *Arterburn* I had made a relatively minor mistake, but in *Lee* v. *Board of Education*, I made a beaut. Elinor Lee, a tenured public school teacher, had been discharged by a town board of education. She appealed to the superior court on the ground that the board had erred in not stating the reasons for its decision. When the matter was assigned to me, I was pleased because I was familiar with teacher tenure law. (As a lawyer I had been general counsel to a statewide teachers union and represented many teachers in discharge cases.) The statute governing procedures for terminating teachers did not require the board to make findings to support its decision. The cases on constitutional law, as I read them, said that although it was desirable for an administrative agency to give reasons for its decisions, it was not mandated by the due process clause. If trial judges were not required to write an opinion in every case, I reasoned, administrative agencies should not have to explain every one of their decisions. So I upheld the education board's discharge of the teacher.

I could not have been more wrong. On appeal, the supreme court found "Error." It agreed that the teacher tenure statute did not specify the form and content of a termination decision by a board of education. But it held "a tenured teacher discharged for cause is entitled, as a matter of constitutional law, to a written statement of the decision reached, the reasons for the determination, and a fair summary of evidence relied on." *Lee* v. *Board of Education* has turned out to be a landmark case in Connecticut administrative law. It is constantly cited and quoted from, each time revealing my blunder.

I have been reversed other times during my fifteen years on the bench—but not so often as to fall into the category of the apocryphal judge who when the lawyer mentioned this was an appeal from his decision, a supreme court justice leaned forward to say, "Do we need any other reason for finding error?"

Actually, judges' "batting averages" before the appeals courts have little effect on their reputation with the bar or their colleagues. The judge with few reversals may take only easy cases and decide them strictly in accordance with black letter law. The judge with many reversals may be willing to take difficult and involved cases, which other judges are eager to avoid, and he may courageously fashion thoughtful opinions that seek to extend the boundaries of the law. A judge of the latter kind is one of the most respected members of the Connecticut trial bench.

Sometimes a reversal is just bad luck, as it was for me in *Paulsen* v. *Manson*. Ronald Paulsen had pleaded guilty to a charge of first-degree assault and been given a long sentence. While in prison he filed a writ of habeas corpus demanding his release on the ground that his guilty plea had been unconstitutionally accepted by the trial court. He relied on a string of Connecticut Supreme Court cases, all of which held that "in order for a plea of guilty to be constitutionally valid, the record must affirmatively disclose that there is a factual basis for the plea." This means the state's attorney must state to the trial judge facts indicating that the accused committed the crime to which he pleads guilty.

In the Paulsen habeas corpus proceedings, I applied that standard to the recital of facts made by the state's attorney at the time of Paulsen's plea. The state's attorney had said: "If Your Honor please, he [Paulsen] was accompanying one David Collins at approximately 11:35 P.M. on June 25, 1976, at or near the Middlebury-Southbury line on Route 84. They were stopped by the police officer, as I mentioned, and the police officer was shot in the right arm by this man's companion, Collins. The police officer returned fire and subsequently apprehended them."

Those facts put Paulsen in the vicinity of the crime committed by Collins, but they did not make Paulsen a participant or accessory. They failed to implicate Paulsen not only in the commission of the crime of first-degree assault for which he pleaded guilty, but in the commission of any crime at all. Consequently I granted the writ of habeas corpus and ordered Paulsen released.

On appeal of my decision, the supreme court acknowledged that I had correctly interpreted its previous rulings but added, "Recent federal case law, however, has provided a clarifying interpretation of due process requirements that is not in accord with that posited by this Court in *State* v. *Eason*." The new federal test was simply whether the plea of guilty was voluntary and intelligent, and a factual basis inquiry was only one way of satisfying that constitutional requirement. The supreme court concluded, "To the extent that our decisions in *Eason, Cutler, Marra*, and *Battle* hold to the contrary, they are overruled." Since I had relied on those cases, the court found "Error."

I did not feel bad about that. As a trial judge I was obligated to follow clear supreme court precedent. When that court decided to change its precedent in my case, I was left hanging.

Another reversal occurred when I attempted to interpret a hopelessly confusing state tax statute. That statute imposes on national corporations, which carry on business in many states, a tax on the part of their total net income attributed to their operations in Connecticut. The tax is calculated by one or the other of two formulas. Which formula is to be applied depends on whether the corporate taxpayer's income is "derived from the use of tangible property" or "*other than* from the use of tangible property." Distinguishing corporations on the basis of which does or does not use property is impossible, for every modern enterprise has typewriters, word processors, telephones, computers, and copying machines.

In the case of *Schlumberger Technology Corporation* v. *Commissioner of Revenue Services,* I attempted to make sense of the statute by interpreting it one way. On appeal, the supreme court interpreted it another way. Both interpretations were guesses of the meaning of the ambiguous law. I did not feel bad about that reversal, either. I had just lost the flip of a coin.

But there is one reversal that still rankles because to this day I feel the supreme court was dead wrong. *Connecticut Bank and Trust Company* v. *Tax Commissioner* did not involve sympathetic parties, but basic fairness was still at stake.

The Connecticut Bank and Trust Company had included the interest earned on state tax-exempt bonds as part of its gross income on its state corporate business tax return and paid the tax on that interest. Discovering what it felt was its mistake, it made a claim to the tax commissioner for a refund of the tax paid on the tax-exempt interest. The claim was denied.

The commissioner acknowledged in his opinion that the statutes authorizing the issuance of the bonds in question provided that the bonds were exempt either "from taxation," "from any taxation," or "from all taxation." But he ruled that the corporate business tax is a franchise tax levied on the privilege of doing business in the state. Although the tax is measured by a corporation's income, it is not a direct tax upon income. Since it was not directly imposed on the bank's tax-exempt interest, the bank was not entitled to a refund.

When the bank appealed to the superior court, I got the case. The commissioner's decision did not make sense to me. It is true the corporate business tax is worded as a franchise tax. But the corporation files an income tax form and calculates its tax on the basis of its net income. From the point of view of the corporation, there is no difference between a franchise tax measured by income and a direct tax imposed upon income. The dollar amount of the tax is the same, and the impact is the same. To make a distinction is to dignify legal fiction over reality.

Moreover, the state had clearly benefited from its promise of a tax exemption on its bonds because it could borrow money at a lower rate of interest. If that promise was illusionary to corporations, they would cease to be purchasers at that interest rate, and the state would lose a substantial market for its bonds. More significant to me, if the state were allowed to renege on its promise, corporations that had already purchased the bonds in reliance on the state acting in good faith would be treated unfairly. So I granted the refund to the bank.

The supreme court would have none of my reasoning. It read the corporate business tax statute literally as imposing a franchise tax for the privilege of doing business in the state, rather than realistically as imposing an income tax. It ignored completely the unfairness of the state requiring a tax be paid on interest that it promised was exempt from taxation.

Damn, I was mad. As a measure of revenge, I wrote a spoof of the high court decision in the local bar association newsletter. But in the end I was, in a way, vindicated. A year or so later the same issue came before the Pennsylvania Supreme Court, and that distinguished body of jurists decided exactly the way I had. My only misfortune was being a trial judge in the wrong state.

High courts in Connecticut do occasionally redeem themselves, however. One case before me challenged the constitutionality of a statute that gave the governor limited power to reduce allotments of funds appropriated by the legislature to state departments in any year that a budget deficit loomed. In a long memorandum of decision, I upheld the law. The supreme court affirmed in *University of Connecticut Chapter, AAUP* v. *Governor*, 200 Conn. 386. Its opinion is replete with, "As the trial court indicated . . ." "As the trial court recognized . . ." and "We agree with the trial court that . . ."

In another case, *Cantor* v. *Department of Income Mainte-nance*, 12 Conn. App. 435, the appellate court affirmed with these laudatory words: "The trial court, *Satter, J.,* filed a complete, well-reasoned, and legally sound memorandum of decision. The trial court's decision so completely articu-lates the issues involved in this appeal and so adequately explains the legal basis for its conclusions that it may be referred to for a detailed discussion of the facts and applica-ble law." Needless to say, that is one of my favorite appeals court decisions.

A delicious experience for a trial judge is to have one of his opinions reversed by an intermediate appellate court and then affirmed by the highest appeals court. This happened to me in *Nardini* v. *Manson,* 207 Conn. 118, in which I denied a habeas corpus application of a convicted arsonist on the ground that he had not established the ineffective assistance of his trial counsel. The appellate court reversed me, and to my delight the supreme court overruled that court and rein-stated my decision. When I next met the judge who had written the appellate court opinion, I said jokingly, "That will larn you to overturn old Bob Satter." He smiled confi-dently because he knew that in the long run he would more often have the last laugh.

Superior court judges are occasionally asked to sit on the higher courts, either to replace a justice who is disqualified from hearing a particular case or to lighten the load of the justices. I have been asked a number of times to both the supreme court and the appellate court. That experience gave me a different perspective of the appellate process. The no-tion of lower court judges that upper court judges are pick-ing on them proved false. When sitting on an appeals court, I never even noticed which trial judge's decision was being reviewed.

The first morning I was to sit on the supreme court, I was exhilarated. The supreme court building is a majestic white stone structure across the street from the state capitol. Tall

Doric columns lend grandeur to its front entrance. I had bounded up the steps and through those columns many times as a lawyer to argue appeals and as legislative counsel to confer with the chief court administrator. This time I entered through a side door leading to the justices' private chambers. I was struck with the quiet of the corridors, so different from the bustle of the superior court I had just left.

In the conference room I was given a friendly greeting by the supreme court justices, all of whom I knew from my legislative days or as former colleagues on the superior court. At exactly ten o'clock we put on our robes and lined up in order of seniority behind the door leading to the courtroom. As the junior member I was last and, when we entered, took the seat on the bench to the far left.

The sheriff exclaimed, "Oyez, Oyez, Oyez. The honorable Supreme Court of the State of Connecticut is now open and in session in this place. All persons having cause or action pending therein will give their attendance according to law." I settled in the high-backed chair. At my place was a neat array of pencils and pads, a water pitcher and paper cups, and a microphone. The winter sun, glistening off the gold dome of the capitol, streamed through the large floor-to-ceiling windows, casting a cheerful light in the courtroom. Painted portraits of former chief justices hanging high on the masonry walls looked gravely down upon us. There I was, at the state's legal summit, supreme court justice for the day.

Justice Arthur Healey, who was senior that day because I was taking the chief justice's place, nodded to the lawyer for the appellate in the first case. The lawyer moved to the lectern and began in the traditional way: "May it please the court . . ." The case involved an important question of tort law. He and his opponent were skillful advocates and made their points well. The justices asked many questions. I followed the argument carefully, jotted down a few notes, and asked a few questions of my own. At the end of an hour we recessed and then heard another appeal on a technical issue of procedure.

When the arguments were over we returned to the conference room. After the mandatory visits to the lavatory, we
gathered around the long conference table. Noticing an in-
viting silver urn on a sideboard, I poured myself coffee in a
delicate blue cup. Only the justices were present—no law
clerks or secretaries. Art Healey turned to me and asked how
I would decide the first case. I knew that the junior judge
went first, so I was prepared. I gave a brief comment and
indicated my vote. In inverse order of seniority, the other
justices gave their votes. The legal issue was a significant
one, and I was surprised at the lack of discussion. As it
turned out, on the first case we all agreed. On the second
case I was the only one wanting to affirm the trial court. I
elaborated on my reasons. Nobody rebutted me, but the
vote stood four to one to reverse.

I left the court pleased with the experience but puzzled by
the deliberative process. Several weeks later a draft opinion
of each case, written by the justice assigned by Healey, came
to me. Then the written comments of the other justices suggesting changes began arriving. It dawned on me that although the justices did not discuss much in conference, they
did express themselves vigorously by memos. It seemed like
an odd way to communicate.

On the second case in which I was alone, I found that I
disagreed even more with the opinion written by Healey
himself. Should I dissent? If I did, would I be asked to sit
again? The heck with it, I thought. I'm going to say what I
think. So I wrote a dissenting opinion. It appears in *Solomon*
v. *Aberman*, 196 Conn. 359, at page 385 and is my attempt to
emulate my judicial hero Oliver Wendell Holmes, the great
dissenter.

I did get asked back several more times. One of the most
memorable cases I sat on was *State* v. *Pecoraro*. The jury had
found William Pecoraro guilty of robbery in the first degree.
Although the evidence against him was overwhelming, he
appealed on the ground that the trial court judge had erred
in an evidentiary ruling. The identity of Pecoraro as the one

committing the crime had been an issue at the trial. The victim of the robbery had gone immediately to the police and identified Pecoraro from two photo boards, each containing eight snapshots of the front and side views of suspects. The boards themselves were offered into evidence with a white slip of paper, stapled at one end only, covering police plac-ards photographed on the chests of subjects, showing the name of the police department and a date. The mug shots of Pecoraro indicated they had been taken on two prior dates. He claimed that because the paper was stapled at only one end and flapped loosely, the jury could see under it easily and infer from the two dates that he had been arrested twice before. Because evidence of prior arrests is not admissible to prove the likelihood that an accused committed the crime for which he is charged, Pecoraro argued that the use of the police photo boards in that condition was error.

At the justices' conference, after the argument, the vote was to uphold the conviction. When I expressed my vote, I also said my research of Connecticut cases indicated that mug shots were admissible in evidence as long as their pro-bative value exceeded their prejudicial tendency. A few days later Chief Justice Ellen Peters assigned me to write the opin-ion. As I worked on it, I realized I should examine the of-fending exhibits. When I observed how easily the jury could see beneath the papers affixed to the photo boards, I had second thoughts about the possibility of unfairness to Peco-raro. I called the chief justice, and she suggested I should express my doubts to all the justices hearing the case. At the reconvened conference, I showed the exhibits. The justices were not impressed with their prejudicial effect. One said, "Jurors know about mug shots. This is harmless error." The others agreed.

That was my first direct experience with the doctrine of "harmless error." The justices were saying that the trial judge may have been wrong in admitting the photo boards, but the mistake was not likely to affect the outcome of the trial, so it did not matter. The doctrine seemed like a flexible way for appellate courts to avoid overturning a conviction when, on all the evidence, the defendant was clearly guilty.

At the conference, when I still seemed doubtful, Ellen Peters considerately asked me whether I still wanted to write the opinion. I thought for a moment and then said I could accept the views of the more experienced justices on the point.

In my opinion, which appears in 198 Conn. 203, 207, I wrote: "Nevertheless . . . the trial court should have required the paper covering the police photos be stapled at both ends. The judge should have been alert to his 'duty . . . to prevent situations from arising during the trial which would prejudice the accused in the minds of the jury.' . . . Our function, however, is not only to identify trial court mistakes but to weigh them. . . . Thus we conclude that the failure of the trial court to adopt the defendant's suggestion was harmless error." I had caught on quickly how to use that handy doctrine.

I also learned from sitting on appeals courts that they take into account the pressures under which trial courts must rule during a trial and make allowances for them. As one appellate judge told me, "If we corrected every mistake we saw in the record, three-quarters of all lower court cases would have to be reversed." To prevent that, appeals courts have developed elaborate rules. One is that a factual determination by a trial court will not be reversed unless it is "clearly erroneous." Another is the doctrine of "harmless error," already mentioned. Still another is that isolated mistakes in a judge's charge to a jury will be ignored, if the charge states the law accurately when "considered as a whole."

These rules of forbearance by appeals courts are reassuring. But they also indicate that when I am reversed, I have made a first-class blunder—at least in the minds of the appellate justices.

17. SUMMING UP

I have had three careers in my life: lawyer, legislator, judge. Of these, being a judge has been the most consuming. When I practiced law or legislated in the General Assembly of Connecticut, I never thought of myself as a lawyer or legislator. But when I ascended the bench I began thinking of myself, deep inside, as a judge. It was not just that the office carried a title and people reminded of my status in and out of court. It was that I felt I had not only assumed a new way of life, but also acquired a new identity. Having donned the robe, I never emotionally shed it.

That transformation of myself carried with it a danger. It increased my susceptibility to certain identifiable maladies that the judicial experience is known to induce. I observed myself succumbing to several with helpless chagrin.

The one judicial affliction for which there is no known cure is ponderousness. That trait developed in me from the beginning. In the course of a trial, because judges must avoid snap judgments, I learned to restrain myself from saying the first thing that came into my head, to think before speaking, and to think a lot before deciding.

Everything a judge says from the bench is taken down by a court reporter. A verbatim transcript is a humbling document, ruthlessly revealing how one really talks—the fractured syntaxes, split infinitives, uncompleted sentences, incoherences. Even off the bench I began speaking as if on the record, self-consciously trying to be articulate and mouthing my words slowly. The stories I told became long in the telling, the jokes, so extended, short in their humor.

Another common judicial malady is assuming an imposing air of self-importance—in short, pomposity. One of my favorite cartoons shows a round, prim judge in his chambers, and on a wall, among the pictures of the judge with famous people, is a framed sign saying, "Pomposity Is Next to Godliness." When a colleague starts to pontificate, his wife sternly tells him to stop being so "judgey." My wife, Ruth, had an equally effective way of dealing with that tendency in me. She delighted in directing me to take out the garbage and added, with a twinkle in her eye, "Your Honor."

The robe a judge dons is symbolic of the impersonality of the law. Like the robe of the pastor, it is designed to transform the wearer into the instrument of a higher power. The risk is that the judge will start thinking that *he* is the higher power. The likelihood increases when he proclaims from the bench to people who cannot differ with him and acquires a complacent confidence in his own view of things. When he starts to believe in those views absolutely, and particularly when he starts to assert his authority insolently, he succumbs to arrogance. I suspect that from time to time I have been arbitrary and bad-tempered. I always regret it afterward. Next to corruption, arrogance is the most unforgivable of judicial sins.

Yet the judicial experience can also induce a profound sense of one's own fallibility. Judge Learned Hand, the great chief judge of the United States Court of Appeals for the Second Circuit, kept under the glass top of his desk the words Lord Oliver Cromwell spoke to the stubborn Scots before the battle of Dunbar: "I beseech ye, in the bowels of Christ, think ye that ye may be mistaken." I quote that line to myself often.

Although judges seem to wield enormous power, I am constantly reminded how limited that power really is. Judges do not control the input of cases into the court system, their progress through it, or their exit out of it.

The police decide who will be arrested, and the prosecutors decide who will be prosecuted. The supply of civil cases is provided by the attorneys who file their writs and complaints in court.

The progress of cases is also out of a judge's hands. Lawyers close the pleadings and claim their matters for trial. Clerks, aided by computers, place the cases on the calendar. Occasionally judges may do some prodding to get cases heard, but for all their threats of dismissal or other dire consequences, lawyers are marvelously adept at inveigling adjournments until they are ready to go to trial.

The disposition of cases is also largely controlled by others. Over 90 percent of all civil cases are settled before or during trial. I can induce settlements by mediation, but the parties and their counsel have to agree. The vast majority of criminal cases also are disposed of by plea bargaining—the defendant agreeing to plead guilty to a lesser charge in exchange for the prosecutor recommending a specific sentence. I do not have to go along but usually do so in order not to bollix up the inexorable operation of the system. They judge best, it seems, who judge the least.

When I do make decisions, the limits of my powers are glaringly revealed when measured against the scope and depth of the issues involved. Americans are compulsive litigators who seek solutions to their problems in the courts, solutions that should be sought elsewhere—in the legislature or within themselves. Even matters that are properly before the courts—such as criminal behavior—induce a sense of helplessness. I know that when I sentence a convicted felon, I am not getting at the broader causes of crime in society, nor perhaps preventing the future criminal conduct of the individual before me. Moreover, my sentence is not even going to be served. Because of overcrowded prisons, for every person incarcerated another must be let go. In fact, in Connecticut in 1989 someone sentenced to *ten years* on a nonviolent drug charge serves on the average only *109 days* behind bars.

This is not, however, to gainsay the importance of the judge's role in conducting trials and making decisions. They establish the quality of justice in the legal system and carve the paths of the law.

Before a trial judge parade the follies, foibles, and frailties of humankind. They exceed the tales of Balzac, Dickens, or Dostoyevski in variety and intensity. Yet there are afternoons when a dull lawyer questions a dull witness in monotones, and the hands of the wall clock seem chained . . . and my eyes close . . . and my head nods . . .

The stresses of the position and the exercise of its powers accentuate both personality deficiencies and strengths of judges. On the bench, a stupid person may become arbitrary, a weak one vacillating, an insecure one tyrannical. By the same token, an intelligent person may become wiser, a sensitive one more compassionate.

A good person does not necessarily make a good judge, because the job requires more than virtue. It also requires intelligence and industry, integrity and temperament. But a good judge—particularly a good trial judge—is usually a good person, because the office requires, above all, compassion and caring. If I were selecting candidates for judgeships, I would look first at the quality of their hearts.

Heeding the admonition of Gloucester in *King Lear*, I would reject anyone

that will not see
Because he does not feel.

.   .   .

Many years have passed since I attempted to dictate a letter to a patient secretary on the fortieth floor of a Wall Street skyscraper. As I look back on my careers, each has had its special appeal to me: advocacy at the bar, politics in the capitol, decision making on the bench. As a lawyer I loved representing my clients, helping them at moments of crisis in their lives, carrying their colors into combat. As a legislator I loved plying the politician's art: developing consensus, forming coalitions, compromising without giving up the essence of measures. As a judge I love grappling with knotty legal issues and perplexing human problems, deciding in accordance with my understanding of the law and my vision of justice. Being a lawyer was the most stimulating, being a legislator the most fun, being a judge is the most satisfying, although the rewards of judging are more internal then external, more cerebral than emotional.

Coming on the bench has been the culmination of my life in the law. My legal and legislative careers enriched my judicial capacity. But every book I have read, every person I have known, every experience I have had—in short, anything that has shaped my notions of society and human nature—has also informed my judicial performance. My deepest fulfillment as a judge has been the merging of life and work into a coherent whole.

Yet it is so hard to measure what I have achieved on the bench. Even Judge Learned Hand, who for forty-two years wrote numerous lucid opinions on the major issues of his day, speculated on whether he might have accomplished more by constructing a boat or building a house. In the end, his magnificent judicial career seemed to him somehow ephemeral and insubstantial.

For me as a trial judge, the feeling of insubstantiality is even greater. Appellate court judges have volumes of printed opinions to document their careers, some of which will shape the law for decades. I have a handful of printed opinions in the law reports, only a few of which are of precedential significance. For me the trial's the thing. In one after another I strive to create an atmosphere that justice is being sought and done. When each trial is over, that atmosphere vanishes like smoke. I am left with a silent, empty courtroom—to try, and try again.

The pursuit of justice is humbling, not only because the ideal is so high, but because it is so ambiguous. All of us can recognize injustice. We know it from the sense of outrage we feel in its presence. As Reginald Heber Smith, the renowned legal aid lawyer, once said, "Nothing rankles more in the human breast than a brooding sense of injustice. Illness we can put up with; but injustice makes us want to pull things down." The vitality of the Sacco-Vanzetti case, after more than fifty years, is clear evidence of the sharp, persistent ache caused by a feeling of injustice.

But what is justice? In *Set This House on Fire,* police sergeant Luigi says, "I think true justice must always somehow live in the heart, locked away from politics, government and even the law." As a judge I cannot be that abstract. I must more practically pursue justice through law. Even if I cannot define it, I discern it in each case to be my sense of what is right, what is fair, what is fitting and appropriate in the law and under all the circumstances. But how do I know if I have achieved it? Bells do not ring and clarion trumpets blow. The scales of the blind lady do not lock loudly into balance.

The ambiguity and elusiveness of justice do not, however, make striving for it less important. Rather, the ultimate challenge and satisfaction of being a judge lie in that constant aspiration. It has always been so for me.

INDEX

accelerated rehabilitation, 171, 172
accused, *see* defendants
administrative agencies, 228–29,
    230
  public utilities and, 64–65
Aetna Surety and Casualty
    Company, 102, 104, 105, 106
  employees of, as jurors, 20–22,
    65–68
Alexander, Donald, 127
alimony, 189, 190–92
American Jury, The (Kalven and
    Zeisel), 131, 133
anti-lapse statutes, 54–60, 62
appeals courts, 24, 64, 71, 78, 92,
    119, 149
  being reversed by, 227–35
  briefs submitted to, 229
  Satter as judge in, 235–39
  see also Connecticut Supreme
    Court

appellate court, 50, 72, 135, 229,
    235, 245
arraignment, 27–28, 143–45
arrest case, 96–97, 118, 123–24
*Arterburn Convalescent Home, Inc.,
    et al.* v. *Committee on State
    Payment to Hospitals*, 228–29,
    230
assault cases, 231–32
  sexual, 17–19, 143, 174–81
automobile accident cases, 124–
    125
  instructions to jury in, 116
  police chase case, 88–89, 115,
    118, 120, 122, 123, 131
  settlement of, 107–8, 109–10

bail, setting of, 142–43
bail commissioners, 142
Bailey, John M., 33, 34
Baldwin, Scott, 127

bank robbery case, 172–73
Bantell, Linda, 219, 220
"best interest of child," 20, 199
bifurcated trials, 138–39
Board of Pardons, 11–12, 13–14
boards of education, 230
Botein, Bernard, 71
briefs, 54–55, 229
burden of proof:
    in civil suits, 116
    in criminal cases, 151, 155, 164,
        165–66
    in extradition, 48
burglary cases, 144, 147, 148, 181–
    182, 183
Burke, Roger, 172–73
Charles Bush estate case, 51–62,
    64

Caldwell, Donald, 154–64, 167,
    168
Caliafiore, Frances, 219, 220
Camus, Albert, 12
Cantor v. *Department of Income
    Maintenance*, 235
capital punishment, 182
    commutation process and, 11–14
    Satter's bill on, 32–33
Cardozo, Benjamin N., 29, 74, 76
Caron, Norman, 96–97, 118
challenges for cause, 65, 66–68
challenges to the favor, 66
child abuse, 202, 207–12
    sexual, 193–94, 210–11
child custody, 59, 190, 192, 195–
    200, 214
    change of, 19–20, 197–200
children:
    constitutional rights of, 203
    see also juvenile court
Children In Placement, 212
child support, 192, 193, 194, 195
child visitation, 192–95
"Chip Smith charge," 120–21
Chisolm, Alfred, 153–69
Churchill, Winston, 134
citizenship, conscientious
    objection and, 31
civil cases, 36, 242
    criminal cases vs., 140–41, 148,
        149

civil court cases, 23, 39–79, 80,
    134, 224
    appeals of, 50
    briefs filed in, 54–55
    conflicts between heart and
        mind in, 51–62
    credibility of witnesses in, 39–
        50
    direct conflict of testimony in,
        39–40, 42–45
    evidential issues in, 41, 53
    judicial decision making in, 63–
        79
    legal principles in, 51–62
    matters heard in, 40
    oral arguments in, 55–57
    settlement of, 40–41, 60–61, 77–
        78
    written opinions in, 78
civil jury cases, 23, 80–139
    assessment of, 126–39
    bifurcated trials proposed for,
        138–39
    burden of proof in, 116
    clarification of testimony in, 94
    damage awards in, 134–39
    epilogues to, 123–25
    instructions to jury in, 81, 115–
        120, 123–24, 127–28, 130, 133,
        134, 136–37
    judge's conversations with
        jurors after, 122–23, 131
    judge's opening remarks in, 83–
        84
    judicial humor in, 90–91, 140
    judicial intervention in, 94–97
    jury deliberations in, 119–21,
        128, 130–32
    jury selection in, 81–83, 128
    matters heard in, 81
    presentation of evidence in, 128–
        129
    reasons for choice of, 81
    role of judge in, 81, 90
    rules of evidence in, 81, 91–93,
        95–96, 149
    settlement of, 99–111, 123, 132,
        137, 138–39
    summations in, 112–15, 130
    unpredictability of jury in, 81,
        111

unprepared or incompetent
  lawyers in, 95–98
verdicts in, 121–22, 123–24, 128,
  130–39
civil rights cases, 31
closing arguments, 112–15, 130,
  163–64
Coastal Air Lines, 113–14, 122,
  123, 124
Columbia Law School, 28–29, 30
common law, 21, 53–54, 127,
  222
Common Law, The (Holmes), 29
comparative negligence doctrine,
  132, 138
conditional discharge, 171
confessions, 147, 148, 150, 182
confiscation without
  compensation, 73–75
Congress, U.S., 31, 54, 131, 184
Connecticut Bank and Trust Company
  v. Tax Commissioner, 233–34
Connecticut Constitution, 142, 166
  statute conflicting with, 72–75
Connecticut Court of Common
  Pleas, 34–37
Connecticut Law Journal, 227
Connecticut state legislature, 32–
  33, 34, 234
Connecticut Superior Court, 36–
  37
  categories of cases heard by, 23
  challenges faced by judges in,
    23–24
  uniqueness of, 22–23
  see also specific topics
Connecticut Supreme Court, 58,
  68, 78, 123
  being reversed by, 227–35
  Satter as judge in, 235–39
conscientious objectors, 31
Constitution, U.S., 142
  Fifth Amendment to, 145–46,
    147, 148, 163, 166, 167
  Fourth Amendment to, 145,
    146–48
constitutional rights, 165, 166
  advising accused of, 27, 141,
    147, 148
  of children, 203
contempt of court, 159

contracts, real estate, 68–72, 216–
  217
contributory negligence doctrine,
  132
corporate taxes, 232–34
court cases, 229
  jury cases vs., 41, 43, 53, 80, 81,
    91
  see also civil court cases
courtroom identifications, 182
criminal cases, 23, 26–28, 36, 140–
  185, 216, 242
  accused as witness in, 149, 164
    165, 166, 175–76, 177
  advising accused of
    constitutional rights in, 141
  arraignment in, 27–28, 143–
    145
  bail set in, 142–43
  burden of proof in, 151, 155,
    164, 165–66
  cathartic purpose of, 150–51
  civil cases vs., 140–41, 148, 149
  court-appointed lawyers in, 141–
    142
  disrespectful behavior of defense
    lawyers in, 149–50
  instructions to jury in, 164–66
  judicial intervention in, 149
  jury selection in, 148
  minority defendants in, 28
  motions to suppress evidence in,
    145–48, 150, 182
  murder trial, 153–69
  opening remarks in, 155
  plea bargains in, 144, 182–83,
    242
  presumption of innocence in,
    141, 143, 165
  rules of evidence in, 145–49,
    237–39
  sentencing in, 17–19, 167, 170–
    186, 242, 243
  summations in, 163–64
  testimony in, 148–50, 155–63,
    174–76
  verdicts in, 151, 167–68
criminal courts, meanness and
  frustration in, 151–52
Criminal Sentences: Law Without
  Order (Frankel), 183

cross-examination, 44, 97, 129
  of rape victims, 175
custody, *see* child custody

damage awards, 134–39
  bifurcated trial proposal and,
    138–39
  randomness of, 135, 139
death actions, 87–88, 113–14, 121–
    122, 123, 124
death penalty, *see* capital
  punishment
decisional law, 133
defendants:
  constitutional rights of, 27, 141,
    145–48, 165, 166, 203
  minorities as, 28
  as witnesses, 164–65, 166, 175–
    176, 177
defense lawyers, disrespectful
  conduct of, 149–50
deficiency judgments, 77–78
delinquency cases, 202, 203–7
Democratic party, 33, 34
Department of Children and Youth
  Services (DCYS), 205, 206,
  207, 209–13
Department of Environmental
  Protection, 72–75
DES cases, 108–9
Dianne DeMartino v. *Parkview West
  Associates,* 97–98
divorce proceedings, 186–201
  alimony awards in, 189, 190–92
  child support awards in, 192,
    193, 194, 195
  child visitation awards in, 192–
    195
  custody awards in, 59, 190, 192,
    195–97, 214
  displays of raw emotion in, 186–
    187
  lawyers as main actors in, 188–
    189
  legal separation and, 188
  long marriages dissolved in,
    187–88
  no-fault law and, 187, 188
  property division awards in,
    189, 190
  step relationships in, 59

drug possession cases, 141, 146–
    148, 243
drunken drivers, 107
due process, 232

Edwards, George, 17–19, 174–
    181
elderly, eviction of, 222–23
electric rates case, 64–65
employment relationship, jury
  selection and, 20–22, 66–68
England, civil jury trials in, 127
environmental cases, 72–75, 109
equity case, 40, 68–72
Esquire, 12
estate case, 51–62, 64
eviction proceedings, 215, 216–17,
    219–20, 221–23, 225
  against physically disabled or
    elderly, 222–23
evidence, 39
  admissibility of, 81, 91–93, 95–
    96
  credibility issue and, 39–50, 75,
    81, 83, 134, 149
  exclusionary rule and, 146–48,
    151
  hearsay, 91–92, 118
  instructions to jury on, 118–19
  motions to suppress, 145–48,
    150, 182
  objections to, 92, 95, 129, 149,
    150, 156
  presentation of, in civil jury
    cases, 128–29
  see also rules of evidence;
    testimony; witnesses
exclusionary rule, 146–48, 151
exhibits, 128, 238–39
expert testimony, 129
  in medical malpractice cases, 85,
    87, 105–6, 133
extradition case, 45–50

facts of case, 39–40, 75, 81, 144
"fair, just, and reasonable
  compensation," 136–37, 139
family court, 23, 186–201
  application for change of
    custody in, 19–20, 197–200
  see also divorce proceedings

family relations officers, 189, 195,
    196, 197, 199
federal district courts, 83, 184
felony cases, sentencing in, 174–
    181, 243
Fifth Amendment, 145–46, 147,
    148, 163, 165, 166
first offenders, sentencing of, 171–
    172
Flaherty, Leo, 155–64, 167, 168
Fletcher, Susan, 19–20, 197–200
For Your Own Good (Miller), 211
foster homes, 211–12, 213
Fourth Amendment, 145, 146–
    148
Frankel, Marvin, 183
fraud, 108, 143

Gault, Gerald, 203
gentrification, 224
Goetz, Bernard, 151
Gold, Mrs., 33–34
Gomez, José, 146–48
Grasso, Ella, 34, 36
Green v. *DeWeese*, 68–72
Griswold, Erwin N., 127
"guilt beyond reasonable doubt,"
    155, 164, 165–66
guilty pleas, 144–45, 182–83, 231–
    232, 242

habeas corpus proceedings, 145,
    231–32, 235
Hand, Learned, 242, 244–45
Hans, Valerie P., 131, 133
"harmless error" doctrine, 238–39
Healey, Arthur, 236, 237
hearsay, 91–92, 118
Holmes, Oliver Wendell, 237
home, divided in divorce
    proceedings, 190
housing code violations, 215, 217,
    219, 222
    sentencing for, 223–24
housing court, 23, 186, 215–26
    development of law in, 224
    establishment of, 217–18
    eviction proceedings in, 215,
        216–17, 219–20, 221–23, 225
    landlord-tenant acts and, 222–
        223, 224

legal aid and neighborhood
    antipoverty lawyers in, 220–22
    staff of, 218–20, 225
housing court sheriffs, 220
housing shortage, 224–25
housing specialists, 219–20, 224
humor, in courtroom, 90–91, 140,
    141
hung juries, 121–22

Immigration Department, U.S., 31
innocence, presumption of, 141,
    143, 165
In re. Gault, 203
insurance companies, 102, 104,
    105, 106, 109, 126, 137, 140
    automobile accidents and, 107,
        108
    employees of, as jurors, 20–22,
        65–68
    as unnamed defendants, 81

James, William, 184
Jubb, Charles, 87–88, 113–14, 121–
    122, 123, 124
judges:
    in court cases vs. jury cases, 41,
        43, 53, 80
    decision making by, 63–79, 199
    differences among, 63
    humorous remarks of, 90–91,
        140, 141
    instructions given to jury by, 81,
        115–20, 123–24, 127–28, 130,
        133, 134, 136–37, 164–66, 229,
        239
    intervention by, in jury trials,
        94–97, 149
    isolation of, 35–36
    jurors' conversations with, at
        close of trial, 122–23, 131
    justice as goal of, 78–79
    lack of indoctrination or training
        for, 26
    limits on power of, 242–43
    most difficult decisions made by,
        213–14
    opening remarks of, 83–84, 155
    pomposity of, 241
    ponderousness of, 240–41
    qualities required by, 243–44

judges (*cont.*)
  research conducted by, 57, 74,
    75–76, 93
  reversals of, 227–35
  robes of, 26, 27, 241
  role of, in civil jury cases, 81, 90
  sentencing by, *see* sentencing
  in settlement negotiations, 40–
    41, 60–61, 77–78, 99–111
  spoken decisions of, 199–200
  transition from lawyer to, 35–38
  values and personality of, 24–
    25, 63–64, 184, 243
  witnesses interrogated by, 94,
    149
  written opinions of, 78, 224, 237,
    238, 239
Judging the Jury (Hans and
    Vidmar), 131, 133
juries:
  bad decisions made by, 132
  in criminal cases, 151
  damage awards made by, 134–
    139
  deliberations of, 119–21, 128,
    130–32
  evaluation of, 133, 134
  evidence presentation and, 128–29
  functions of, 81
  impartiality of, 20–22, 65, 68
  instructions to, 81, 115–20, 123–
    124, 127–28, 130, 133, 134,
    136–37, 164–66, 229, 239
  judge's conversations with, at
    close of trial, 122–23, 131
  "lawless" decisions of, 132
  note taking by, 129–30, 133
  polling of, 122
  questioning by, 129, 134
  questions about efficacy of, 126–
    127
  right to trial by, 80
  settlements during trial and,
    110–11
  swearing in, 154
  unable to reach unanimous
    verdict, 120–21
  unpredictability of, 81, 111
  verdicts of, 110–11, 121–22, 123–
    124, 128, 130–39, 151, 167–68
  written questions from, 120

jury selection:
  in civil cases, 20–22, 65–68, 81–
    83, 128
  in criminal cases, 148
  employment relationship in, 20–
    22, 65–68
  in federal court, 83
  voir dire in, 82–83, 128, 148
jury trials, 229
  court cases vs., 41, 43, 53, 80,
    81, 91
  relevant law in, 53
  see also civil jury cases
justice, 78–79, 245
juvenile court, 23, 186, 202–14
  constitutional rights of children
    protected by, 203
  delinquency cases in, 202, 203–7
  neglect cases in, 202, 207–14
  origin of, 202–3
  plea bargains in, 204
  termination proceedings in, 212–
    214

Kalven, Harry, Jr., 131, 133
Kant, Immanuel, 184–85

landlord-tenant acts, 222–23, 224
larceny cases, 172, 204–7
law:
  three broad categories of, 53–54
  see also legal principles
law clerks, 57
lawyers:
  in appeals, 229
  cases lost by, 228
  competency of, 95–98
  court-appointed, 141–42
  in court cases vs. jury cases, 41,
    80
  disrespectful conduct of, 90,
    149–50
  in divorce proceedings, 188–89
  legal aid and neighborhood
    antipoverty, 220–22
  summations of, 112–15, 130,
    163–64
  susceptibility of, to settling, 109
Lee v. *Board of Education*, 230
legal aid lawyers, 220–22
legal positivists, 64

legal principles, 23, 24
  competing, 72–75, 76
  and conflict between heart and
    mind, 51–62
  in housing court, 224
  judge's instructions to jury on,
    81, 115–20, 123–24, 127–28,
    130, 133, 134, 136–37, 164–66,
    229, 239
  judge's values and, 64–79
  narrow interpretation of, 75–
    76
  research on, 57, 74, 75–76, 93
legal realists, 64, 68
Leidenfrost, Eric, 31
libel, 108
Lieberman, Joseph, 61
Long Lane School, 205, 206

Magna Carta, 80
manslaughter charge, 154–55, 167
medical malpractice cases, 84–87,
    90, 109, 117–18, 119, 121, 123
  damage awards in, 135, 137
  expert testimony in, 85, 87, 105–
    106, 133
  insurance company employees
    as jurors in, 20–22, 65–68
  settlements in, 100–107, 123
Meskill, Thomas, 34
Miller, Alice, 211
Miller, Charles A., 76
minorities, as defendants, 28
Miranda v. Arizona, 147
misdemeanors, sentencing for,
    171–74
Morgan, Brian, 20–22
Morgan Street courthouse, 26–27
Morgan v. Saint Francis Hospital, et.
    al., 65–68
mortgage foreclosures, 77–78
mug shots, as evidence, 238–39
murder, as charge, 154–55
murder trial, 153–69
  defendant as witness in, 164–65,
    166
  instructions to jury in, 164–66
  opening remarks in, 155
  summations in, 163–64
  testimony in, 155–63
  verdict in, 167–68

Nardini v. Manson, 235
National Commission on the
    Constitutional Rights of
    Children, 211
Nature of the Judicial Process, The
    (Cardozo), 29, 74, 76
neglect cases, 202, 207–14
  termination proceedings in, 212–
    214
negligence, 116–17, 132, 134, 138
Newman, Jon, 57
no-fault divorce law, 187, 188
Northeast Utilities Corporation,
    96–97, 118
nuisance suits, 107–8

objections, to presentation of
    evidence, 92, 95, 129, 149, 150,
    156
objections for cause, 83
opening remarks, 83–84, 155
oral arguments:
  on admissibility of evidence, 93
  in civil court cases, 55–57
  see also summations
Oviedo, Alvaro, 20–22

"pain and suffering," 138
Paradoxes of Legal Science (Cardozo),
    76
parental rights, termination of,
    212–14
Paulsen v. Manson, 231–32
Pecoraro, William, 237–39
Pennsylvania Supreme Court,
    234
peremptory challenges, 65, 82
perjury, 44
personal injury cases:
  step relationships in, 59
  see also civil jury cases
Peters, Ellen, 238, 239
physically disabled, eviction of,
    222–23
plane crash case, 87–88, 113–14,
    121–22, 123, 124
plea bargains, 144, 182–83, 204,
    242
pleading, 143–45, 171, 172
  guilty pleas in, 144–45, 182–83,
    231–32, 242

police chase case, 88–89, 115, 118, 120, 122, 123, 131
Pound, Dean Roscoe, 76, 132
poverty, 28, 211
  housing matters and, 215–26
Prange, John, 88–89, 115, 118, 120, 122, 123, 131
precedents, 64, 73–74, 75–76
presentence reports, 176, 178, 182
presumption of innocence, 141, 143, 165
principal challenges, 66–68
probate courts, 52
probation, 171, 181
product liability cases, 109, 133
property division awards, 189, 190
property rights, 72–75, 222
prosecutors, in sentencing process, 182–83
public defenders, 142, 204
public housing, 224
public utilities, 64–65
punishment:
  purpose of, 170–71
  see also capital punishment; sentencing
purse snatching cases, 142, 174

Raffone, Salvatore, 153–69, 177
rape cases, 17–19, 143, 174–81
real estate contracts, 68–72, 216–17
"reasonable doubt," 155, 164, 165–166
"Reflections on the Guillotine" (Camus), 12
Reid, Benjamin, 11–15
rent subsidies, 224–25
research, 57, 74, 75–76, 93
reversals, 227–35, 239
Rhode Island Supreme Court, 65
robbery cases, 149–50, 237–39
robes, judicial, 26, 27, 241
Romano v. Costello, 39–45
Rosado extradition proceeding, 45–50
Ross v. Ross, 196–97
rules of evidence, 81, 91–93, 95–96
  in court cases vs. jury cases, 41, 53, 91
  in criminal cases, 145–49, 237–39
  on hearsay, 91–92

Sacco-Vanzetti case, 245
St. Francis Hospital, 20–22
Satter, Robert:
  appointed judge, 34
  appointed to housing court, 218
  first judicial assignment of, 26–28
  first law job held by, 29–30
  housing court left by, 225–26
  law partnership of, 30–32, 33–34, 240, 244
  legal profession entered by, 28–29
  political career of, 32–33, 34, 240, 244
  reversed decisions of, 228–35
  sitting on Connecticut Supreme Court, 235–39
  in transition from lawyer to judge, 35–38
Satter, Ruth, 36, 60, 241
Schlumberger Technology Corporation v. Commissioner of Revenue Services, 233
search warrants, 145, 146–48
second offenders, sentencing of, 172–73
Sentence Review Board, 183–84
sentencing, 17–19, 167, 170–86, 214, 242
  disparities in, 183–84
  in felony cases, 174–81, 243
  of first offenders, 171–72
  for housing code violations, 223–24
  judicial discretion essential in, 184–85
  and maximum terms set by statute, 177
  for misdemeanors, 171–74
  presentence reports and, 176, 178, 182
  prosecutors' role in, 182–83
  public reaction to, 177–78
  and purpose of punishment, 170–71
  of second offenders, 172–73
  seminars on, 183
  standardization of, 184
  in U.S. vs. other Western countries, 177

Sentencing Commission, U.S.,
    184
separation, legal, 188
Set This House on Fire (Styron), 245
settlements, 99–111, 123, 132, 137,
    138–39, 242
  in civil court cases, 40–41, 60–
    61, 77–78
  clients' willingness for, 109
  in complicated cases, 108–9
  as compromise, 111
  difficult cases for, 107
  easiest cases for, 107
  impossible cases for, 108
  individual lawyers' susceptibility
    to, 109
  judge's individual style and, 100
  in medical malpractice cases,
    100–107, 123
  of nuisance suits, 107–8
  pressure for, 99
  during trial, 110–11
sexual abuse, of children, 193–94,
    210–11
sexual assault cases, 17–19, 143,
    174–81
shading of truth, 44
shoplifting case, 173
Shore, Richard, 147, 148
Smith, Reginald Heber, 245
Solomon v. *Aberman*, 237
Spatta, Dawn, 86–87, 100–107
spoken decisions, 199–200
standards of proof, 48
state legislatures, 54
  of Connecticut, 32–33, 34, 234
State v. *Eason*, 232
State v. *Pecoraro*, 237–39
State v. *Raffone*, 153–69
State v. *Smith*, 120
statutes, 54, 64, 133
  anti-lapse, 54–60, 62
  constitutional provision
    conflicting with, 72–75
  on corporate taxes, 232–34
  on landlord-tenant relations,
    222–23, 224
  maximum sentences set by, 177
  with more than one meaning,
    75–76
  on teacher tenure, 230

step relationships:
  in divorce law, 59
  in estate law, 52–62
  in tort law, 59
Styron, William, 11–16
summations, 112–15, 130, 163–64
Supreme Court, U.S., 34, 147, 203,
    230
suspended sentences, 171

Taborsky, Joseph, 13, 14
Targett (Aetna manager), 102, 104,
    105, 106
tax cases, 232–34
teacher tenure statute, 230
termination proceedings, 212–
    214
testimony, 39
  clarification of, 94, 149
  in criminal cases, 148–50, 155–
    163, 174–76
  direct conflict of, 39–40, 42–45,
    75, 83, 89, 129, 131
  expert, 85, 87, 105–6, 129, 133
  judge's instructions on, 118
  rehearing of, 120
  see also evidence; witnesses
tort law, 133
  step relationships in, 59
  see also civil jury cases

University of Chicago, 130–31
*University of Connecticut Chapter,
    AAUP,* v. *Governor,* 234
University of Connecticut School
    of Law, 38
"unreasonable searches and
    seizures," 145, 146–48

verdicts:
  in civil jury cases, 121–22, 123–
    124, 128, 130–39
  in criminal cases, 151, 167–68
  damage awards in, 134–39
  judge's decision making process
    and, 63–79
  mock, in cases settled during
    trial, 110–11
  not accepted by judge, 122, 123–
    124
  overturning of, 119, 227–35, 239

verdicts (*cont.*)
  setting aside of, 135, 167
  unanimous, inability to reach,
    120–21
victims, in sentencing process, 18,
  176–77, 178, 179
Vidmar, Neil, 131, 133
visitation rights, 192–95
vocational training, 206
voir dire, 82–83, 128, 148

Wallas, Graham, 76
Watson, Lori, 117–18, 119, 121,
  123
Weaver, Jack, 142
welfare fraud cases, 143
White, Robert, 143
Wigmore, John Henry,
  44
witnesses, 129

accused as, 149, 164–65, 166,
  175–76, 177
conflicting testimony of, 39–40,
  42–45, 75, 83, 89, 129, 131
credibility of, 39–50, 75, 81, 8?.
  134, 149
cross-examination of, 44, 97,
  129, 175
interrogated by judge, 94, 149
lack of background information
  about, 44–45
see also evidence; testimony
written opinions:
  in civil court cases, 78
  of Connecticut Supreme Court,
    237, 238, 239
  on housing law, 224

Zeisel, Hans, 131, 133
Zenger, John Peter, 151